Charging for government

User charges and earmarked taxes are methods by which people pay directly for the services they receive from government. As such they are frequently supported by those who oppose increased taxation, who argue that they are more like market transactions than traditional forms of taxation. This book explores the cogency of these arguments in the light of public choice analyses of political processes.

The twelve chapters in this book examine the possible conflict between arguments for user fees and earmarked taxes and public choice analyses which explain how political outcomes reflect the operation of self-interest. Hence the reality of user fees and earmarked taxes may diverge sharply from the common justifications. Furthermore, the extent of such divergence will depend on the nature of the constitutional rules that constrain and shape political processes.

The contributors to this volume include several prominent members of the public choice school, most notably the Nobel Laureate James Buchanan. The editor, **Richard E. Wagner**, has written extensively on public choice and constitutional economics. He is currently Harris Professor of Economics and Chairman of the Department of Economics at George Mason University.

Charging for government

User charges and earmarked taxes in
principle and practice

Edited by
Richard E. Wagner

London and New York

336,16
C4722

First published 1991
by Routledge
11 New Fetter Lane, London EC4P 4EE

Simultaneously published in the USA and Canada by
Routledge
a division of Routledge, Chapman and Hall Inc.
29 West 35th Street, New York, NY 10001

© 1991 Richard E. Wagner

Typeset in Times by
NWL Editorial Services, Langport, Somerset

Printed and bound in Great Britain by
Biddles Ltd, Guildford and King's Lynn

UB

All rights reserved. No part of this book may be reprinted or
reproduced or utilized in any form or by any electronic,
mechanical, or other means, now known or hereafter invented,
including photocopying and recording, or in any information
storage or retrieval system, without permission in writing from
the publishers.

British Library Cataloguing in Publication Data
Charging for government: user charges and earmarked taxes
  in principle and practice
  1. United States. State governments & local authorities.
Revenue
I. Wagner, Richard E.
336.0273

  ISBN 0–415–06463–5

Library of Congress Cataloging in Publication Data
Charging for government: user charges and earmarked taxes
  in principle and practice / Richard E. Wagner, editor.
    p. cm.
Includes bibliographical references and index.
ISBN 0–415–06463–5
1. User charges. 2. Revenue. 3. Special funds.
I. Wagner, Richard E. II. Title: Earmarked taxes.
HJ5001.C48 1991   90–24731
336.1'6 – dc20   CIP

Contents

Figures		vii
Tables		ix
The contributors		xi
Preface		xiii

1 **Tax norms, fiscal reality, and the democratic state: user charges and earmarked taxes in principle and practice** 1
Richard E. Wagner

2 **The fiscal significance of user charges and earmarked taxes: a survey** 13
Gary M. Anderson

3 **User charges, rent seeking, and public choice** 34
Bruce Yandle

4 **The political economy of user charges: some bureaucratic implications** 60
Dwight R. Lee

5 **Subjective cost, property rights, and public pricing** 75
Richard E. Wagner

6 **The practice and politics of marginal cost pricing: the case of the French electric monopoly** 90
Henri Lepage

7 **The political economy of tax earmarking** 110
Dwight R. Lee and Richard E. Wagner

8 **Rent seeking and tax earmarking** 125
Dwight R. Lee and Robert D. Tollison

University Libraries
Carnegie Mellon University
Pittsburgh, Pennsylvania 15213

 9 **Tax earmarking and the optimal lobbying strategy**   141
    Mwangi S. Kimenyi, Dwight R. Lee, and Robert D. Tollison

10 **The constitutional economics of earmarking**   152
    James M. Buchanan

11 **Excises, earmarked taxes, and government user charges in a
    rent seeking model**   163
    Fred S. McChesney

12 **User fees and earmarked taxes in constitutional perspective**   179
    Richard E. Wagner

    Index   195

Figures

3.1 Analysis of user fees   47
3.2 Effects of liability rule   48
4.1 Niskanen's model of bureaucracy   63
4.2 Inefficient bureau output   66
4.3 Bureau financed by a user charge   67
5.1 Marginal cost pricing dilemma   78
5.2 Monopoly pricing by a public enterprise   80
8.1 Tax earmarking with hostile interest group, I   129
8.2 Tax earmarking with hostile interest group, II   130
8.3 Tax earmarking with hostile interest group, III   130
8.4 Tax earmarking with favourable interest group   131
8.5 Efficient rate of tax earmarking   134
8.6 Interest group pressures on tax earmarking   138
11.1 User charges and social welfare   165
12.1 The social dilemma   180

Tables

9.1 Regression results for the determinants of
LRFEDR (1933–82)   147

9.2 Regression results for the determinants of
LPRPEDR (1933–82)   148

9.3 Regression results for the determinants of
LRFEDR and LPRPEDR (1933–82)   149

The contributors

Gary M. Anderson is Professor of Economics at California State University at Northridge. His work has appeared in such journals as the *Journal of Political Economy*, the *Journal of Law and Economics*, the *International Review of Law and Economics*, and *Public Choice*.

James M. Buchanan is University Distinguished Professor of Economics at George Mason University, and recipient of the Nobel Memorial Prize in Economic Science for 1986. His major books include *The Calculus of Consent* (with Gordon Tullock), *Public Principles of Public Debt*, *The Limits of Liberty*, *Democracy in Deficit* (with Richard E. Wagner), and *The Power to Tax* (with Geoffrey Brennan).

Mwangi S. Kimenyi is Associate Professor of Economics at the University of Mississippi. His work has appeared in such journals as *Public Choice*, the *Yale Journal Regulation*, and the *Journal of Population Economics*.

Dwight R. Lee is Professor of Economics and holder of the Bernard B. and Eugenia A. Ramsay Chair of Private Enterprise at the University of Georgia. He is the author of three textbooks in economics, and his work has appeared in such scholarly journals as the *Atlantic Economic Journal*, *Economic Inquiry*, the *Journal of Political Economy*, and the *Southern Economic Journal*.

Henri Lepage studied economics at the London School of Economics, and then became a well-known journalist in France. His book *Demain le capitalisme* became a highly regarded explanation of economic liberalism for French readers and subsequently became a widely acclaimed best-seller in English translation, *Tomorrow, Capitalism*. Formerly President of the Institut de l'Entreprise, he is now Director of Research for Euro 92.

Fred S. McChesney is Robert Thompson Professor of Law at Emory University. His work has recently appeared in such professional journals as the *University of Pennsylvania Law Review*, the *Journal of Legal Studies*, the *Yale Law Review*, the *University of Connecticut Law Review*, and the *Journal of Legal Studies*.

Robert D. Tollison is Duncan Black Professor of Economics and Director of the Center for study of Public Choice at George Mason University. He is the co-author of a best-selling textbook *Economics* (with Robert B. Ekelund), and has written a dozen other books in addition to having published over 200 articles in professional journals.

Richard E. Wagner is Holbert L. Harris Professor of Economics and Chairman of the Department of Economics at George Mason University. He is co-editor (with Viktor J. Vanberg) of the new journal *Constitutional Political Economy* and includes among his recently published books *To Promote the General Welfare*, *Public Choice and Constitutional Economics* (with James D. Gwartney) and *Smoking and the State* (with Robert D. Tollison).

Bruce Yandle is Alumni Professor of Economics at Clemson University and Senior Research Scholar with the Center for Policy Studies. Among his recent publications are articles appearing in the *Journal of Energy Development*, *Social Science Quarterly*, the *Journal of Labor Research* and *Public Choice*.

Preface

There is a long-standing principle in public finance scholarship, the 'benefit principle', which says that it is a good idea to place the costs of public services upon those who use them, and in a way that those who benefit more also pay more. The main, generally acknowledged exceptions to this principle are cases where the redistribution of income is thought to be a significant justification for the service being provided, as with various welfare services. But in cases where efficiency and not redistribution is thought to be the primary object, the benefit principle is generally thought to be applicable. Despite this general applicability in principle, the practical applicability of the benefit principle is also often thought to be limited to those cases where it is easy to identify beneficiaries and to charge them directly for their use of public services. These practical considerations lead to the suggestions for *user charges*, where beneficiaries are charged directly for their use of public services, and to *tax earmarking*, which can be viewed as an indirect form of user charging, and which operates by taxing something closely related to the public service being supplied and earmarking the revenues collected for support of the public service.

With the development of the body of scholarship known as public choice, scholars are coming increasingly to recognize that actual political or fiscal practice may diverge, and sometimes sharply, from the justifications or principles advanced in support of particular measures. The essays in this book examine user charges and earmarked taxes from such a perspective. These instruments are justified in terms of their ability to promote economic efficiency, through placing the cost of public services upon those who benefit from their provision. However, the theory of public choice suggests that actual governmental choices concerning user charges and earmarked taxes will emphasize not so much the promotion of economic efficiency as the promotion of

political success. Actual policies concerning user charges and
earmarked taxes will tend to promote the political interests of dominant
interest groups pertinent to the issue at hand, and the resulting
consequences of these policies may often be inequitable and inefficient,
as judged by the standards of the benefit principle.

The first two chapters are introductory. Chapter 1, by Richard
Wagner, describes the benefit principle of public finance and notes how
user charges and earmarked taxes would seem to be congruent with that
principle, and then considers how actual fiscal practice may diverge from
these requirements of fiscal principle. Chapter 2, by Gary Anderson,
surveys the importance of user charges and earmarked taxes in existing
fiscal systems. Chapters 3–6 provide a unit on user charges. Chapter 3,
by Bruce Yandle, illustrates the potential disparity between common
justifications for user charges and the actual practice, with particular
attention given to environmental protection under the American
'Superfund' programme. Chapter 4, by Dwight Lee, examines how the
actual operation of government bureaux is influenced by user charges,
and builds upon some of the issues treated by Yandle in the process.
Chapter 5, by Richard Wagner, extends the preceding two chapters by
exploring how the economic principles of subjective cost and property
rights explain why it is essentially impossible for public enterprises to
institute economically efficient prices, even if the officials in charge of
those enterprises should desire to do so. Chapter 6, by Henri Lepage,
examines electricity pricing in France, which has been widely heralded
as an illustration of economically efficient user charging in operation –
and which is a claim that Lepage shows to be false.

Chapters 7–10 comprise a unit on tax earmarking, which also is
organized in terms of developing the distinction between traditional
justifications and actual practice. Chapter 7, by Dwight Lee and Richard
Wagner, describes the standard, normative theory of tax earmarking as
an indirect form of user charging and then examines how the arguments
in support of earmarking may evaporate once the realities of tax politics
are taken into account. Chapter 8, by Dwight Lee and Robert Tollison,
explores in greater detail the political and economic consequences of
the link that tax earmarking creates between those who are being taxed
and those who are beneficiaries of the services provided by the
earmarked revenues. Chapter 9, by Mwangi Kimenyi, Dwight Lee and
Robert Tollison, examines the impact of earmarked taxes on the
incentives that interest groups have to lobby for higher taxes within
democratic budgetary processes. Chapter 10, by James Buchanan, who
is responsible for the recent intellectual interest in tax earmarking,
summarizes and extends the preceding three chapters, by relating tax

earmarking to alternative models of governmental process – showing how different models of government give different insights into the properties of tax earmarking.

Chapter 11, by Fred McChesney, examines the possibility that legislatures can use threats to impose user charges or earmarked taxes as a form of political extortion that, among other things, will elicit higher campaign contributions from the 'threatened' parties to the members of the legislative committees that rule on such legislation. Chapter 12, by Richard Wagner, surveys the divergencies between rationale and reality concerning user charges and tax earmarking that have been laid out in the previous chapters and explores the possible institutional and constitutional requirements for and limitations on budgetary and political processes that would be necessary to bring the justifications more closely into line with the reality.

Support for the research that went into this book has been provided by the Tobacco Institute and by the Lynde and Harry Bradley Foundation. To both I am exceedingly grateful.

1 Tax norms, fiscal reality, and the democratic state

User charges and earmarked taxes in principle and practice

Richard E. Wagner

Fiscal scholars have not been shy in setting forth criteria for good systems of taxation. Nor have they been hesitant to criticize existing tax systems. Adam Smith's four maxims of taxation – that taxes should be, first, based on the benefits that people receive from governmental services; second, imposed in certain and not arbitrary fashion; third, levied in a convenient manner; and, fourth, easily administered – are found in most texts on public finance. The subsequent scholarly literature led to the refinement of two main principles of taxation, represented by the respective claims that taxes should be based on individual evaluations of (or benefits from) public services and that they should be based on individual abilities to pay.[1]

To be sure, these alternative principles of normative public finance would seem, at base, to represent two sharply different approaches to the subject matter and to the presumed relationship between citizen and state.[2] The ability-to-pay approach represents a transcendental approach to evaluation, in that the criteria of evaluation are presumed to have merit independently of what individuals may agree to. Government, in other words, is treated as being prior to people and their rights of person and property; what constitutes a good tax system is defined independently of what a group of people may agree to and, indeed, stands in judgment of what those people actually do agree to.

In contrast, the benefit principle represents an immanent approach to evaluation. People are treated, normatively, as being prior to government. A good tax system thus depends on what people want to accomplish in common, and cannot be determined independently of what those people agree to. The benefit principle, in other words, does not specify any substantive content as to what constitutes a good tax system, and rather posits that a good tax system is that which accomplishes what the citizenry agrees to accomplish. To be sure, it is possible to restate the ability-to-pay approach in terms of the benefit approach, by arguing that one of the things people want is a tax system that distributes burdens in the light of abilities to pay.[3] But any such redefinition of terms should not obscure the need to be clear about the dependence of any particular approach to fiscal evaluation on political presuppositions.

In terms of intellectual foundations, the benefit approach is surely more congruent with a democratic political order, just as the ability-to-pay approach is more congruent with an absolutist order, for an absolutist order has a place for an external judge or evaluator but a democratic order does not. Indeed, the benefit principle of public finance follows directly from various contractarian theories of the state, where the purpose of government is seen as being to protect people's rights and to advance their interests through collective projects that they could not advance, at least not very effectively, through market processes. On the surface, the growing recent interest by governments in user charges and earmarked taxes would seem to represent a reaffirmation of the benefit principle as a guide to public finance, for the use of charges in place of taxes would seem to be a way of charging people for government according to the use they make of services provided by government and, hence, would represent an expansion in the extent to which contractual relationships guide governmental conduct.

The articulation of normative principles does not, however, by itself ensure that those principles will be implemented. Even if there were agreement to accept the general framework of the benefit principle as an approach to the evaluation of fiscal systems, it does not follow that actual fiscal outcomes will mesh with that normative principle, for a logic of collective action might clash with a logic of welfare economics; the outcomes of actual political processes might diverge from those envisioned by the normative arguments. Indeed, the contemporary scholarship on public choice has sought to explain how processes of fiscal politics in democratic political systems may bring about fiscal outcomes that diverge, sometimes sharply, from the norms that underpin and legitimize those democratic systems.

To be sure, the extent of such divergence can to some extent be controlled – or at least this presumption is central to the contemporary scholarship in public choice and constitutional economics – for the extent of this divergence is a matter of the incentives contained within existing political systems, and those incentives can to some degree be modified through changes in constitutional rules.[4] User charges and earmarked taxes are typically justified as means of placing the cost of government on those who use governmental services, but to advance this justification is not automatically to deny that those instruments might be used instead as means by which politically dominant groups place costs on others. In turn, the extent of any divergence between justification and reality, a logic of collective action would suggest, depends upon the strength of incentives that different constitutional rules give to participants in political processes.

1 THE BENEFIT PRINCIPLE AND THE CONTRACT THEORY OF THE STATE

The contract theory of the state sees people and their rights, normatively, as prior to government. Whether represented by King or Parliament, government is seen not as a source of rights but as a reflection of people's use of their rights. Governments are instituted to preserve and protect rights and not to create them or to rearrange them for the benefit of some people at the expense of others.

The benefit principle represents an effort to extend the principle of consumer sovereignty to the conduct of government, and holds that budgetary choices should reflect individual valuations in essentially the same manner that a market economy reflects those valuations. Within the normative vision of the various contract theories of the state, citizens are seen as making contributions to the state with the taxes they pay and receiving services they value from the state in return. This vision is essentially the same as that which governs market relationships, where consumers receive services of value in exchange for their payments. The normative legitimacy of a market economy represents a general accept-ance of liberal values, which in turn emphasize individual autonomy within a framework of law, exercised to the extent that such exercise does not infringe on the recognized rights of others.[5] The benefit principle of public finance assesses the use of resources by government against the same liberal value of individual autonomy; citizen sovereignty in the public economy is complementary to consumer sovereignty in the market economy.

In principle it is simple to test whether particular fiscal choices adhere to or violate the benefit principle, for the contractual metaphor suggests that state actions will be agreeable to the citizens who constitute the state, as Knut Wicksell (1896) noted in his seminal contribution to the benefit principle of public finance.[6] A proposal to increase the gasoline tax and to earmark the resulting revenue to support mass transit rather than to support highways will, if it is consistent with the benefit principle, be able to command the assent of *all* taxpayers – those who drive cars as well as those who ride mass transit. In other words, the benefit principle looks to taxpayer evaluations in judging whether or not it is being violated. Taxes are assessed in terms of their agreeability to taxpayers. Should there be taxpayers who object to the proposed tax, this is evidence against the proposition that the benefit principle is being followed.

But such objection is not conclusive evidence, for if people are able successfully to oppose taxes by claiming that the services to be provided are not worth the taxes they are being asked to pay, people will have an incentive to understate their evaluation of public services. This free rider dilemma can arise whenever individual tax liabilities are made to vary directly with taxpayer declarations about their evaluations of public services. By declaring a lower than 'truthful' valuation, recognizing there is no way for any third party to determine what truly constitutes a truthful valuation, a taxpayer can bring about a significant reduction in personal tax liability. But because one taxpayer's contribution to total tax collections is but a pittance, in all but the least populous of governments, that understatement of valuation would produce practically no reduction in government spending.

The possibility of such free riding clearly trumps any argument that the presence of individual claims not to receive good value in exchange for their tax payments demonstrates a violation of the benefit principle. For people would have some direct financial incentive to make such claims even if those claims were false. The possibility of such free riding is typically used to justify some degree of coercion in taxation, as in denying people the ability to contest their tax liabilities on the grounds that they are not receiving worthwhile service in return for their money. But once people are prohibited from disputing their tax liabilities on the ground that the services they receive are not worth what they are being asked to pay, an opportunity for forced carrying arises. Whereas free riding refers to someone failing to carry a proper – truly agreeable – tax burden, forced carrying refers to someone being made to carry a tax burden that is heavier than proper, as judged by the contractual perspective of the benefit principle.[7]

2 THE BENEFIT PRINCIPLE AS COMPUTATIONAL OBJECTIVE

At least two versions of the benefit principle can be found in the fiscal literature. One version is more local in nature and looks to specific governmental projects where the principle can be implemented by well-meaning third parties. The emphasis in this case is on end-states or fiscal outcomes. Most of the discussion of user charges and tax earmarking falls within this perspective. The other version is global in orientation, and looks not for computational techniques suitable for use by third parties but for principles and procedures for political and fiscal organization that, if followed, would produce outcomes that would correspond to the requirements of the benefit principle. The emphasis in this case is on the rules or processes according to which fiscal choices are made. The benefit principle as possessing a local, computational orientation is found in a variety of instances, especially in financing local governments. A city extending sewer lines or street lights to a new area might finance them by special assessments imposed on the owners of adjacent property. In such cases as these it might seem to be comparatively straightforward to charge beneficiaries directly for the services they receive. The cost of the sewer extension can be billed to the property owners who get the service, rather than being absorbed within the general fund.

But there exist many cases where such straightforwardness does not seem to be present. An improvement to a neighbourhood park might seem to benefit neighbourhood users, and so be suitable for special assessment. But there is surely ambiguity about the extent of the neighbourhood. Usage would typically vary directly with proximity to the park. Residents who live nearby would on average make more use of the park than residents who live farther away. But there would also typically be residents close by who make less use than residents who live further away.

Even a well-meaning city official, who was dedicated to trying to impose charges and special assessments on contractarian terms would encounter an impossible situation presented by the inherent subjectivity of the data that inform choice. In actual market settings people are faced with options and in the light of those options they make their choices. Someone can choose to enter a park at a fee of $1 and refuse to do so at a fee of $2, or can choose to use the park twenty times per year when the admission fee is $1 and only eight times per year when it is $2. Information about personal evaluations is revealed as a by-product of the market process within which the provision of park services is organized.

But in the absence of that market process the well-meaning city official has no process available by which information about evaluations can be directly acquired. In the absence of a market process through which people can reveal through their choices their evaluation of alternative park options, the city official must resort to some alternative technique. One technique might be surveys, another might be hearings, a third might be econometric estimates made from data taken from other areas that do organize parks through market processes. But regardless of technique, accuracy will be reduced and, perhaps more significantly, the scope for creativity that arises within market processes will be curbed. In short, the well-meaning public official would either recommend the replacement of surveys, hearings, and estimates with a genuine market process, or, if that were judged inadvisable because it was thought that problems of non-exclusion and free ridership would interfere, he would recommend the construction of some process for making collective choices for which there was good reason to think the benefit principle would aptly characterize its outcomes.

3 THE BENEFIT PRINCIPLE AS OUTCOME OF PROPER POLITICAL PROCESS

So long as the benefit principle is viewed as offering computational advice its range of applicability will be quite limited. The inherent subjectivity of the data that inform economic choice means that even computational uses of the benefit principle to guide such things as special assessments for street lighting will be fraught with difficulty. But, still, the task of third-party assessment is simpler and more constrained in this case than it is in most cases. Special assessments for street lighting are surely simpler to compute than are evaluations for educational programmes.

In its broadest interpretation, the benefit principle is not limited to particular divisible services supplied by government but can be applied to the full range of governmental activities. A proposal to increase the general fund allocation for road maintenance is as capable of being subjected to the benefit principle as is a proposal to install curbs and sidewalks along a single block. The difference in settings is more apparent than real, at least with respect to the applicability of the benefit principle. With curbs and sidewalks along a single block the beneficiaries are readily identifiable, for the most part, and it seems comparatively easy to develop a set of assessments to be charged to the adjoining property owners that would be agreeable to them. But it is really no different for a proposal to increase the general level of maintenance expenditures. To be sure, the set of beneficiaries is larger, and those beneficiaries may have a more difficult time envisioning the consequences of alternative maintenance budgets than envisioning the consequences of curbs and sidewalks along their streets. None the less, in both cases a judgment is formed about the anticipated value of the public service to be provided in relation to the anticipated cost. The benefit principle merely holds that expenditure decisions should reflect individual evaluations.

How those decisions might come to reflect those evaluations, or the degree to which they might do so, is a complex matter that is addressed by much of the literature on public choice.[8] In short, different political and fiscal rules that set the framework within which fiscal choices are made will influence the extent to which those choices are consistent with the benefit principle. Knut Wicksell advanced one set of proposals for implementing the benefit principle. Public choice scholars have in recent years examined the properties of different forms of voting in terms of the ability of those rules to lead to outcomes that reflect individual evaluations for public services.[9] Regardless of the particular details of those various scholarly contributions, the main point to note is that the benefit principle can be applied to the entire range of governmental activities, once it is realized that this principle can be approached from a procedural instead of a substantative or computational perspective.

4 USER CHARGES, IN PRINCIPLE AND IN PRACTICE

In these days of increased resistance to taxation, increasing attention is being given to 'user charges' as a way that governments can raise revenues without violating pledges not to increase taxes. To a substantial extent user charges are perceived as being largely voluntary, while taxes are presumed to be compulsory, hence a greater use of charges would seem to reduce the range over which compulsion is practised. There might thus seem to be a categorical distinction between taxes and charges as methods of government finance.

While such a categorical distinction is accepted by many, that acceptance cannot be based facilely on the claim that charges are voluntary payments while taxes are compulsory extractions, for the amount of taxes that people pay is to some extent voluntary. People can affect the amount of cigarette tax or alcohol tax they pay by varying the amount of those products they buy. Income tax liability can likewise be affected by varying the amount of labour supplied. Alternatively, there may be little or no practical alternative to paying user fees. While a fee for a driver's licence can be avoided by choosing not to drive, this is a practical option for precious few people. It might well be easier to avoid paying cigarette taxes or income taxes than to avoid fees for driver's licences.

The possible categorical distinction between charges and taxes might seem rather to rest on the point that charges involve a direct connection between making a payment and receiving a service from government. A charge placed upon cattle producers to finance the grading of beef might be one such illustration, and a 'tax' on gasoline earmarked to build and maintain highways might serve as another such illustration. In these cases, and in others that could be depicted, the people who pay the charge or the earmarked tax are the same people who receive the service that the revenues generated are used to supply.

With tax finance there is no direct connection between personal tax payments and services received in return. Tax revenues go into a general fund, appropriations from which are made according to a process that makes no effort to connect the two sides of the budgetary process. Payments made under an income tax or a cigarette tax simply form part of a general pool of revenues, with the services to be financed by those revenues determined within an appropriations process that is unconnected with the revenue-raising process.

User charges might thus seem to represent an effort to place government more directly and immediately on a contractual footing than might characterize general-fund financing. In this way charges could represent a programme to implement more fully the benefit principle of public finance, through getting people to pay for the services they receive from government. After all, if the state is viewed, normatively, as simply a nexus of contractual relationships among inhabitants, people should pay for government only to the extent to which it is agreeable to them, which, in turn, produces some direct link between people's tax payments and their evaluations of the services government provides. Indeed, there is certainly strong argument in support of the proposition advanced by Richard Epstein that something like the benefit principle was incorporated into the American constitutional order.[10]

But no matter how strong such arguments might be, merely to articulate them does nothing to assure that those principles actually characterize contemporary fiscal processes. The fiscal choices that emerge within democratic regimes may diverge sharply from the characterizations that would seem to be implied by the benefit principle. A tax on beef where the revenues are used to finance the inspection and grading of beef may well receive the approval of beef producers and consumers and thus be consistent with the benefit principle, but a tax on beef with the proceeds earmarked to finance coronary bypass operations might also pass political muster, perhaps even accompanied by supporting arguments about beef and cholesterol, and yet violate the benefit principle severely.

Actual fiscal practice may diverge significantly from the dictates of the benefit principle, as the remaining chapters in this book explore along several dimensions. Merely to advocate user charges, accompanied by claims that those charges truly represent a network of contractual relationships among citizens, with government acting merely as an agent acting on behalf of the common interest of all of those citizens, is not itself evidence of the veracity of that advocacy or those claims.

5 EARMARKED TAXES, IN PRINCIPLE AND IN PRACTICE

The same possible divergence between principle and practice holds for the use of earmarked tax revenues to finance particular government services. The common justification for tax earmarking in place of general-fund financing is that earmarking serves to concentrate the cost of public services on particular groups of beneficiaries. The earmarking of revenues from a tax on gasoline to finance highways is an oft-cited example of how earmarked taxation can create a kind of quasi-pricing of governmental services.

To be sure, some people have suggested that the technology now exists to price highways directly, through a system of transmitters and receivers embedded in roads and installed in cars. Such a system would allow highways to be priced directly to individual users according to their usage, and could even vary the charge according to the time of day. But absent such direct charges, earmarked gasoline taxes can be seen as a form of quasi-charge, for the consumption of gasoline is positively correlated with the use of highway services: it is generally accurate to say that people who consume more gasoline also make greater use of highways. Hence, the earmarking of revenues from a tax on gasoline to finance highways can be seen, alternatively, as a form of charging users for their consumption.

Granted, this indirect form of quasi-charging would not operate identically to direct charging. For one thing, a gasoline tax cannot take into account the time of day when highway consumption takes place, whereas direct charging could vary with the time of day, and such peak-load pricing would in turn economize on the use of highways, lowering congestion in the process. A gasoline tax cannot create variations that might come about because of differences in the costliness of different roads and highways. None the less, absent direct charging, it is surely reasonable to think of a gasoline tax, with the revenues earmarked for highways, as an indirect form of user charging, as distinct from a tax that is used to provide revenues for a general fund that will be spent through some appropriations process.

But what if some of those tax revenues were used not for highways but to subsidize mass transit in urban areas? The analogue with user pricing surely becomes less clear, though it cannot be said with certainty that such an analogue disappears. Such a diversion of revenues from a gasoline tax would seem on the surface to represent the imposition of a tax on consumers of gasoline (users of highways) to subsidize those who use mass transit instead. Rather than illustrating the benefit principle in operation, this portion of the gasoline tax would illustrate instead a process of income redistribution through government, in sharp contradiction to the spirit of the benefit principle.

None the less, it is possible to argue, to the contrary, that shifting some gas tax revenues to the provision of mass transit falls within the spirit of the benefit principle. What would be necessary in this case would be to argue that the provision of mass transit is a more economical approach to reducing highway congestion than is the expansion of highways, at least over some ranges and margins of choice. In other words, the users of highways would be better off as a result of some diversion of gas tax revenues to mass transit than they would be if those revenues were spent on highways.

Anything can be rationalized, of course, but there is a test of whether or not a particular rationalization is correct. This test is *agreement* among the taxpayers. If the diversion of gas tax revenues to the provision of mass transit is consistent with the benefit principle, highway users themselves will approve that diversion: a proposal to divert such revenues will secure a consensus among those who pay gasoline taxes. But should such diversion fail to command such a consensus the rationalization would have to be rejected and the diversion would have to be explained alternatively as part of a political process of income redistribution from losing groups of people (highway users) to winning groups (mass transit users).

One particularly interesting case arose in California in a referendum that passed in November 1988. This referendum proposed to increase the cigarette tax by 25 cents per pack and to earmark those revenues for a variety of educational and medical programmes. Could this referendum be seen as one particular implementation of the benefit principle, in which people agree to tax themselves to finance services they value? The two-thirds majority the referendum commanded might seem to indicate a fairly high degree of consensus for the programme, which would suggest the tax could reasonably be viewed instead as a quasi-user charge.

However, the degree of support for the tax was similar to the proportion of non-smokers in the population (around 30 per cent of adult Americans smoke), and this suggests the programme could be seen alternatively as a form of income redistribution, in which a majority voted to award benefits to itself, financed by tax burdens it chose to impose on a minority. The ultimate test of whether a particular programme of tax earmarking is properly viewed as an indirect form of user charging is whether those who pay the taxes approve of the programme. Suppose it were found that the preponderant number of people who buy gasoline support gasoline taxes earmarked for highways, while the preponderant number of smokers opposed cigarette taxes earmarked for educational materials in public schools. It could thus be concluded that the gasoline tax operates much as a user charge, but that the cigarette tax violates the benefit principle and represents instead wealth redistribution through political processes.

6 WELFARE ECONOMICS, PUBLIC CHOICE, AND CONSTITUTIONAL ORDER

For the most part, the analysis of taxation has has been pursued from within the normative perspective of welfare economics. Only recently have economists begun to analyse taxation in terms of positive theories of collective action and fiscal politics. And when this is done what often emerges is a realization that actual fiscal outcomes diverge significantly from the characterizations of normative analysis. The standard justifications for user charges and earmarked taxes may have little to do with the actual operation of such practices.

Yet the degree of correspondence between principle and practice is itself a variable that can be influenced by the constitutional rules within which political processes operate. This point was, as noted earlier, central to Knut Wicksell's seminal work on democracy, public finance, and constitutional order. In short, the more fully constitutional rules operate to require the consent of taxpayers, such as is envisioned by the benefit principle and as is justified by arguments for user charges and earmarked taxes, the more closely principle and practice will correspond. Regardless of particular analytical details, the incorporation of public choice insights into a normative concern with tax policy in a democratic political order places in the foreground the constitutional framework within which political and fiscal choices are made.

NOTES

1 For a valuable survey of both the benefit and the ability-to-pay approaches to fiscal principle, see Musgrave (1959: 61–115). And in referring to the literature 'subsequent' to Smith, I would certainly not want to leave the impression that the articulation of maxims of taxation began with Smith. For it did not, as Musgrave explains. For a careful survey of ideas on this topic, see Mann (1937).
2 These perspectives are contrasted in Wagner (1985).

3 This approach characterizes the approach to income redistribution taken by the literature on 'Pareto optimal redistribution', initiated by Hochman and Rodgers (1969).

4 It is also true that there are political incentives to create constitutional rules that solidify particular political positions and interests, thereby giving constitutional protection to favoured positions.

5 For a significant effort to recast welfare economics in terms of a commitment to liberalism, see Rowley and Peacock (1975).

6 Knut Wicksell's work became pivotal in the subsequent development of constitutional economics, initiated in Buchanan and Tullock (1962) and summarized in Buchanan (1987).

7 Brubaker (1975) uses the term 'forced riding', but 'carrying' seems more apt than 'riding'.

8 For a thorough survey of this scholarship, see Mueller (1989).

9 See, for instance, the literature on demand-revealing processes, the essential ideas behind which are laid out in Tideman and Tullock (1976).

10 See Richard Epstein (1985). Essentially the same argument is advanced in Vincent Ostrom (1987). The British sources of this perspective are examined in, among other sources, Bernard Bailyn (1968) and Arthur Hogue (1966).

REFERENCES

Bailyn, B. *The Ideological Origins of the American Revolution.* Cambridge: Harvard University Press, 1968.

Brubaker, E.R. 'Free rider, Free revelation, or golden rule?' *Journal of Law and Economics* 18 (April 1975): 147–61.

Buchanan, J.M. 'The constitution of economic policy'. *American Economic Review* 77 (June 1987): 243–50.

Buchanan, J.M., and Tullock, G. *The Calculus of Consent.* Ann Arbor: University of Michigan Press, 1962.

Epstein, R.A. *Takings: Private Property and the Power of Eminent Domain.* Cambridge: Harvard University Press, 1985.

Hochman, H.M. and Rodgers, J.D. 'Pareto optimal redistribution'. *American Economic Review* 59 (September 1969): 542–57.

Hogue, A.R. *Origins of the Common Law.* Bloomington: Indiana University Press, 1966.

Mann, F.K. *Steuerpolitische Ideale.* Jena: Gustav Fischer, 1937.

Mueller, D.C. *Public Choice,* 2nd ed. New York: Cambridge University Press, 1989.

Musgrave, R.A. *The Theory of Public Finance.* New York: McGraw-Hill, 1959.

Ostrom, V. *The Political Theory of a Compound Republic: Designing the American Experiment,* 2nd ed. Lincoln: University of Nebraska Press, 1987.

Rowley, C.K. and Peacock, A.T. *Welfare Economics: A Liberal Restatement.* New York: John Wiley, 1975.

Tideman, T.N. and Tullock, G. 'A new and superior process for making social choices.' *Journal of Political Economy* 84 (December 1976): 1145–59.

Wagner, R.E. 'Normative and Positive Foundations of Tax Reform'. *Cato Journal* 5 (Fall 1985): 385–99.

Wicksell, K. *Finanztheorie Untersuchungen.* Jena: Gustav Fischer, 1896.

2 The fiscal significance of user charges and earmarked taxes

A survey

Gary M. Anderson

'User fees' are the fiscal panacea of the 1990s. The employment of 'non-tax revenue enhancement' has become popular with politicians of both major parties as a potential cure for the federal deficit, which sometimes refers more generally to the goal of somehow spending *more* while taxing *less* – meaning less tax *revenue*, not merely lower tax *rates*. For many years, the idea that revenue can *increase* even though 'taxes' remain the same or even *decrease*, received relatively little attention from politicians. After the late 1980s this neglect suddenly ended.

The new-found enthusiasm for user fees is not limited to politicians. A Fortune 500/CNN Moneyline survey in December 1988 of 225 chief executive officers found that 66 per cent favour increasing user fees as a means for reducing the federal budget deficit; if tax increases were necessary the CEOs preferred tax increases that would affect smokers, drinkers, drivers, and well-to-do Social Security recipients – in other words, those excise taxes which most closely resemble (and are some-times called) user fees.[1] Another recent article claims that surveys of taxpayers have shown that local voters much prefer special fees to general tax increases as devices to fund local government expenditures.[2]

A *Los Angeles Times* poll in November 1987 found that 64 per cent of voters polled opposed raising taxes to cut the federal deficit.[3] The notion that revenue can somehow be increased without raising taxes is therefore very attractive. On the other hand, the idea of earmarking specific tax revenues to 'worthy' causes has widespread appeal. A Gallup poll taken in May 1989 found that more than 80 per cent of respondents in California believed that the revenues from Proposition 99 tax increases on cigarettes should be earmarked to health care.[4]

User charges have been especially popular among conservatives and advocates of the 'privatization' of government services. Savas (1982: 131–2) endorses the replacement of 'taxes' by 'user fees', because the latter can 'reveal fully the true cost of service, thereby creating the . . .

opportunity of making comparisons and devising alternatives'. Both the Reagan Administration and now the Bush Administration have endorsed the use of user charges as a revenue-raising device which eliminates the need for new taxes.

The purpose here is to examine the details of this apparent shift towards user fees as a means of raising government revenue. The replacement of taxes with fees has many advocates, but it is difficult to define precisely just what such advocacy implies – the difference between a 'user fee' and a simple 'tax' is shrouded in murk, if not mystery. An examination of the actual practice of governments which employ user fees is especially revealing. American government has demonstrated a very 'creative' streak in its efforts to raise new revenues by way of user fees. In fact, some of the relevant users would be surprised that they were receiving any 'benefits', and might have assumed that they were actually paying 'fines'. The political economy of contemporary user fees requires an excursion through the looking glass.

The present paper is organized into five sections. Section 1 discusses the theory of user fees and considers the problems associated with distinguishing fees from taxes, specifically earmarked and otherwise. Section 2 reviews the fiscal significance of user charges and specifically earmarked taxes in the United States at the federal, state, and local levels, and discusses some examples of similar measures in other countries. Section 3 provides a more detailed look at various selected user fees in actual practice in the United States. Section 4 explores some proposed, but so-far unimplemented, charges which 'stretch the envelope' of the user-fee paradigm. Finally, Section 5 summarizes and concludes the argument.

1   A TAXONOMY OF FISCAL DEVICES: USER FEES AND TAXES COMPARED

Curiously, the precise difference between a 'user fee' and a 'tax' is difficult to discern. Many public finance texts argue in favour of 'user charge' finance on various grounds, but the exact difference between 'fees' and 'taxes' is left unclear. Textbook discussions traditionally refer to the close temporal connection between the collection of the fee and the disbursement of the service, and to the earmarking of the revenues generated by the user charges to the provision of the service upon which the charge is based. User fees are said to be more efficient if they more closely resemble market prices, in such a way that the marginal benefit of using the service is equal to the marginal cost of providing it. User fees promote economic efficiency by inducing appropriate marginal decisions on the part of consumers of public goods. Efficient user charges will equal the marginal cost of providing the service to the consumer.[5]

To the extent that user fees are to be distinguished by these characteristics – i.e., identifiable beneficiaries paying for the marginal cost of providing the benefit – the difference between taxes and user fees would be left reasonably clear. A 'pure user fee' is simply a charge by a government agency in exchange for the goods that the agency provides to consumers; an efficient pure user fee would equal the marginal cost of the service provision. However, various economists have insisted that some deviations from marginal cost pricing can be justified if externalities are present, or perhaps when asymmetric information renders direct transfers infeasible.[6] Recent articles by Bird and Slack (1983) and Krashinsky (1981) argue that deviations from strict marginal cost pricing can represent a 'second-best' solution for some distributional goal in cases where the donor lacks information about the amount of resources an individual donee requires to attain some 'minimum' level of well-being.[7] Singh and Thomas (1986) argue that when the federal government partially funds some local project which generates positive externalities outside the local community, a user charge requirement may provide the incentive for the local authority to behave efficiently.[8]

Theoretically, the notion that external benefits and/or costs should be taken into account when establishing the level of user charges has great merit. Unfortunately, implementing this sensible-sounding notion runs into an enormous problem. Externalities are, in effect, exchanges which *did not actually happen*. Therefore, 'estimates' of externalities are necessarily based on guesswork. While the concept is theoretically sensible it fails to provide a firm ground for real estimation. If user charges are to be set at an 'efficient' level in the presence of externalities, we must first estimate the value of those externalities.

Methodological quibbles aside, governments typically sidestep the issue altogether. Although some real-world user fees pay lip-service to the presence of some sorts of 'externalities', in fact the charges are set without any reference to *any* calculation of the actual extent of the externalities. Real-world user fees, like taxes, are determined as the result of a political process (whether in the legislature or at the bureaucratic level), and rarely – if ever – even by reference to estimates of the *marginal costs* of providing the relevant services

Despite these difficulties (both theoretical and political), there is a considerable economic literature devoted to arguing for user fees on efficiency grounds. Economists are first and foremost price theorists, and since prices are such relatively efficient rationing devices it is not surprising that, where feasible, economists tend to favour 'price-like' user fees over taxes. For example, Small and Winston maintain that efficiency in highway infrastructure investment requires the 'immediate adoption of user charges based on the short run marginal cost of highway wear'.[9] A vast number of additional articles make similar arguments for various forms of user fee. Pechman (see Klott 1987) questions whether there is any economically important difference between a user fee and an excise tax. Economics textbooks typically avoid the issue of the precise distinction (if any). Both forms of revenue collection require payment at a specific point-of-purchase; both can be avoided to the extent that the consumer is free to choose other consumption options (and are therefore 'voluntary payments'); and both payment devices may be a primary (or even the sole) source of revenue used to cover the costs of providing specific relevant 'services'. For example, an excise tax on cigarettes might be described as a user fee imposed on smokers, who are defined to be 'users' of government-subsidized health-care services to which the 'tax' is earmarked.

However, if *excise taxes* can be considered user fees then why not sales taxes more generally? If one argues that a specific excise imposed on cigarettes is a user fee because cigarette smoking purportedly makes smokers sick, and that they consequently impose a financial burden on government, similar arguments are available in principle for sales taxes on many other kinds of goods – for example, on restaurant meals (which often tend to be fatty and unhealthy), or automobile sales (which lead to more costly car accidents), etc. Since in 1985, 20.8 per cent of revenues at all levels of government was collected from sales and gross receipts taxes, the potential domain for user fees is enormous.[10] Pechman does not explain why he does not regard his arguments as applicable beyond specific excise taxes.

The 'earmarking' of taxes refers to the specific designation of funds to some particular end use. This is to be contrasted with general fund financing, which involves the expenditure of revenues collected in terms of consolidated receipts.[11] The restriction of expenditures from revenues collected from a gasoline tax to highway construction would be an example of earmarking. The earmarked tax is claimed to be *like* a user charge, in that beneficiaries of the governmentally provided good or service are required to pay a tax designed to partially reimburse government for the costs of provision, but is sometimes referred to as a 'proxy' for user charges, a 'second-best' solution.[12]

The problem is that precise criteria for the distinction between user fees and earmarked taxes have not been defined, let alone generally accepted. The use of both is usually justified according to the 'benefits principle', the notion that efficiency is improved to the extent that the financing of public goods is borne by those who actually receive the benefits from the expenditure. But with the relatively minor exceptions of charges for admission to certain public parks, library fines, and other examples of charges which closely approximate market prices for services, few governmentally imposed 'charges' link the rate charged to the actual marginal cost of providing the service. Most charges commonly referred to as 'user fees' would, on this ground alone, be considered a variety of 'earmarked taxes'. (I will explore this ambiguity in detail in Section 3.) As it happens, in the United States 'earmarked taxes' is a term rarely used by governments to describe revenue collection devices; 'user fees' has become the catch-all term used to refer to all cases where there is some (alleged) link between the beneficiaries of the services provided and the source of the funding. Therefore, in the first place, the precise difference between a 'user fee' and an 'earmarked tax' is poorly defined; and, second, the former term has usurped the latter in actual use by politicians and officials.

A final problem that rarely receives much attention is the relationship between the user fee as a price and the monopoly nature of much governmental service production. For example, many local governments collect user fees in the form of water rates and utility charges, which result from the fact that, by law, those local governments hold a pure monopoly in the production of those goods within the given jurisdiction. Thus, many user fees are charges imposed by a monopoly; we would ordinarily expect that a profit-maximizing monopolist would extract monopoly rent from consumers by charging higher prices, and supplying a lower quantity of the good or service, than would a competitive industry.

However, in typical cases consumers face another problem as well. Governments are *not* profit-maximizing firms, and are notorious for providing goods and services inefficiently by comparison with private suppliers. In other words, this particular monopolist's cost curves are likely to be significantly *higher* than those in a profit-maximizing, privately owned and operated industry. In short, when the government charges a consumer a user fee in many cases it is simply making an offer the consumer cannot refuse. Even if, for some reason, the government charges a user fee limited to the amount of the marginal cost of providing the service, this marginal cost may be much higher than would have been the case if the service was privately provided, and not a governmental monopoly.

Regardless of these seemingly daunting conceptual problems, the redefinition of excise taxes as 'user fees' or at least 'like' user fees is becoming increasingly popular among advocates of excise tax increases. The basic rationale would seem to be that if an excise tax (for example, on cigarettes or beer) can be defined as a 'user charge' designed to compensate government for additional costs, such as health care expenditures purportedly caused by the consumption of the goods subject to the 'tax/charge', voters who are not actually consumers of the goods in question will be more likely to support increased rates.

For example, in November 1988 California voters passed Proposition 99, a cigarette tax increase measure that specifically links revenues to health-care projects, and was widely labelled to be a 'user fee' imposed on smokers. Recent advocates of increases in federal taxes on beer and other alcoholic beverages have argued that such excise taxes are really user fees.

The basic idea that 'sin taxes' really represent user charges has been accepted with few reservations in the economics literature. For example, a recent article by Phelps and Cook (1988) argues that taxes on alcoholic beverages are 'user fees' because they increase highway safety and reimburse government for part of the expense supposedly caused by drunk drivers (for example, the hospital costs of drivers on welfare).[13]

If the distinction between a 'user fee' and a 'tax' is somewhat ambiguous in the economics literature, the real difference becomes even more problematic in the realm of actual practice by government. Take, for example, a highway toll, a typical user charge. Motorists who wish to drive along a particular stretch of highway must pay a toll designed to partially defray the expense of building and operating the road. This resembles a market price insofar as the individual paying the fee has voluntarily chosen to consume the service in question. However, unlike a market price, the user charge represents the outcome of a political process and most likely bears little relationship to the marginal benefit associated with each use, nor is it set by a profit-maximizing firm with an incentive to establish an economically efficient level of output.

Furthermore, the highway is a public monopoly, and quite possibly motorists face very poor substitutes; there may be no competing roads connecting the point of departure to the destination, or at least the available alternatives may be poor. In one sense, the user fee is, in part, a charge for provision by government of the 'service' of coercively restricting competition from potential private suppliers (in this case, of highways), a dubious benefit to drivers. It seems to be functionally identical to an excise tax charged to the user of the road. Moreover, in practical fact, a 'user fee' is whatever government says it is.

2 THE RELATIVE IMPORTANCE OF USER FEES AND EARMARKED TAXES

For the federal, state, and local governments taken as a whole, there has been a relative increase in the reliance on non-tax revenue sources in the past twenty-five years. Non-tax revenues represented 17.6 per cent in 1970, 21.8 per cent in 1980, and 24.7 per cent in 1985 (Tax Foundation 1988: 15). Naturally, taxpayer opposition to revenue collection that can be plausibly claimed to be based on something other than tax is slight.

Of the various non-tax revenue sources the largest is 'current charges'. The Tax Foundation defines this to include 'amounts received from the public for performance of specific services benefiting the person charged; includes fees, toll charges, tuition, other reimbursements for current services, gross income of commercial-type activities, etc'. 'Current charges' are, in other words, various forms of user fees. Current charges have grown from 7.9 per cent of total revenue in 1970 to 9.6 per cent in 1985. The 1985 percentage represents $135.496 billion in revenue. Not included under current charges, but probably classifiable as user fees, are receipts from locally operated utilities, payments made to public employee retirement funds, payments made for veteran's life insurance, and revenue from liquor stores owned and operated by state or local governments. Adding these other revenues to current charges produces a figure of 16.9 per cent of total government revenues (Tax Foundation 1988: 15).

Classified as 'taxes' but often defended as 'user fees' (or at least, 'like' user fees) are levies on motor fuel, alcoholic beverages, and tobacco. In 1985 the respective percentages of total revenue accounted for by each of these taxes were 1.8, 0.6, and 0.6 (for a total of 3 per cent).

If (following Pechman) we were to classify all excise taxes as essentially 'user fees' the total across all levels of government would be 19.9 per cent of total revenue collected in 1985. In the limit, tax earmarking will be a perfect substitute for user fees.[14] In fact, the difference between the two possible revenue-raising devices is extremely ambiguous. Most accounts of earmarked taxes imply that such devices rely on the collection of revenues which are not closely linked to the marginal benefits or marginal costs associated with the consumption of specific services provided by government; the taxes are collected from the general group benefiting from the provided service, but do not approximate individual 'prices'. User fees, on the other hand, are 'prices' charged by government to consumers of specific services, which are based on the marginal cost of providing the service. But if, as we noted above, user fees may be taken to reflect other considerations than the marginal cost of providing individual direct beneficiaries with the service (for example, if they take into account 'externalities') those same fiscal charges could also be described as 'earmarked taxes'. Since real-world user fees are rarely, if ever, assigned on the basis of strict marginal cost estimates, such fees and earmarked taxes are generally not clearly distinguishable in practice.

The federal government does not employ the term 'earmarking' in its budget. However, the federal government does earmark some revenue (in effect) by directing certain revenues into various trust funds, from which those funds are later drawn to cover the expenses of particular, designated programmes. For example, the federal gasoline tax is directed into the Highway Trust Fund and is restricted to spending for highway improvement/repair-type purposes.

The largest earmarked tax source in the federal budget, by far, is Social Security. The Old-Age and Survivors Insurance portion, tax revenue estimated for the fiscal year 1990 at $259.615 billion, is the largest part. These taxes (paid by both employees and employers) are unavailable for any other purpose, although the federal government occasionally 'borrows' from the Social Security Trust Fund for limited periods. Disability insurance taxes, the other component, are estimated at $27.035 billion for the fiscal year 1990. The other major trust funds in the federal budget are Highways, Airport, Black Lung Disability, Inland Waterway, Hazardous Substance Response (i.e., 'Superfund'), and Aquatic Resources. These additional trust funds are expected to receive $22.264 billion of designated tax dollars in the fiscal year 1990. Adding this subtotal to the subtotal for Social Security produces a total of $308.914 billion in earmarked tax revenues in the fiscal year 1990 federal budget. This represents 27.7 per cent of total estimated federal revenues for FY 1990.[15]

Governments in many developed countries employ similar user fees as a substitute for regular taxes. Recent studies have examined the systems of highway user charges in Britain and Japan.[16] Member nations in the Organization for Economic Cooperation and Development (including Australia, Canada, New Zealand, Japan, and Western Europe) have aggressively expanded the employment of 'user charges' against polluters.[17] Even governments in less developed countries find user charges an attractive alternative to traditional taxation, in part because administrative costs tend to be relatively low.[18]

If Western Europe is any indication, environmental user fees – so-called 'green taxes' – promise to expand rapidly in the 1990s elsewhere, the United States included. Sweden taxes carbon dioxide emissions (as do Finland and Holland) and nitrous oxide (emitted by large power plants), and plans to tax heavy metal waste discharge. Norway taxes chlorofluorocarbons (CFCs), which are claimed to harm the earth's ozone layer. Denmark has imposed taxes on rubbish produced. In Finland, the 'environmental' taxes and charges represent nearly 1 per cent of total government revenue. West Germany taxes automobiles on the basis of their exhaust fumes and noise. Italy has imposed a 100-lire (8-cents) tax on plastic shopping bags (a kind of 'land-fill use fee') and plans an extensive system of taxes on non-biodegradable industrial waste. Britain, Ireland, France, and Belgium are considering similar kinds of environmental taxes.[19]

3   A SURVEY OF PRESENT AND FUTURE USER FEE SCHEMES

Whatever the economic ambiguities, the *legal* distinction between user fees and taxes was firmly established by the US Supreme Court in a sweeping ruling announced in late April 1989. A coalition of groups (including the US Chamber of Commerce, the National Taxpayers' Association, and the National Association of Manufacturers) had submitted a brief to the Court, in which they argued that the US Constitution does not permit legislators to hide behind bureaucrats or regulators but requires them to pass actual *laws* to impose new taxes. The brief insisted that user fees were a form of disguised taxation which allowed elected politicians to avoid politically unpopular new taxes while at the same time enjoying additional revenues. In response, the US Supreme Court cut the Gordian Knot, ruling unanimously that user fees are not taxes. The opinion, written by Justice Sandra Day O'Connor (*Skinner* v. *Mid-America*, 87–2098), argued that Congress has the responsibility for defining the difference between user fees and taxes.[20] The decision appears to be unambiguous: a user fee is different from a tax, because Congress has decided that the two are different. The challenge to user fees on constitutional grounds was rejected. Newspaper accounts of the decision placed considerable weight on the total revenues which might have been affected by the Court's ruling – $22 billion per annum.[21] As has been the case on many other issues, in this instance the Court may have concluded that practicality (in the form of supposed fiscal necessity) outweighed constitutional technicalities.

The federal agency which has been the most aggressive in promoting, and implementing, user charges as a budgetary supplement is the Department of Transportation (DOT). In the fiscal year 1990 (the last submitted by the Reagan Administration), approximately 75 per cent of the Department of Transportation's total budget was financed from earmarked user fees of various sorts. This percentage represented approximately $18.750 billion in revenues (Cushman 1989: B14 [Local]). The largest single component in this total is the $13.5 billion in revenues from the federal gasoline tax, which is allocated to the Highway Trust Fund. Certain DOT programmes are entirely funded by earmarked user fees. For example, the Federal Pipeline Safety Programme is entirely financed by charges on oil and gas transmission lines ($9 million per annum). The DOT is currently proposing a new railroad user fee (to be borne by the railroad industry) in order to defray the expense of railroad safety programmes (Cushman 1989: B14 [Local]).

In the usual discussion in economics textbooks the assumption is made that in order to have a user fee there must be a 'beneficiary' paying the charge. Actual governmental practice is sometimes based on a different assumption. An excellent example of a user fee in actual practice that imposes charges on individuals who might better be described as *victims* rather than beneficiaries are the fees on imported goods charged by US Customs. These are described as a means of direct payment for Customs services provided to importers, such as inspection, registration, and monitoring of imports and the associated collection of tariffs. These fees are based on the value of the imported goods. As such, they seem economically equivalent to tariffs, with the exception that the revenues collected are earmarked for use by the Customs Service and do not flow into general revenues. It is hard to understand why ordinary tariffs could not just as easily be described as 'user charges', and this objection has been raised at meetings of GATT and has formed the basis for strong objections to the practice from the European Economic Community and other foreign countries that export to the USA. However, similar fees are also charged to *exporters* based on the value of exported goods, in a manner reminiscent of seventeenth-century restrictions on exports in mercantilist England. At present, these charges are quite low – in general, amounting to less than 1 per cent of the estimated value of goods shipped – but since there is no well-defined limit on the value of Customs' 'services' to importers/exporters, there seems to be no well-defined 'ceiling' on the charges either.[22]

Perhaps the latest fashion among advocates of user fees has been to argue for 'charges' to the regulated for the 'benefits' of regulation. For example, the Environmental Protection Agency has recently decided that by reviewing new products for safety it provides a service for which the applicant must pay a user fee. These 'administrative user fees' are collected to recover EPA administrative costs from processing applications. The EPA has also instituted user fees for non-compliance with its pollution decisions, which equal the amount of the estimated excess profit the firm in question supposedly earned by failure to comply, plus a punitive component.[23]

The legal constraints on new user fees appear to be gradually relaxing, making this form of revenue enhancement increasingly attractive to federal agencies. In the course of the previously mentioned April 1989 decision, the US Supreme Court ruled that the Secretary of Transportation had the authority to impose user fees for the purpose of covering the expenses of federal pipeline safety programmes. Previously, the federal regulatory agencies had been restricted to charging user fees only in cases where special benefits were rendered to identifiable entities. The Supreme Court eliminated this restriction and allowed federal agencies to charge user fees in order to recover regulatory costs which were *not* related to specifically identified benefits. In other words, federal agencies can now impose user fees in cases where the benefits exist only in theory and are unmeasured, and where the users are not identifiable individuals or firms.[24]

This decision neatly skirts the most fundamental question involving 'public goods': how do we determine whether the commodity or service being provided by government is a 'good', and how valuable it is to consumers? The users of government regulation (i.e., the regulated firms) have traditionally been assumed to be subject to regulation in order to *constrain their behaviour*, and not for their *benefit*. Thus, government agencies may impose user fees on victims of involuntary transactions. The term 'user fee' has become positively Orwellian.[25] In medieval Europe convicted heretics were forced to pay court costs before they were burned at the stake.[26] Presumably, these were also user fees.

The redefinition of regulatory penalties and fines as 'user fees' is not restricted to the federal level of government. The City of Phoenix, Arizona, conducts an annual User Fee Review which has been the subject of a recent study.[27] Phoenix may be taken as typical of many municipalities in its employment, and definition, of such charges. User fees include such things as charges for publicly provided airline hangers, for the use of public golf courses, tennis courts, and other 'private good'-type services. But it also lists things like 'Building Safety Inspections and Plans Review', a Drinking While Intoxicated Fee (i.e., a fine paid by drunk drivers), 'Engineering Inspection and Plans Review', Business, Liquor, and 'Privilege' (i.e., retailers) licences, the Dog Licence Fee, and Alcohol Permits (allowing the sale of drinks at bars). Most of these services are not 'goods' from the perspective of the individuals making the payments, but presumably 'bads'.

An additional, and rather pure, example of a government regulation user fee is to be found in a plan currently under consideration in Congress to impose fees as a part of new pension-reporting requirements. Under ERISA, employers providing employees with pension benefits are required to file a 'Series 5500' report every year which lists the number of currently covered employees and other pension data. The House Education and Labor Committee would set a fee of $100 for plans covering fewer than 100 employees, rising to $500 for plans with 500 or more employees; the Senate Labor and Human Resources Committee's version would mandate filing fees ranging from $250 to $1000. Further, both Committees have approved provisions that would require employees to pay 'exit fees' of $200 per participant when filing to terminate pension plan coverage.[28] These user fees are to be charged for the 'consumption' of government regulatory functions which are required by law. But if the relevant difference between a user charge and a tax is that the former is directly linked to the receipt of benefits purported to arise from the provision by government of a commodity or service, then such payments would indeed qualify as fees and not taxes.

4   EXPLORING THE OUTER EDGES OF THE ENVELOPE: PROPOSED USER FEES

A bewildering variety of potential new user fees have been suggested. The federal government has been the source of perhaps the most creative proposals – however peculiar many may sound to economists. Some of these proposed charges would appear to be rather ordinary, insofar as readily identifiable direct beneficiaries of various services would be required to pay fees purportedly based on the marginal cost of service provision. But many others would seem to qualify as user fees, as opposed to taxes, only under the US Supreme Court's liberal definition: that a user fee is whatever government says it is. Some of these proposed schemes sound like 'fiscal doublespeak'.

A proposed user fee that generally accords with the usual rationale for charges over taxes is the Department of Transportation's proposed 'user fee' to be attached to the purchase of licences to boaters. The reasoning behind this particular fee is that the Coast Guard, an agency under the jurisdiction of the Department of Transportation, provides protection to boaters in general, and that those beneficiaries should be made to pay for those benefits. Neither the DOT nor anyone else has considered any device designed to determine exactly what 'benefit' is received by each individual boater each year; this is probably just as well, because beyond the competitive prices voluntarily paid in the marketplace there is no direct metric for establishing the value of such benefits. The most recent version of this proposed fee would charge all boaters a flat $25 per annum, to be allocated by the Department of Transportation for boating-related services.[29] The actual cost of providing services to individual boaters would not be considered. Still, it seems reasonable to argue that most boaters enjoy some positive value from Coast Guard protection, even if the most careful and responsible boaters enjoy the least (i.e., they will avoid dangerous situations in the first place), so such a user fee is in closer accordance with the benefit principle than many other payment schemes (for example, placing the tax burden for Coast Guard protection of boaters on, say, Iowa farmers). But, on the other hand, if such a revenue collection scheme is to be regarded as a user fee rather than just a tax then many other revenue devices which have traditionally been regarded as simple taxes might just as easily be described as charges, too. For example, since a proportion of personal income tax revenues goes to defray the cost of national defence, and all income taxpayers benefit (to some extent) from national defence, is the income tax not a user fee? The Department of Transportation's plan to impose a user fee on boaters was narrowly defeated in Congress in July 1989, but is likely to be reintroduced.[30]

Some proposed user fees are based on the weakest possible links between 'service' and 'charges'. In the example of a fee on boaters discussed previously it at least seems reasonable to claim that most boaters *do* benefit to some measurable extent from the services in question, even though the proposed fee bears no relationship to any measure of the actual marginal costs of providing the service to particular individuals. But other schemes even abandon the connection between the fee and benefit altogether.

An interesting example of this abandonment of any link between payment and benefit involves a Federal Communications Commission licence sale user fee, proposed in 1987 by Senator Ernest Hollings (D-South Carolina). Since 1923 the federal government has claimed that the airwaves are a public resource which fall under the jurisdiction of the national government. Private radio and TV broadcasters may 'rent' selected portions of the public airwaves, by purchasing licences from the FCC for particular frequencies. Given that the number of legally usable frequencies has been fixed, the total number of licences available is also fixed. In extraordinary circumstances the FCC can legally revoke licences from commercial users, but this has occurred only rarely. Practically speaking, if a new entrant into the broadcasting industry desires to obtain a licence for use of a particular broadcast frequency, that firm must purchase an existing licence from an existing broadcaster. In other words, the Federal government has 'nationalized' the airwaves, and has artificially restricted the total number of airwaves available for broadcasting use.

Senator Hollings proposed that every time a business with an FCC licence is sold the seller must pay a user fee based on the sale price of the business-plus-licence. Because FCC licences cannot legally be sold, broadcasting industry transactions normally take the form of the sale of a bundle consisting of a broadcasting station and its equipment *including* the operating licence – the last usually constituting by far the most valuable component part of the package. The businesses subject to this fee would include cellular radio and paging services, microwave and satellite services, and TV and radio broadcasters.[31]

For most sellers, the fee would be 2 per cent of the resale price. The fee would rise to 4 per cent in cases where the seller had held the property for less than three years. This rising fee schedule was justified on the grounds that it would help to limit the 'trafficking' in licences, and restrict the 'absentee landlordism' that 'hurts the public interest'. Newspaper accounts at the time failed to explain the exact reasoning behind these claims. The conventional rationale offered for nationalized airwaves involves the claim that frequencies are a 'common property resource', and therefore the 'owner' (i.e., the public, represented by government) will act to protect 'its' interests from malfeasance on the part of the 'users' (i.e., the broadcasters). The federal regulation of the airwaves is truly an island of pure socialism in the American market economy.

The fees were intended to go into a Public Broadcasting Trust Fund, which would then direct the revenues towards defraying the expenses of the Corporation for Public Broadcasting (Rockefeller 1987). Obviously, if the user fee itself represented direct payment for some service, regulatory or otherwise, then there should be no 'surplus' available for a trust fund. But since legally a user fee is whatever Congress says it is, this paradox is of solely intellectual interest.

This scheme was narrowly avoided in July 1989, when both Houses agreed to defer the idea for the time being. The principal source of opposition was based on objections to the Public Broadcasting Trust Fund aspect.[32] The really peculiar aspect of the proposed fee – that no service was being provided and that the individuals liable to pay the fee were really being fined, not charged for the cost of providing them with any benefit – was ignored.

Many recent proposed user fees seem indistinguishable from fiscal instruments which have traditionally been called 'taxes'. These fees tend, upon closer examination, to resolve into simple coercive levies, and to bear little resemblance to market prices arising from voluntary transactions. But since user fees seem more politically palatable to the electorate than 'new taxes', such relabelling has become extremely popular.

For example, the Department of Transportation proposed a $1 user fee per ticket for passengers on airlines and cruise ships taking international trips. The service that the customer was to be paying for with the fee was not explained, and the charge would appear to be identical in form to the existing federal excise tax on air tickets.[33]

A similar user fee was proposed in 1986, ostensibly to aid airline inspection, which would have charged each traveller entering the United States $5. Curiously, the inspection this fee would have been imposed to cover was inspection of the baggage of *outgoing* travellers; the baggage of disembarking passengers travelling *to* the USA is not subject to inspection upon arrival. This particular fee was never actually imposed, although it would appear that the peculiar employment of the term 'user fee' for a fee imposed only on *non-users* of the service (i.e., the baggage inspection) was not itself found to be objectionable.[34]

However attractive the concept of user fees is to vote-maximizing politicians by comparison with (new) taxes, more attractive still is the idea of a 'free lunch': providing voters with benefits in cases where the cost of those benefits is sufficiently small to hide elsewhere in the federal budget. Ironically, some of the potential user fees which seem least popular politically involve examples which most economists would recognize as textbook illustrations of what user fees are *supposed* to be.

A case in point is the user charges which were briefly imposed on tourist visitors to the Statue of Liberty. According to an April 1987 newspaper account, 'the Senate indignantly told the Reagan Administration to take its dollar sign off of the Statue of Liberty', and voted to revoke the $1-per-person fee that had been instituted by the National Park Service in February 1987 to help cover costs of maintenance at the Statue.

The week before, the House of Representatives passed broader legislation (subsequently approved by the Senate) prohibiting entrance fees at all national parks and monuments for which admission had not been charged in the past. Again, the rhetoric emphasized the 'priceless' nature of our nation's heritage, and so on.[35] The Park Service had expressed concern about the possibility that charging user fees for park admission might decrease park attendance, a predictable concern given the relationship between the Park Service annual budget and attendance figures.[36]

This is an example of a peculiar fact: the kinds of user fee economists would normally think of as representing models of efficient pricing are usually those most strenuously opposed by politicians and bureaucrats. From the perspective of the latter groups, the primary economic 'virtue' of such forms of user fee – i.e., that the charges are voluntarily paid by clearly identifiable individual beneficiaries, and are therefore analogous to positive market prices – is simultaneously a major defect. This is because the demand curves of consumers for such publicly provided goods (which may or may not have some 'public' goods characteristics) *slope downwards*. The demand curves for many such goods, like library books and visits to national parks, are highly elastic (consumers confront many close substitutes in the marketplace). Charge a positive price, regardless of whether it is below marginal cost, and the quantity demanded will decrease to some extent. Forcing consumers to pay the marginal cost of the provided service would be efficient, *ceteris paribus*. But the jobs and salaries of park rangers, librarians, and many other public employees who actually produce the relevant services are a function of attendance figures – the number of bodies passing through the park gates or checking out books, etc. Hence, it is a curious fact, however predictable, that many public librarians continue to oppose vigorously the implementation of user fees in those domains where economists would argue most strongly for them.[37]

However, the most peculiar user fee/earmarking schemes seem to grow up around cigarette taxation. For some reason, the allocation of tax revenues collected from smokers amounts to the 'Twilight Zone' of tax designation: fiscal opportunism is completely unrestrained by the absence of plausible rationalization. California's Proposition 99 is probably the leading example of a cigarette tax earmarked to a particular form of spending (in this case, 'health' related). Proposition 99 was designed to earmark its revenues to such 'tobacco-related' programmes as cancer research, medical care for alleged smoking-related diseases, and anti-smoking education. Obviously, cancer research benefits cancer patients generally, non-smokers and smokers alike; diseases of smokers may, or may not, be caused by cigarettes; and anti-smoking campaigns do not directly benefit smokers. Thus, even if Proposition 99 worked as originally advertised, it would constitute a dubious 'user fee.' But, in fact, Proposition 99 revenues have yet to be spent for the ostensible 'smoking-related' purposes; in October 1989, the Governor signed a bill allocating Proposition 99 funds for use in subsidizing hospital trauma care (an allocation completely unrelated to illnesses claimed to be smoking related).[38]

But for all the attention Proposition 99 has received, it is far from the high end of the creativity scale. In October 1988, Senator Warren Rudman (R-New Hampshire) proposed a 2-cent-per-pack increase in the federal cigarette excise tax in order to help fund the War on Drugs. Although the measure was defeated it is interesting to note that it contained no explanation of any purported connection between the revenue source and the spending goal.[39] An Indiana law earmarks revenues from a portion of the state cigarette tax to subsidized day-care for school-age children. The scheme, which provides about $600 thousand a year to day-care, is not based on any argument that the revenue source and the spending goal are in any way related. (Indiana is currently considering a similar earmarked tax on liquor to supplement the revenue spent on day-care.)[40] Finally, the city of Chicago earmarks a portion of its cigarette tax revenues to aid for the homeless. Smokers are not alleged to be destroying the housing stock, nor is any other argument apparently offered to justify the strange link between the tax and the spending goal.[41]

5 CONCLUSION

User fees are an important contributor to government revenue in the United States and seem to be popular with both voters and politicians. Both liberals, who believe that the consumers of certain goods (for example, cigarettes and alcoholic beverages) should pay for the 'social costs' their behaviour purportedly imposes, and conservatives, who argue that involuntary taxes are inferior to voluntary charges as a revenue device, agree that user fees should be more extensively utilized by government.

Despite the growing popularity of user fees as a revenue-raising device across all levels of government in the United States, the precise difference between such charges and *taxes* is left dangling in the realm of public finance theory, and becomes virtually unfathomable in the realm of public policy. In practice, the term user fee generally describes a source of government revenue which is claimed to have some, perhaps only vague, relationship to the cost of providing the 'service' to the 'user'. But as we showed above, many 'users' required to pay fees would object to being classified as 'beneficiaries' at all, and would almost certainly regard themselves as 'victims' instead.

Eventually, the semantical aspects of the use of the term 'user fee' – i.e., the problems associated with distinguishing fees from 'taxes' – will become more widely appreciated by the general public, and support for fees based on 'fiscal illusion' (the idea that 'good' fees and 'bad' taxes are intrinsically different) will rapidly erode. But in the meantime, the redefinition of yesterday's taxes as tomorrow's 'user fees' will continue to be a popular political pastime.

NOTES

1 See Kirkpatrick (1989). The CEOs indicated that they viewed user fees as a superior alternative to raising capital gains tax, corporate income taxes, and personal income taxes for the purpose of closing the deficit.

2 See Novack (1988). The article argues that state and local taxpayers are increasingly sympathetic to the use of user fees to cover the costs of government activity, and that in many cases the same fiscal devices which have traditionally been referred to as 'taxes' have achieved better acceptance after being relabelled 'charges'.

3 See Skelton (1987).

4 See Spiegel (1989).

5 For example, see Stiglitz (1988: 126).

6 See Singh and Thomas (1986).

7 See Bird and Slack (1981).

8 See Bird and Slack (1981).

9 See Small and Winston (1986: 168).

10 See ACIR (1989: 38).

11 See Teja (1988: 523).

12 See Teja (1988: 527).

13 See Phelps and Cook (1988). Incidentally, the article maintains that current levels of alcohol taxation are inefficient because they are *too low*.

14 See Wagner (1983: 161) for a discussion.

15 Calculated from data provided in OMB (1989).

16 For Britain, see Newbery (1988); for Japan see Fujii (1989).

17 See Barde (1989).

18 For example, Kenya and Peru both rely on user fees to finance the provision of government health care, and have been the subjects of recent studies. See Ellis (1987) on Kenya; and Gertler and Sanderson (1987) on Peru.

19 See *The Economist* (1990: 47).

20 The Court was ruling on an appeal of a district court decision made in Oklahoma during 1988. See Savage (1989: 4).

21 See Savage (1989: 4).

22 See *Wall Street Journal*, 24 November 1987: 44; 'Customs User Fees Cause Global Furor', *Journal of Commerce and Commercial Exchange* 369, 22 August 1986: 1A; and 'Customs Fees Called Threat to US Exports', *Journal of Commerce and Commercial Exchange* 381, 14 August 1989: 38.

23 See 'Environmental User Fees', *Regulation* 12, 1 (1988): 4–5. The article argues that the EPA user fees are set 'incorrectly', and should equal the cost of 'environmental damage' resulting from non-compliance. The problem of how, exactly, to measure the value of 'environmental damage' is not addressed.

24 See Norris (1989).

25 The modern economic literature on regulation suggests that, in many cases, incumbent firms *do* benefit from industry regulation because that government activity serves to organize and maintain a *cartel* amongst those firms. Assuming a public choice model of government regulation, describing charges imposed on regulated firms for purposes of covering the cost of regulation makes a kind of sense: the recipients of cartel rents are paying for the governmental cartel management services. However, employees of

federal regulatory agencies normally deny that *their* agency's activity serves to produce rents for interest groups.
26 See Lea (1956: 503).
27 See Flanagan and Perkins (1987).
28 See Fisher (1989: 23).
29 See Cushman (1989). The 1989 proposal replaced a 1987 proposal which would have imposed a sliding-scale fee system, with fishing boats paying as much as $1000 while pleasure boaters paid $5 or $10. Strong lobbying from the boating industry and the fishing industry helped to defeat the earlier version, that had the picturesque title of 'Coast Guard User Fee and Free Ride Termination Act of 1987'. See *Boating Industry* 50, June 1987: 15.
30 See *Congressional Quarterly Weekly Report* 47, 15 July 1989: 1771.
31 See Rockefeller (1987). Rockefeller is described as a former Chairman of the Corporation for Public Broadcasting, and currently a member of the Board of the Public Broadcasting System.
32 See Pytte (1989).
33 See Klott (1987).
34 See 'User Fee Proposed for Entering US,' *Washington Post*, 20 August 1986: A15.
35 See 'Senate Liberates Miss Liberty of $1-a-person Admission Fee', *Washington Post*, 10 April 1987: A11.
36 The simple economic explanation for bureaucratic resistance to user fees in cases like this is generally ignored. One recent article in the marketing literature 'explains' the hostility of US Forest Service employees to recreation user fees by reference to their 'shared organizational values' – i.e., they don't like fees because they don't like fees. See Badovick and Beatty (1987).
37 An interesting example is Dubberly (1986). The author examines various techniques librarians can use for resisting pressures to impose user fees, which are implicitly regarded as somehow unethical, if not actually illegal. Given that any price above zero for the loan of a book would almost certainly reduce circulation, and therefore reduce the need for librarians, this hostility to user fees on the part of librarians seems rational.
38 See Paddock and Weintraub (1989).
39 See Rasky (1988).
40 See Lewin (1988).
41 See 'Cigarette Tax Aids Homeless (in Chicago)', *New York Times*, 30 June 1989: A7 (national).

REFERENCES

Advisory Commission on Intergovernmental Relations. *Significant Features of Fiscal Federalism: 1989 Edition*. Washington, D.C.: ACIR, 1989.
Anonymous. 'Where There's Muck There's Brass'. *The Economist* 314 (17 March 1990): 46–7.
Badovick, G.J., and Beatty, S.E. 'Shared Organizational Values: Measurement and Impact Upon Strategic Marketing Implementation'. *Journal of the Academy of Marketing Science* 15 (Spring 1987): 19–26.
Barde, P. 'The Economic Approach to the Environment'. *OECD Observer* (June–July 1989): 12–15.

Bird, R. M., and Slack, E. 'Urban Finance and User Charges.' In G.F. Break (ed.). *State and Local Finance*. Madison: University of Wisconsin Press, 1981.

Cushman, J.H., Jr. 'Fees for Federal Services: Is the Sky the Limit?'. *New York Times*, 16 February 1989: B14.

Dubberly, R.A. 'Managing *Not* to Charge Fees: With Commitment and Good Management, 'Extra' Services Can Be Delivered Without User Charges'. *American Libraries* 17 (October 1986): 670–4.

Ellis, R.P. 'The Revenue Generating Potential of User Fees in Kenyan Government Health Facilities'. *Social Science and Medicine* 25 (1987): 995–1002.

Fisher, M.J. 'Pension Plan "Fees" Proposed in Congress'. *National Underwriter: Property and Casualty/Risk and Benefits Management* (28 August 1989): 23, 42.

Flanagan, J.A., and Perkins, S.J. 'Annual User Fee Review Program of the City of Phoenix, Arizona'. *Government Finance Review* 3 (June 1987): 13–18.

Fujii, Y. 'User Charges, Cross-Subsidization, and Public Subsidy – the Case of Expressways in Japan'. *Transportation Research* 23 (January 1989): 7–12.

Gertler, P., Locay, L., and Sanderson, W. 'Are User Fees Regressive? The Welfare Implications of Health Care Financing Proposals in Peru'. *Journal of Econometrics* 36 (September-October 1987): 67–88.

Kirkpatrick, D. 'CEOs to Bush: Raise Taxes Now'. *Fortune* 119 (16 January 1989): 95–6.

Klott, G. 'A User Fee: What's That?'. *New York Times*, 13 October 1987: D2.

Krashinsky, M. *User Charges in the Social Services*. Toronto: University of Toronto Press, 1981.

Lea, H.C. *A History of the Inquisition of the Middle Ages: vol. 1*. New York: Russell, 1956.

Lewin, T. 'Letting Smokers Pay for Child Care'. *New York Times*, 24 October 1988: A10 (local).

Newbery, D.M. 'Road User Charges in Britain'. *Economic Journal* (15 March 1988): 161.

Norris, J.E. 'The Assessment of User Fees to Recover Generic Regulatory Costs'. *Public Utilities Fortnightly* 123 (22 June 1989): 42–45.

Novack, J. 'But Don't Make Them Hiss.' *Forbes* 142 (14 November 1988): 159–60.

Office of Management and Budget. *Historical Tables: Budget of the United States Government, Fiscal Year 1990*. Washington, D.C.: Government Printing Office, 1989.

Paddock, R.C., and Weintraub, D.M. 'Prop 99 Funds OKd for Trauma Care Units'. *Los Angeles Times*, 3 October, 1989 I: 3.

Phelps, C.E., and Cook, P.J. 'Death and Taxes: An Opportunity for Substitution'. *Journal of Health Economics* 7 (March 1988): 1–24.

Pytte, A. 'FCC Broadcast Fees Avoided in $450 Million Package.' *Congressional Quarterly Weekly Report* (29 July 1989): 1946.

Rasky, S.F. 'Senators Reject Efforts to Pay for Drug War.' *New York Times*, 7 October 1988: p. A19.

Rockefeller, S.P. 'A Boon For Broadcasting.' *New York Times*, 13 November 1987: 27.

Savas, E.S. *How to Shrink Government: Privatizing the Public Sector*. Chatham, New Jersey: Chatham House, 1982.

Savage, D. 'Justices Rule User Fees Are Not Taxes, Averting $22 Billion Budget Headache'. *Los Angeles Times* 108, 26 April 1989: 4.

Singh, N. and Thomas, R. 'User Charges as a Delegation Mechanism'. *National Tax Journal* 39 (1986): 109–13.

Skelton, G. '64% Oppose Raising Taxes to Cut Deficit'. *Los Angeles Times*, 5 November 1987: I: 1.

Small, K.A., and Winston, C. 'Efficient Pricing and Investment Solutions to Highway Infrastructure Needs'. *American Economic Review* 76 (May 1986): 165–9.

Spiegel, C. 'More Spending for Health Supported in Poll'. *Los Angeles Times*, 11 May 1989, I: 3.

Stiglitz, J.E. *Economics of the Public Sector*, 2nd ed. New York: W.W. Norton, 1988.

Tax Foundation *Facts and Figures on Government Finance*. Washington, D.C: Tax Foundation, 1988.

Teja, R.S. 'The Case for Earmarked Taxes'. *International Monetary Fund Staff Papers* 35 (September 1988): 523–33.

Wagner, R.E. *Public Finance: Revenues and Expenditures in a Democratic Society*. Boston: Little, Brown, & Co., 1983.

3 User charges, rent seeking, and public choice

*Bruce Yandle**

In the last few years public-sector budget managers and deficit-weary politicians have become increasingly determined to find new sources of revenue. Hoping current tax revenues can be maintained, these managers and politicians quite naturally have developed a fondness for adopting fees to be paid by citizens who use such government facilities as parks and landfill as well as for implementing taxes that are based on the use of such governmentally supported and maintained resources as highways, rivers, streams, and territorial waters.

In a 1989 Supreme Court decision (*Samuel K. Skinner, Secretary of Transportation* v. *Mid-America Pipeline Co.*) the Court upheld the power of the Department of Energy to assess user charges or fees to operators of pipelines in order to recover the Department's adminis- trative cost of running two energy pipeline safety programmes.[1] The Department's mandate for recovering those costs through user charges was included in the Consolidated Omnibus Budget Reconciliation Act of 1985. In a related action that followed the March 1989 Valdez oil spill, President Bush proposed the creation of an oil-spill clean-up fund that would be funded by a 1.3-cent tax on each barrel of oil imported and produced in the United States. Members of Congress were already considering including that kind of user fee in pending legislation.[2]

For decades, economists have argued the pros and cons of such user fees, generally accepting the notion that user fees have a solid theoretical foundation.[3] Like the price system that calmly allocates billions of items across as many people, a properly designed system of user fees, or what can be termed corrective taxes, can link the user to the cost he imposes on society and cause him to ration his consumption while logically considering substitute activities that may be less costly. Charging a price for something that can be metered across individuals seems to induce efficient behaviour. All else equal, if the budgets of public-sector managers are linked, even partly, to the proceeds of such revenues, they too become tied to the power of economic incentives, at least theoretically.

Although most economic literature on user fees and taxes originates in the 1920s, user charges are themselves a feature of feudalism. Indeed, they may be thought of symptomatically as the antithesis of capitalism. After all, the presence of a user fee indicates collective and not individual ownership, which in turn generally implies the absence of a separate market for the product or service. The interaction of a feudalistic device employed in a capitalistic economy that is managed by a republican form of government generates interesting dynamics. The property rights specification is part of the problem; respecification may have much to do with the solution.

This chapter focuses on user fees and corrective taxes employed by government to affect the behaviour of consumers and producers. In so doing, the political economy of user fees is an important part of the story, since the public-choice aspects of user fees may deflect them from their efficiency-enhancing path. The first major section examines user fees in the context of the feudal system and illustrates how a limited scope of individual freedom and property rights gave rise to a thorough-going system of user fees. The rise of markets, individual liberty, and the price system displaced the older feudalistic institutions, at least partly; Section 2 discusses the potential problems that may emerge when user fees are developed and operated by representative government. Section 3 discusses major contributions to the economic literature on user fees, and therefore necessarily examines the work of A.C. Pigou (1920), the name most frequently associated with the concept. In addition to refreshing memories about Pigou's ideas, the section goes on to describe alternative prescriptions to problems Pigou attempted to solve with taxes and fees.

Since an appropriate discussion of user fees and Pigovian taxes must consider political behaviour, Section 4 concentrates on a public-choice analysis that introduces strategic behaviour on the part of the demanders and suppliers of political action. It is here that certain perverse outcomes are illustrated. Section 5 applies the earlier discussion to environmental use and focuses on the management of toxic wastes in the United States, which is associated with a user fee system. Predictions drawn from the theoretical discussion are found in this section. A few final thoughts conclude the chapter.

1   USER CHARGES: FROM FEUDALISM TO CAPITALISM

Trade and purposeful behaviour

The notion that members of a community are purposeful economic agents has limited meaning in the absence of the general freedom for community members to buy, sell, and hold defined bundles of property rights. As the scope of property rights expands to include a larger number of items and relationships, and freedom is held constant, the operational meaning of purposeful behaviour becomes richer. But when this scope contracts, so too does purposeful behaviour become more limited in scope.

Under the feudal system that dominated England and parts of Europe in the eleventh century and before, freedom and property rights were limited across all classes of people.[4] The scope of purposeful behaviour was also limited. Peasants in a manor community had certain rights and duties but hardly any scope to engage in trade. For example, the peasant had use rights to certain strips of land but could not transfer those rights to other peasants. Nor could he arbitrarily pass them along to another member of his family. Failure to use the strips of land could also result in their being forfeited to another peasant. Those who used the land, fished in the rivers and ponds, or hunted the lord's game, paid in-kind user charges. Ownership over and transferability of property were non-existent. By comparison, the liberty and scope for exchange enjoyed by the lord of the manor were quite large. Though the lord did not enjoy fee simple rights to his estate, it being the property of the king, he could reallocate the uses of manor property across the peasant population. Under the feudal system, land and most property of any importance was owned by the king, who in turn rewarded his faithful knights by assigning large parts of it to them. The king and his knights determined the user fees to be charged to peasants and others who worked and lived the manor life.

It took centuries for the institutions of liberty, property rights, and alienability to evolve. Along the way, money payments replaced many in-kind transfers, and market-determined prices replaced administratively set payment schemes. As trade expanded across resources and relationships, the scope of purposeful human behaviour was enlarged. At some point, the market system, where private decision making dominated transactions, handled one part of the allocation process. Along with political systems, where collective decision making dominated and other services were allocated, the two systems displaced the authoritarian feudal system. Even so, important vestiges remained fastened to the new social clothing. Like sandspurs fastened to the trousers of those who travelled the historic path, user fees survived into the twentieth century.

Modern-day user fees are among the more visible vestiges of feudalism in capitalist societies. Though now the exceptional way for allocating resources across individuals, rather than the rule, they are found at every level of government and are applied to a wide variety of resources and relationships. Like their feudalistic counterparts, administratively determined user fees indicate that property is controlled by the 'lord of the manor', government, and not by free men. The property rights are public, not private, and therefore limit the scope of purposeful individual action in certain directions. However, unlike their earlier counterparts, each case where allocation is guided by user fees today is theoretically a candidate for replacement by allocation through private markets.

Comparisons of old and new user charges

Visitors to Yellowstone Park pay an entrance fee, just as they do at Six Flags Over Texas. At Yellowstone the charge is set and collected by government. At Six Flags the price is determined by competition. If the management of Yellowstone is delinquent in its duties and runs a deficit for a long period or allows the resource to be destroyed by fire, the lord of the manor provides more resources or reduces the level of services. The property rights are not transferred to someone else. If the same thing occurs at Six Flags the spur of competition closes the doors, and the property rights are transferred to someone else. To be sure, there is no reason in principle why Yellowstone Park could not be leased, or even sold, to a private operator, who in turn would be subject to market forces.

In Tudor and Stuart England, kings were paid tonnage and duties, set administratively, by operators of ships for the purpose of defraying the cost of protecting the shipping lanes (White 1979: 100). In modern America, operators of automobiles pay gasoline taxes to defray government's cost of maintaining the highways. Similarly, the price of an aeroplane ticket includes a fee paid to government for operating the air traffic control system. If the expenditures on highways or air traffic control exceed user fee revenues the fees are generally adjusted. The 'lord of the manor', no longer an authoritarian ruler, still does not allow for property transfers. Arguably, the air traffic control system could be privatized. But similar arguments for highways are much less compelling.

User fees survived the trip from feudalism to capitalism, but the massive institutional change that occurred along the way altered significantly the process through which the charges were designed and implemented. When despots ruled supreme, user fees often impoverished the peasants. When markets dictated prices the community flourished. Today, republican forms of government provide an expanded arena in which purposeful human behaviour exerts itself. Actions driven by private interest are no longer isolated to narrowly defined markets. The modern politician, who is the symbolic lord of the manor, be he rent seeker or efficiency seeker, can be voted out of office by the peasants, which is admittedly a much less costly and more desirable social endeavour than rebellion.

Modern economists offer politicians strong arguments in support of feudalistic user fees, usually assuming the body politic is dominated by efficiency seekers. Enamoured with markets and recognizing the responsiveness of individuals to unit pricing, as opposed to lump-sum taxation, the partisan economist examines government allocation of resources and sees the fields white unto the harvest. Unfortunately, many of the advocates assume implicitly that their advice is being heard by a benevolent lord of the manor and not by a representative body that answers to a heterogeneous group of rent seekers. This heroic assumption about political economy leads the analyst to quicksand.

2   OTHER THOUGHTS ON USER CHARGES AND TAXES

How do user charges differ from revenue taxes?

Before considering some of the analytical roots of governmentally imposed user charges, some thought should be given to what distinguishes a politically determined charge for a service from taxes that must be paid by all citizens. In a brief but useful paper, Marchetti (1980) focuses on the salient differences between charges and taxes that are predominant in the fiscal literature. One of these is the presumption that while taxes are mandatory, user charges are voluntary. Hence, charges are like market prices, in that those who use the service pay, while those who avoid using the service do not pay. A second difference is the presumption that while taxes do not yield a specific benefit to those who pay them, charges are linked directly to beneficial consumption on the part of those who pay the charges.

After reviewing these presumptions, Marchetti suggests that the distinctions are more symbolic than real. For example, a corporate income tax could be viewed alternatively as a charge for incorporation privileges and services, just as charges could be viewed as incremental taxes. Indeed, a polluting firm that does not pay its user fee will be shut down, perhaps more surely than a firm that fails to pay its income taxes. In any event, there are generally penalties associated with non-payment in either case.

What appears to be distinguishing features that set apart conventional taxes from user fees can easily become blurred as one ponders the two devices. However, focusing too much on the similarities may cause one to overlook small but important differences. It is clear that when user fees are set to vary directly with usage, different behaviour is induced on the part of consumers of public-sector services. If a person receives garbage removal services as a part of a bundle of things paid for by property taxes there will be no intelligent way to link the production of garbage to the level of and change in property taxes. As a result, those who produce large quantities of garbage will generally be subsidized by those who produce very little. But if, by contrast, an individual is charged incrementally for garbage removal, with an absence of garbage meaning an absence of charge, a marked difference in behaviour and revenues can be expected to result.

Legal challenges of user charges brought by industries subject to them focus on the intent of government when levying the charges (Rothchild 1988). As it turns out, questioning intent offers a useful way of differentiating between taxes and charges. Intent to ration use among competing users and thereby recover identifiable costs is viewed as the legal rationale for user fees. Intent to obtain revenues is seen as the logic for taxes. In recent years, Congress has unquestionably moved towards revenue enhancement.

Arguments about intent and constitutional authority were made in 1988 before the US Court of Appeals in *Florida Power and Light* v. *NRC*, when petitioners challenged the legality of the Nuclear Regulatory Commission's expanded use of user fees (Rothchild 1988: 87). One question turned on intent: Was the agency after revenues or was the agency seeking cost reimbursement? The unlawful delegation of Congressional taxing authority to a regulatory agency was a related issue. The court upheld the NRC's authority in the face of the challenge.

Although matters of intent may appear to have little relevance to the economics of user charges something of importance comes from the logic. If a government agency, like the NRC, exercises its monopoly power when setting charges, it can be challenged by citizens on the grounds that the agency lacks taxing authority. Since the NRC funds 45 per cent of its operations from user fee revenues and Congress has toyed with raising that to 100 per cent, there is always a risk that the agency,

and others like it, will engage in monopoly pricing. Legal challenges
based on intent and delegation of powers may be the only safeguard
available to citizens.

Why public-sector production of metered services?

Where it is simple for governments to produce appropriate levels of
some service and collect efficient user fees for services rendered, as in
the provision of drinking water and garbage-removal services, it is
difficult to justify public-sector delivery of the service in the first place.
Government production is generally supported theoretically where it is
quite difficult, if not impossible, for appropriate user fees to be
determined. All this follows from the fact that private firms can replace
any government body that prices its services to individuals on the basis
of incremental cost, provided there are sufficient revenues to cover
costs. It can also be generally concluded that private firms will produce
at lower cost.

The question of why the public-sector engages in the production and
sale of services that could be produced alternatively through
private-sector activities has not escaped the scrutiny of economists. A.C.
Pigou (1947: 24–9), an important name, to be discussed later, in the
development of user fees, raised the question and offered some answers.
The public-sector may become engaged or remain engaged in such
activities when it is likely that a private firm would become a monopolist
or when some minimal level of the service is to be allocated to all
citizens, even those who do not pay, which, in other words, is counten-
anced when government is seen as a legitimate redistributor of income.

The concern about monopoly expressed in Pigou's public utility
justification is somewhat ironic. After all, if the state takes over production of a service, a monopoly will result – one that will be unlikely to
be broken in the future. But when private firms hold a monopoly
position that does not result from state licensure, competitive forces can
still affect the firm's pricing behaviour, for in this case there still exists
the prospect that technological change will bring about the entry of new
firms, which is much less likely in the presence of government
enterprise. Even if the state assumes the responsibility of providing
some service and billing users it is not clear why the state would produce
directly instead of contracting out. As Sir Edward Chadwick noted long
ago, competition for the field can substitute for competition within the
field.[5] In this kind of setting there is much scope for user fees to be
influenced heavily by market-determined prices.

Buchanan and Flowers (1975: 364) examine public funding of

highways today, which are supported by user fees in the form of gasoline taxes, and report that in the early days roads were generally available to everyone. At this time they were supported by general tax revenues, but they could not have been provided economically by private firms. However, once automobile and truck transportation replaced horses and rail passenger transportation, highways became congested and could then have become a private-sector activity. This possibility was presented because the public institutions were already in place. The current system of user fees bridges the past and present.

To be sure, private firms would have difficulty surviving should they engage in the production of goods and services that cannot be packaged so as to allow consumption by those who pay while withholding it from those who do not. This is the public goods problem. How to set price appropriately and collect revenues sufficient to cover costs is the issue. Since governments have the power to tax all beneficiaries they can survive, but not if they seek to fund the same public good solely with normal user fees. The difficulty of the problem becomes intensified once it is recognized that what truly matters is something like the quality – not the quantity – of water in lakes and rivers.

The distinction between the manor operator and the capitalist emerges again in this discussion of how to set appropriate user charges. A manor operator and the administrator in a system of market socialism can attempt to mimic a capitalist firm in setting prices for services that can be metered across individuals. However, the absence of the spur of competition introduces the risk that public-sector managers will never find the efficient price and will have, instead, simply an incentive to raise revenues to the maximum. The legal safeguard mentioned previously may become exceedingly important in such cases.

The search for additional sources of revenue during times of fiscal stress provides another rationale for applying new user fees to public-sector production as well as for increasing older fees. Mercer and Morgan (1983) analysed such a situation in California during the time when Proposition 13 was limiting the ability of local governments to expand their taxing power. The two researchers first developed a metric to determine if the user fee was approximately equal to the average cost of various services they studied. They then examined thirty-four California cities and twenty-two counties. In the majority of cases user fees were lower than the average cost of production. Users were being subsidized, which is Pigou's point. However, after Proposition 13 was in effect for a while, the charges increased, all the while getting closer to the average cost of producing the services. Proposition 13 provided the stimulus to use existing user charges for revenue enhancement. The convergence of fees with average cost found by Mercer and Morgan suggests that the Proposition 13 stimulus may have contributed to efficient pricing. However, before drawing such heroic conclusions the determination of cost must be examined carefully.

There are enough pricing and other controversies associated with governmentally imposed user fees for services that are metered across citizen-consumers to make it difficult to conclude that such fees are unambiguously desirable on efficiency grounds, though they may be desirable simply for raising additional revenue. However, hardly anyone would argue that public-sector charges for drinking water, garbage-removal services, and sewer services frequently billed to citizens on the basis of use should be replaced by lump-sum taxes. But, as with most public-sector actions, there is political economy to consider before accepting user fees *carte blanche* as efficiency enhancing.

3   PIGOU, CORRECTIVE TAXES, AND STRATEGIC BEHAVIOUR

The Pigovian prescription

Oddly enough, there seems to be less controversy on the use of fees to correct the behaviour of firms that generate third-party costs in the normal production of goods and services, which raises the subject of externalities. The story goes this way: in the absence of property and liability rules, it is possible for a producer of steel, let us say, also to produce large volumes of effluent that is discharged into a river. The discharge reduces downstream property values, but the mill owners face no recourse. If the stream is collective property managed by government, public-sector agents can consider imposing a tax to be paid by the mill operators for the use of the environment. By doing so, the operators recognize the costs they are imposing and adjust their behaviour.

The name of A.C. Pigou (1920) is immortalized by a tax designed to adjust the behaviour of economic agents, like the steel mill just mentioned, who impose more cost on society than they recognize in their decision making. Among the first to claim on technical grounds that the invisible hand of the market might fail to generate efficiency, Pigou argued for fiscal encouragements and discouragements to exploit opportunities for Pareto moves.

Pigou's prescription, stripped of all institutional and political considerations, goes like this: if the all-knowing economist finds a situation where private cost is not equal to social cost, which means there is an opportunity for a Pareto move, a proper equilibrium can be attained by taxing the producer of the social cost at an amount equal to the previously unrecognized marginal cost imposed on society. In effect, the producer pays a user fee.

Just why such opportunities might abound is not fully explained by Pigou. The institutional side of the Pigovian situation, to be discussed later, was left for others to contemplate. However, one point seems clear. If there are no enforceable property rights and rules of liability related to the assets that affect cost and benefits, and if the parties to the controversy are unable to communicate with each other, Pigou's problem may emerge. The question of why there are no property rights, however, is simply begged in the typical formulations.

Like other efficiency-based arguments put forward in an institutional vacuum, Pigou's prescription sparkles with morgue-like logic. If politicians are all dead, and if rigor mortis has set in and frozen the relevant supply-and-demand curves, the prescription will work. Efficiency will be attained just as surely as the solar system – comprised of dead bodies – will move in predictable ways.[6]

Pigou's argument from the 1920s about smoke control continues to be repeated to this day. For example, a recent item in issue 1 of *Regulation* magazine put the argument this way:

> If the EPA decides to limit lead in gasoline, or acid rain, or chlorofluorocarbons, then user fees are an efficient solution. They force firms to pay for the damage done to the environment or for the scarcity value of the resources they consume.
>
> (1988: 5)

The revisionists

But reactions to the analytics of environmental user fees identified some fatal flaws. First off, Turvey (1963) and then Cordes (1980) described post-equilibrium bargaining, the situation that occurs predictably after the appropriate Pigovian tax is placed on the producer of specified emissions, say smoke, that can be monitored. Allow me to couch Turvey's argument in the language of political economy. To be sure, a tax on the emissions of smoke will not emerge until politically effective people demand action. Suppose such action does emerge, as represented by political pressure, lobbying, or some other costly political-influencing activity of the sort described by Cordes (1980). This means that there are private individuals who demand political action in the form of a tax on smoke emissions. The effects of the noxious smoke on these people and their economic fortunes are normally shown as a rising marginal cost that is not registered in the decision making of the polluting firms. Given the identification of that cost function, the all-knowing Pigovian economist calculates the appropriate marginal tax, and the politicians – seeking to serve the public interest – impose the tax on smoke-producing firms. The equilibrium is achieved where marginal social cost is equal to the demand by those firms for getting rid of smoke. The demand for alternative smoke-removal services becomes meaningful when it is likely that environmental user fees will be charged to polluting firms.

But Turvey and Cordes tell us this equilibrium will not hold. To demonstrate the point, they subtract the marginal tax from the firms' demand for smoke emissions, giving a net marginal benefit curve. Just as Pigou and the recent writer in *Regulation* indicate, the polluting firms produce to the point where the net marginal benefit is zero. Returning to the demanders for political action, analysts remind us that individuals will seek reductions in pollution until the net marginal benefit to them from doing so is also zero. While lobbying activity is no doubt costly, those who demand political action do not face a marginal tax for each unit of emission reduced. But suppliers of smoke must pay an incremental fee. Furthermore, the presence of the regulatory institution formed to set and collect the environmental tax reduces the cost of political lobbying. There is a political focal point where pressure can be applied.

In the small numbers setting contemplated here, the demanders of environmental purity demand even more smoke reduction once the Pigovian tax is put in place. When lobbying costs are introduced to the analysis it is possible that the demanders of purity will be satisfied with a smoky world. They will undertake lobbying actions so long as there are gains from so doing.

Without addressing institutional arrangements and the necessary political intermediaries, Turvey couches his behavioural analysis in terms of post-equilibrium bargaining, where the polluter is bribed to reduce pollution beyond the amount that coincides with the Pigovian tax. He indicates that a sub-optimal amount of smoke will be produced. In this setting, environmentalists demand more purity than Pigovian politicians provide. Introducing a costly political mechanism where purity lovers must compete in a political economy with industrialists and an unorganized but none the less important group of consumer/ taxpayers obviously brings discipline to the analysis.

James Buchanan and William Craig Stubblebine (1962) also analysed the Pigovian problem and carefully defined and analysed the problem of externality. Dressed in efficiency-enhancing clothing, they described an appropriate equilibrium in a world where smoke producers valued the opportunity to discharge smoke and receivers of smoke suffered economically from its discharge. Again, there is an absence of property rights to the use of the environment and no apparent liability rule. Their prescription implied that a Pigovian tax should be imposed on both sides of the transaction, a point enlarged upon by Hugh H. Macaulay (1972). If the receivers of smoke, just as producers, have to pay for marginal benefits they obtain as reflected in an improvement in their environment and the rents that accompany it, their demand will be satisfied by the appropriate user fee. There will be smoke in the final equilibrium, but there will be no post-equilibrium bargaining.

Theoretically, at least, Congress can impose the appropriate tax on all parties and having performed that miracle go on to do greater things. Following the final resolution of the problem the environmental lobbyists will retire. Of course, we have yet to hear of a bilateral user fee. We are more disposed to think in terms of right and wrong, somehow knowing that smoke producers are wrong and must be punished.

Breaking the institutional vacuum

Ronald Coase (1960) became as famous as Pigou, if not more so, for his contribution to the debate. Using a rich institutional model under theoretical circumstances less severe than those specified by Pigou, Coase argued that social cost just does not exist in a world where contracts can be written and property rights defined and enforced at negligible cost. All problems of social cost are really private problems. If there is a problem labelled 'social cost', such as an abundance of smoke, it implies either that property rights will soon emerge and opportunity cost along with them or that the cost of contracting through the external effect is just too high.

One interpretation of Coase's theoretical point implies that it is better to bear the cost of living with or avoiding smoke than to incur the cost of controlling it. Another interpretation asks that the cost of exercising government's police powers be compared with the private transaction costs for dealing with the problem. If the cost of government regulation is less than private party bargaining costs a case is made for environmental regulation, where government becomes the implicit owner of certain rights to the use of a resource. In effect, a new landlord enters the picture, but, as discussed previously, severe difficulties are encountered when the political incentives of politicians become intermingled with regulation.

A final interpretation carries us to rules of liability, which are

generally present under common and statute law and are implied in
Coase's property rights' analysis. Legal actions can generally be brought
against firms that reduce the value of the property of others, whether
that property be public or private. If a steel mill damages a downstream
property owner or interferes with water use the owners of the mill must
be prepared to defend themselves in court and to bear the cost of
damages as well as the loss of brand-name capital associated with such
frays. The expectations of that cost will enter into the calculations of the
firm's management, which is to say the external costs are internalized.

Quite often firms and individuals will purchase liability insurance
coverage to insure against such actions. Competition drives the related
premium to equal the expected value of damages plus the administrative
costs of operating the insurance programme. When it is added to other
operating costs the insurance premium causes the firm to recognize
third-party effects. Firms that misbehave pay a higher premium or lose
their insurance. Firms that seldom have a claim pay lower premiums.
The charge is modulated to account for the external effect. It is only
where there is no liability rule and no well-defined property rights, or
where those institutions are in a state of flux, that governmentally
imposed corrective taxes can be justified fully on the basis of external
costs. That is, the justification is made in an institutional vacuum.

All this leaves a puzzle. If institutions that force decision makers to
consider all costs fail to emerge we must ask why this failure results. The
generic response says that transaction costs are too high. If government
steps in because of the absence of those institutions, we must ask if those
institutions will ever emerge. The generic response says most likely not,
because the transaction costs associated with private institutional
development are raised, not lowered, by the presence of government
regulation.

A diagrammatic treatment

The analysis contained in this review is illustrated in Figure 3.1, which
contains the familiar marginal benefit from discharge by the polluter,
MB, and the marginal cost imposed on smoke receivers, MC. Pigou calls
for a marginal tax, T, to be imposed on the polluter, anticipating an
equilibrium quantity of smoke, OE.

Turvey's net marginal benefit function, NMB, is also shown in the
figure, along with the implied final equilibrium quantity, OB. Following
Turvey, the polluter pays OTAE in taxes and receives up to BCAE in
bribes for post-equilibrium adjustments. However, political economy
suggests that payment would go to politicians or at least be shared with

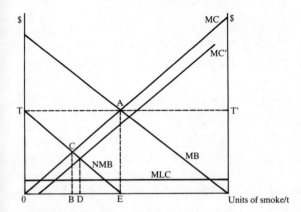

Figure 3.1 Analysis of user fees

them. The diagram also shows a bilateral tax, with T imposed on polluters and T′ charged to the demanders of smoke reduction. The equilibrium OE holds in this case. There is no economic force calling for further adjustment.

We can explore what happens when the demanders of purity face explicit lobbying costs. Introduction of a constant lobbying cost function, MLC, and subtracting it from MC, which is the inverse of the smoke receivers' marginal benefit curve, yields MC′, a net marginal cost function. The intersection of MC′ and NMB yields another equilibrium solution, with OD amount of smoke being emitted. Unless misguided, the demanders of purity would not engage in costly lobbying if that activity brought less smoke reduction than was attained with the tax and no lobbying activity. We also can picture what might happen if government subsidizes the purity lovers while taxing the polluter. The adjusted net MC curve would shift to the left, calling for more reductions.

But why might the government choose to use some of the user tax revenues, or other revenues, to subsidize the purity lovers? The purity lovers can identify new pollutants or new dimensions of the old pollutant and thereby strengthen the regulatory hand of government. If government announces that additional features of smoke discharge are to become subject to taxation the polluter must then consider alternative ways to control the newly specified pollutants. Any positive opportunity cost for controlling pollution generates an addition to the polluters' marginal benefit to discharge. (The polluter must either

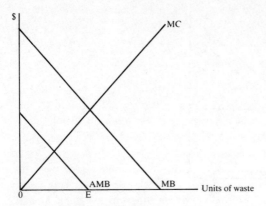

Figure 3.2 Effects of liability rule

change its production technique, such as or discharge pollutants and pay the tax.) An increase in the marginal benefit function can allow for increases in the Pigovian tax, or at least generate more revenues from the current tax. An interesting interaction between user charges and regulation results from all this, with revenues becoming an important feature of the analysis. However, the active participation/resistance of the regulated, a point to be introduced later, further complicates the analysis.

Figure 3.2, which is similar to Figure 3.1, illustrates the standard externality problem in the presence of a liability rule. This time, we see two marginal benefit curves for the firm, one adjusted for liability insurance, AMB, and one not adjusted. The unadjusted curve, MB, is identical to that in Figure 3.1. The difference between the two curves reflects the insurance premium. Having assumed that cost, the firm assigns smaller benefits to using the environment to get rid of smoke. As a result, the equilibrium between the adjusted curve, AMB, and MC, the incremental cost imposed on neighbours, is the appropriate one. All costs have been internalized. There is no reason to impose a corrective tax on the firm.

Even so, it should be noted that pollution costs are being imposed on unrelated individuals by the firm. In a politically charged environment, where individuals are told they have a right 'to breathe clean air' without specifying how clean is clean, the individuals might organize and lobby for even cleaner air.[7] Since they are not connected to the insurance programme and bear no direct incremental cost for the clean air they do enjoy, it is likely that the implied equilibrium will not hold. The latter part of the analysis discussed along with Figure 3.1 becomes pertinent once again at this point.

What about the revenues?

It is interesting that what becomes the more salient part of the user fee question from a public-choice perspective – the revenues raised by the tax or fee, and what might be done with them – is generally dismissed in the debates about the fees. Efficiency analysts see revenue consider-ations as a totally different question, unrelated even to the central point about the merits of the fees themselves. But as revealed in the work by Mercer and Morgan (1983), public choice economists expect politicians to assign a positive value to alternative tax revenues, especially in an age of government deficits and public opposition to direct taxation. Given constraints on the normal means of taxation, the mistaken efficiency trait of user fees can be put forward in efforts simply to find more money to fund special interest programmes. Once the fees are in place the politicians will predictably seek ways to increase demand for the fee-generating activity.

Of course, neither Pigou, Buchanan and Stubblebine, Turvey, nor Coase were reflecting on the literature of public choice when they prepared their analyses of user fees. At the time they were writing, that literature did not exist in a defined form. As it turns out, Pigou's prescription suffers under public-choice scrutiny. Buchanan and Stubblebine's point continues to hold water, as do the insights of Coase and particularly Turvey, as amended by Cordes, since those analyses were predicated upon rational human behaviour in political settings. At best, however, the valuable public-choice insights registered in those earlier years were important scratches on the surface of the problem.[8]

4   NEW PUBLIC-CHOICE PERSPECTIVES

Deeper analytical cuts were made when public choice economists began to investigate why user fees are seldom used. Widely advocated by economists, efforts to impose a tax on the sulphur content of coal, so as to reduce sulphur dioxide emissions, by the Nixon administration were frustrated by Congressional committees (Downing [1984: 211–12] and Irwin and Liroff [1974: 126–34]). Environmental issues were handled by one committee, Ways and Means dealt with taxes, and both committees had bigger fish to fry.

Buchanan and Tullock (1975) pointed out why none of the

demanders for control, those who might have lobbied the Public Works Committee, wanted taxes. Spokesmen for industrial firms knew they were against taxes on pollution. Already being required to install pollution-control devices, they wanted subsidies. As they saw things, placing a tax on post-control pollution added insult to injury. The Ways and Means Committee sympathized. Its members did not want to see a more valuable tax initiative become bogged down in debates about pollution taxes. The politicians could arguably earn more rent dealing with income tax reform than from such small fry as a sulphur tax on the burning of coal.

But what about the technology-based regulation that ultimately became the flagship of American environmental regulation? Why didn't the environmental lobbyists go for Pigovian taxes? Heavily funded by EPA, the environmentalists worked for rules that promoted the agency.[9] Taxes collected by the IRS do not do this. Popular rhetoric at the time added a nice veneer to their arguments. User fees were described as giving a licence to pollute. Since zero pollution was the official goal why fool around with taxes, unless the taxes were high enough to reduce pollution to zero (US Congress 1971).

But there is more to the story. As Buchanan and Tullock tell us, and later empiricists support (Maloney and McCormick 1982), industrialists can gain from command and control regulation. It cartelizes existing firms by limiting entry and coordinating output across firms in the same industry. Sadly for special interest groups, user fees tend to maintain competition and generate no rents for industrialists. If there is to be environmental control the industrialists predictably side with the environmentalists and call for command and control. Like bootleggers and Baptists, the two groups argue separately for rules that restrict output.

The case for revenue-generating user fees is weakened significantly by three distinctly different forces. First, environmentalists view the sale of the right to pollute as being immoral. Second, as cost minimizers, industrialists have nothing to gain by paying more taxes, but can gain from technology-based standards that restrict entry and raise competitors' costs. Finally, political agents can gain by providing regulatory outcomes that are valuable to environmentalists and industrialists.

There are two additional public-choice explanations of why command-and-control regulation is preferred to economic incentives, such as user fees. Viewing Congress as a rent-maximizing organization, Fred McChesney (1987) has shown how political bodies will logically propose regulations that inspire affected groups to organize and lobby against the rules, thereby increasing their support of the relevant politicians. Once the rules are in place, McChesney argues, Congress can play the same game in reverse, in effect auctioning off regulatory reform to members of the same group. His analysis suggests Congress would entertain the use of environmental user fees and in doing so extract payments for moving away from that mechanism. Once command-and-control regulation is in place Congress can gain political contributions by tinkering with the rules.

Yandle and Young's (1986) analysis of environmental regulation supports the McChesney argument. They state that the current practice of command-and-control regulation is highly discriminatory across firms, industries, and regions. The actual rules are designed for industry subcategories, and have different levels of stringency and varying levels of enforcement. Congress can price discriminate across firms as though the rules were being auctioned to political agents.[10] Pigovian taxes, on the other hand, tend to be uniform, and the IRS is generally interested in collecting taxes, not campaign contributions. The political bargaining discussed here does not take place in a fiscal vacuum. The general populace may face high transactions costs that limit political action, but at some margin we would expect all interest groups to become aware of the deadweight loss and loss of revenues associated with the regulatory institutions that emerge. Given competing and growing demands for government services and the relative burden of existing taxes, Congress would find occasions where command-and-control regulation would be modified and augmented by user fees. However, public-choice predicts that the tax revenues will then be used in strategic ways to reward special-interest groups and the political brokers who serve those interests.

Three propositions unfold from a public-choice analysis of environmental taxes. First, unilateral taxes for controlling external effects will not generate a stable equilibrium in a political economy where individuals have the right to petition and influence political representatives. Second, command-and-control regulation will generally be preferred to taxes and other economic incentives. Authoritarian rules enable political agents to achieve other important goals. When they are used, perhaps for reasons having to do with fiscal stress as opposed to efficiency, taxes on environmental use will be applied in ways that inspire the organization of interest groups, who then support the expansion of bureaucracies. Third, the additional revenues from environmental taxes, which relieve pressures for the use of general tax revenues, can be important enough to overcome their otherwise unattractive features, especially when the fees are included in a regulatory package.

5   TAXES AND EPA'S SUPERFUND

An opportunity to consider these propositions is found in the US Environmental Protection Agency's Superfund programme. Superfund was established when the Comprehensive Environmental Reclamation and Clean-up Act was passed on 11 December 1980 (*Environmental Law Handbook*, 1985). It is important to recognize that the legislation established a regulatory scheme that included a $1.6 billion clean-up fund that was to receive 87.5 per cent of its revenue from taxes on petroleum stocks and forty-two specified chemical feedstocks. The balance was to come from general revenues.

The Pigovian logic

The logic of the feedstock tax appears to be partly Pigovian, at least in its origins. In March 1979, before debating the control of hazardous wastes and passing the Superfund legislation, Congress had been considering a proposal from the Coast Guard to place a tax on imported oil that would account for the external costs imposed when oil spills occurred in coastal and inland waters.[11] As noted before, one decade later Congress is now debating the same proposition. Going beyond the Pigovian prescription, the proceeds from the fee were to go into a fund that would then be used to repair damages and compensate damaged parties, so as to eliminate litigation. At about the same time, Love Canal entered the picture, and EPA joined the Coast Guard and the Justice Department in recommending a larger fund.

In a purely theoretical way, the underlying notion of placing an environmental user fee on producers of chemical wastes would seem to be straightforward. Hazardous waste products found in unmanaged, mismanaged, and neglected dumps are the result of chemical production. The producer unwittingly imposes costs on society that are not included in the prices paid for inputs. Taxes based on production will fund necessary future clean-up actions that restore the affected sites. In this way the taxes indirectly cause firms to recognize external costs imposed on innocent third parties.

Missing the Pigovian mark with political economy

While the Superfund tax concept appears to follow Pigovian logic its design misses the mark. As is frequently the case, the tax is not a user fee set equal to the marginal social cost generated by any particular producer. In fact, all producers using the same feedstocks pay the same marginal tax rate without regard to their present and past behaviour. The cleanest and most careful chemical firm pays the same unit tax as the most delinquent and vicious polluter. None the less, the tax comes as close to the Pigovian prescription as anything we might expect to find north of the Potomac. As Turvey and Cordes both suggested, passage of the initial legislation did not end the struggle by environmentalists and others who worked the halls of Congress.

Close examination of the Superfund tax reveals other public choice predictions. Disregarding risk assessment and marginal social cost, the 1980 law required that EPA specify at least 400 clean-up sites (about one for each Congressional district) and that each state would have its worst site – no matter how risky in a relative sense – included in the 400. Put differently, the law had the immediate and politically valuable effect of generating excess demand for Congressional services. This inspired new local-interest groups to organize lobbying efforts. McChesney's point comes through.

Going on, the law specified that all firms presumed to have contributed to a Superfund site will bear joint and several liability for the cost of clean-up. Before that, firms were liable for their actions under common law and generally used liability insurance as the mechanism to manage the risk. The insurance premium, or the opportunity cost of internal reserves if they self-insured, was a proxy for the expected costs imposed on the environment.

The legislative move to joint and several liability superceded the Common Law rule of contract that allows individuals to write their own liability agreements, and tied together all producers of hazardous waste who might have participated in the development of a waste site. Those who disposed of one pound of waste could be liable for the clean-up of tons of waste. Theoretically, the firm with the deepest pockets and largest amount of brand name capital at risk can bear all the cost, even though its waste contribution is slight. All visions of Pigovian efficiency are quickly replaced by political rent seeking.

There is a saving grace in all this, for some firms. The joint and several liability feature led to the sudden demise of privately provided environmental liability insurance, an institution that previously functioned to internalize the cost (Katzman 1985)! Private insurers cannot estimate the risk faced by a particular firm, since the firm may be found liable for another firm's actions. Chemical firms have little choice but to self-insure, which provides an advantage to large firms (US General Accounting Office 1987). Superfund has the effect of restricting output and limiting entry. The theoretical point made by Buchanan and Tullock (1975) is now observed in application.

Like most large environmental endeavours of the past, the Superfund programme became ensnared in bureaucratic red tape and management problems. The culmination of that was seen when Rita Lavell, the EPA director of Superfund programmes, was convicted of perjury before Congress after being charged with allocating Superfund dollars in ways that promoted the political fortunes of Republican candidates for Congress (Florio 1986). Pigou would turn over in his grave.

Empirical evidence on the fund operation

The allocation of Superfund resources through EPA's designation of sites has been studied by Barnett (1985) and by McNeil *et al.* (1988). Barnett built a statistical model for predicting the level of Superfund expenditures across the fifty states, in which he used elements of EPA's criteria for ranking the riskiness of sites with respect to surface water, air pollution, and ground water, and where he included other variables having to do with state support of remedial action as well as regional variables. Barnett reports one puzzle. Where the risk of ground water contamination is high, EPA has allocated a smaller amount of its budget. Ground water contamination was one of the chief reasons for establishing Superfund.

McNeil *et al.* examine the relationship of contributions to Superfund from in-state industries and the redistribution of those funds through Superfund. If contributions are risk-based one would expect this to be reflected by use of Superfund dollars for the repair of sites in those states where large amounts of fees are collected. After all, the pollution in question does not migrate great distances. The research, however, finds nothing of the sort. For the most part, Superfund payments are highest in the South-west, where the petrochemical industry is concentrated. Superfund expenses are highest in the North-east. It turns out that payments to the fund are not related to state personal income, past problems with hazardous waste sites, or to funds obligated to the state through the programme. The research suggests Superfund is a complex system for redistributing funds in a hazardous waste framework.

Revisions and adjustment

The tensions between bureaucrats who allegedly allocated funds on a political basis and elected politicians who see redistribution as their domain, as well as other Superfund problems, led to the Superfund Amendments and Reauthorization Act of 1986, which tightened the leash on EPA, increased appropriations and the taxes to fund the programme, expanded the coverage of sites and the list of harmful pollutants, and required that chemical producers provide detailed information to local communities on the chemicals used and produced in each and every plant.

As if recalling Turvey's point and going one better, the 1986 law authorizes private parties to petition EPA to perform risk assessments on any site, whether or not the site has earned a priority standing. The law also provides funds to private parties to sue EPA when the agency fails to classify a site as being hazardous. There is a post-equilibrium subsidy in place, one which assures an increase in demand for Superfund action (see Figure 3.1).

In March 1988 the average cost of cleaning Superfund sites was approximately $25 million ('Current Developments' 1988). At that rate, some $20 billion will be needed to handle the 951 sites now listed for clean-up. There is $8.5 billion in the fund and 27,000 additional candidate sites waiting to be included in the programme. When we recall that those who wish to make use of the programme pay no fees, indeed are subsidized, it is little wonder that the quantity of services they demand would increase, along with the tax on feedstocks. To cap it all, EPA has expressed concern about the logic of the programme on risk reduction grounds (US EPA 1987). It seems that other far more crucial and less costly problems have been pushed to one side by Congressional interest in the politically more appealing Superfund programme.

The Superfund story is just one episode involving taxes based on environmental use, hardly enough to serve as convincing evidence that fees will always be perverted in the political process. However, it is a major episode, one involving billions of dollars and the entire US economy. Yet while we might be cautious in drawing general conclusions from this one episode, Congressman James J. Florio, a major supporter of the programme, is not so bashful. After writing extensively about the experience with Superfund, Mr Florio said this: 'When issues are brought before Congress, disagreements quickly become political and sensible environmental policy may be lost in the process' (Florio 1986: 379). Mr Florio could just as well have said that efficiency arguments always tend to give way to special-interest demands for redistribution.

6 CONCLUSION

This chapter has examined user fees and corrective taxes and traced their evolution from the feudal system to market capitalism; it has focused on the political economy of user fees and used public-choice analysis as a vehicle to examine purposeful behaviour induced by the fiscal device. As indicated theoretically and by application, there are potential distortions that enter what might ordinarily be viewed as a pricing technique for enhancing government efficiency. If there is a major message contained here, it is this: before applying economic ideas developed in institutional vacuums that characterize social science laboratories, the policy maker should consider what happens when the vacuum is broken.

The political economists who viewed the world before Pigou were keenly aware that human beings always strive within systems of incentives, including those that evolve politically. The dawning of the natural sciences, the age of rationalism, and the Enlightenment nudged the social scientist into the deep recesses of his laboratory, away from the messy world of political action and reaction. Perhaps due to the extraordinary growth of governments in the twentieth century's last half, or perhaps for other reasons, political economy has once again surfaced as a viable method of explaining the way the real world works. The work of public-choice scholars has been a part of this return to the roots of economics.

In conclusion, this chapter draws pessimistic conclusions for advocates of user fees who seek efficient outcomes for controlling external effects. The prospects for user fees as prices for services has a more optimistic sheen. However, there are still serious considerations to ponder before unambiguously endorsing the political use of fees. When making such assessments, one must ask: relative to what? There are competing institutional arrangements for internalizing costs and providing citizen services. An unambiguous endorsement of user charges implies that all other viable institutions are inferior. As indicated in this chapter, it is highly unlikely that anyone would arrive at such a far-reaching conclusion.

NOTES

* The author expresses appreciation to Cora Moore and Jody Lipford for research assistance. Portions of this chapter are based on Yandle (1989).

1 See 'Supreme Court Upholds Pipeline User Fees' (1989: 44).

2 See 'Administration Proposes Oil-Spill Clean-up Fund' (1989: 1117).

3 For a sampling see Balcher (1980), Barnett (1980), Baumol (1972), Buchanan (1969), Downing (1973), Meade (1952), and Plott (1966).

4 For discussion of legal arrangements and later changes, see Hume (1778, vols I and II) and Thorne (1979: 13–29, 197–210).

5 The ideas of Sir Edward Chadwick are examined in Crain and Ekelund (1976), and Ekelund and Hebert (1983: 184–97).

6 The necessity for rigor mortis is discussed (not in those terms) by Hamilton

et al. (1989). Their analysis illustrates the difficulty of attaining efficiency through Pigovian taxes even under the most extreme assumptions. They describe behavioural adjustments that confound the apparent effectiveness of the tax.

7 This statement was included in President Bush's 12 June 1989 environmental message. (See Bush 1989.)

8 It is interesting to consider revenue-enhancement parallels from the feudal years. During the time of Henry VIII, the Crown began charging tonnage fees to owners of shipping vessels to defray the cost of protecting shipping lanes. The user charge practice was continued to the seventeenth century, but along the way, at the time of James I and his son Charles, the fees were raised in the hope that additional revenues would be generated for the Crown. Unfortunately for the Crown, price elasticity of demand precluded the desired revenue increase. (For discussion, see Hume 1778: 207 and White (1979: 100.)

9 For pertinent details on this, see Downing (1984: 263–8) and Bennett and Dilorenzo (1985: 137–72).

10 A related argument is made by Pashigian (1982) regarding the political use of environmental regulation to affect regional development and the protection of industry in one location from competitive entry and exit.

11 On this and additional discussion of White House strategizing, see White (1981: 145–59, especially p. 147).

REFERENCES

'Administration Proposes Oil-Spill Clean-up Fund'. *Congressional Quarterly.* (13 May 1989): 1117.

Balcher, Y. 'Taxation of Externalities: Direct versus Indirect'. *Journal of Public Economics* 13 (1980): 121–9.

Barnett, A.H. 'The Pigovian Tax Rule under Monopoly'. *American Economic Review* 70 (December 1980): 1037–41.

Barnett, H.C. 'The Allocation of Superfund, 1981–1983'. *Land Economics* 61 (August 1985): 255–62.

Baumol, W.J. 'On Taxation and the Control of Externalities'. *American Economic Review* 62 (June 1972): 307–22.

Bennett, J.T., and Dilorenzo, T.J. *Destroying Democracy: How Government Funds Partisan Politics.* Washington: Cato Institute, 1985.

Buchanan, J.M. 'External Diseconomies, Corrective Taxes, and Market Structure'. *American Economic Review* 59 (March 1969): 174–77.

Buchanan, J.M., and Flowers, M.R. *The Public Finances: An Introductory Textbook,* 4th ed. Homewood: Richard D. Irwin, Inc., 1975.

Buchanan, J.M., and Stubblebine, W.C. 'Externality'. *Economica* 29 (November 1962): 371–84.

Buchanan, J.M., and Tullock, G. "Polluters' Profit" and Political Response: Direct Controls versus Taxes'. *American Economic Review* 65 (March 1975): 139–47.

Bush, G. 'Remarks by the President in Announcement of the Clean Air Act Amendment'. Office of the Press Secretary, The White House (12 June 1989).

Coase, R.H. 'The Problem of Social Cost'. *Journal of Law and Economics* 3 (October 1960): 1–44.

Cordes, J.J. 'The Relative Efficiency of Taxes and Standards'. *Public Finance* 36 (1981): 339–42.

Crain, W.M., and Ekelund, R.B. 'Chadwick and Demsetz on Competition and Regulation'. *Journal of Law and Economics* 19 (April 1976): 149–62.

'Current Developments'. *Environment Reporter*. (25 March 1988): 25.

Downing, P.B. 'User Charges and the Development of Urban Land'. *National Tax Journal* 36 (December 1973): 631–7.

Downing, P.B. *Environmental Economics and Policy*. Boston: Little, Brown & Company, 1984.

Ekelund, R.B., Jr and Hebert, R.F. *A History of Economic Theory and Method*, 2nd ed. New York: McGraw-Hill Book Co., 1983.

Environmental Law Handbook, 8th ed. Rockville, Md: Government Institute, Inc., 1985.

Florio, J.J. 'Congress as Reluctant Regulators: Hazardous Waste Policy in the 1980s'. *Yale Journal on Regulation* 3 (Spring 1986): 351–82.

Hamilton, J.H. Sheshinski, E., and Slutsky, S.M. 'Production Externalities and Long-Run Equilibria: Bargaining and Pigovian Taxation'. *Economic Inquiry* 27 (July 1989): 453–71.

Hume, D. *The History of England*, vols. I and V. Indianapolis: Liberty Fund, Inc. reprint 1983 (orig. ed. 1778).

Irwin, W.A., and Liroff, R.A. *Economic Disincentives for Pollution Control: Legal, Political and Administrative Dimensions*, EPA–600/5–74–026. Washington: US Environmental Protection Agency, 1974.

Katzman, M.T. *Chemical Catastrophes: Regulating Environmental Risk through Pollution Insurance*. Homewood, Ill. : Richard D. Irwin, Inc., 1985.

Macaulay, H.H. 'Environmental Quality, the Market, and Public Finance'. In R.M. Bird and J.G. Head, eds *Modern Fiscal Issues*. Toronto: University of Toronto Press, 1972: 187–224.

McChesney, F.S. 'Rent Extraction and Rent Creation in the Economic Theory of Regulation'. *Journal of Legal Studies* 16 (January 1987): 101–18.

McNeil, D.W. Foshee, A.W. and Burbee, C.R. 'Superfund Taxes and Expenditures: Regional Redistribution'. *Review of Regional Studies* 18 (Winter 1988): 4–9.

Maloney, M.T. and McCormick, R.E. 'A Positive Theory of Environmental Quality Regulation'. *Journal of Law and Economics* 25 (April 1982): 99–123.

Marchetti, P.K. 'Distinguishing Taxes from Charges in the Case of Privileges'. *National Tax Journal* 33 (June 1980): 233–6.

Meade, J.E. 'External Economies and Diseconomies in a Competitive Structure'. *The Economic Journal* 62 (March 1952): 54–67.

Mercer, L.J. and Morgan, D.W. 'The Relative Efficiency and Revenue Potential of Local User Charges: The California Case'. *National Tax Journal* 36 (June 1983): 203–12.

Pashigian, P.B. 'Environmental Regulation: Whose Self Interests Are Being Served?' Center for the Study of Economy and the State, University of Chicago, 1982.

Pigou, A.C. *The Economics of Welfare*. London: Macmillan & Company, 1920.

Pigou, A.C. *A Study in Public Finance*, 3rd ed. London: Macmillan, 1947.

Plott, C.R. 'Externalities and Corrective Taxes'. *Economica* 33 (February 1966): 84–7.

Rothchild, T. 'User Fees at the Nuclear Regulatory Commission'. In T.D. Hopkins, ed. *Federal User Fees: Proceedings of a Symposium*, Administrative Conference of the United States, Washington, DC, 1988: pp. 84–9.

Thorne, S.E. *Essays in English Legal History*. London: The Hambledon Press, 1979.

Turvey, R. 'On Divergencies Between Social Cost and Private Cost. *Economica* 30 (August 1963): 309–13.

US EPA 'Unfinished Business: A Comparative Assessment of Environmental Problems: Overview Report'. Washington: US EPA (February 1987).

US Congress. *Hearings on Economic Analysis and the Efficiency of Government*. Joint Economic Committee, 1971.

US General Accounting Office. 'Hazardous Waste: Issues Surrounding Insurance Availability', GAP/RCED–88–2. Washington: US General Accounting Office, October 1987.

White, L.J. *Reforming Regulation: Processes and Problems*. Englewood Cliffs, NJ: Prentice Hall, 1981.

White, S.D. *Sir Edward Coke and 'The Grievances of the Commonwealth,' 1621–28*. Chapel Hill: The University of North Carolina Press, 1979.

Yandle, B. 'Taxation, Political Action, and Superfund'. *Cato Journal* 8 (Winter 1989): 751–64.

Yandle, B. and Young, E. 'Regulating the Function, Not the Industry'. *Public Choice* 51 (1986): 59–69.

4 The political economy of user charges

Some bureaucratic implications

Dwight R. Lee

Given the advantages of market prices it is not surprising that economists are almost unanimous in their recommendation to impose political prices in the form of user charges in many situations where market prices are absent. In cases where price-excludable goods and services are being publicly provided at little or no charge (for example, airport landings), or where economic activity generates significant social costs (for example, polluting activities), politically imposed user charges are seen by economists as efficiency-enhancing alternatives to market prices.

Under certain circumstances it is surely the case that improvements in efficiency will result from a programme of governmentally imposed user charges. Certainly, user charges are capable of rationing goods and services among competing users in ways that increase the total value they provide. Also, the voluntary payment consumers make when charges are imposed provide information on the relative value they place on the good or service under consideration, and provide the financial resources and the motivation to provide more of that which consumers value most. But even granting the general advantages of pricing goods and services, the circumstances under which user charges are efficiency enhancing are more restrictive than most economists realize. Important problems can arise precisely because user charges for government services are determined and imposed by the political process. There are fundamental differences between the prices that emerge from market transactions and those that are imposed by the political process.

The claimants against the revenue raised by a market price are typically well specified, as is the extent of their claims. On the other hand, the revenue raised by a political price typically goes into a common pool (the general fund) with the claimants to these revenues not well specified. In principle, general fund revenues belong to all citizens, and are to be used for the general benefit. In practice, however, organized interests are actively involved in efforts to lay claim to these revenues, with the success of these efforts determined on the basis of political competition. The difference between market competition and political competition in the claims on revenues has important efficiency implications. Recipients of revenues generated by political prices stand to gain or lose on the basis of how well they use resources to influence political decisions; this is a use of resources that generally does more to redistribute existing wealth than to create new wealth. Recipients of revenues raised by a market price stand to gain or lose on the basis of how efficiently they use resources to respond to the preferences of consumers; this is a use of resources that creates wealth.

The tenuous connection between the amount of revenue received from politically imposed user charges and the efficiency of the response to the consumers' preferences for the goods and services being charged for is a problem that exists even when the user charge is set at the efficient level. Unfortunately, in the absence of transferable property rights and market exchange, the information necessary for choosing the efficient charge is not available. And even if the information were available there may be little motivation to set the user charge at the efficient level, given the political incentives that will often dominate the pricing decision. Consumer groups will favour a low user charge, as will private producers of goods that are complementary to the public service subject to the charge. The public agency providing the service will also often prefer to keep the user fee low in order to maximize the number of citizens who are anxious to have the service provided, and therefore anxious to have the agency well funded. On the other hand, there will often be organized groups which want to restrict the use of a government service (for example, access to wilderness areas) and so will push for a high user charge. So rather than being determined through the interplay of supply and demand, the determination of user charges will be heavily influenced by the interplay of special-interest political pressures.

In the present paper some of the above problems will be considered with an emphasis on the response of the bureaucratic supplier of the publicly provided service that is subject to a user charge. The basic analytical framework will be that of the Niskanen model (1971) of bureaucratic budget maximization. Because the supply response to a user charge by the bureaucratic providers of a service will typically be only remotely connected to the demand response of consumers to the charge, the ability of user charges to enhance efficiency is shown to be limited, and possibly non-existent.

1   THE BUREAUCRATIC ENVIRONMENT

In private firms, with a well-defined residual claimant controlling management decisions, strong incentives exist to produce the firm's output at least cost and to price it in such a way as to maximize net revenues. There is no motivation to expand output beyond the point where the cost of producing the marginal unit is equal to the revenue received from so doing. For to produce beyond this point would be to reduce the profit going to the residual claimant without creating any compensating benefit. In the case of the modern corporation, in which there is separation of ownership and management, the incentives to produce the profit maximizing output at least cost are less compelling than in the owner-managed firm. Managers, as imperfectly controlled agents of the stockholder-owners, possess some latitude within which to capture personal benefits by increasing output and costs at the expense of shareholder profits. Because of this latitude, such economists as Penrose (1959), Baumol (1959), and Marris (1964) have justified the assumption of sales and growth maximization in models of firm behaviour. But even in these models, minimum profit constraints are imposed because of the recognition that managerial discretion is limited in private firms. And more recent work, exemplified by that of Fama and Jensen (1983a, 1983b) and Demsetz (1983), have pointed to corporate arrangements that serve to reduce significantly, though not eliminate, the agency costs associated with the separation of ownership and management.

It is within bureaucratic agencies providing government services that one finds the most extreme cases of managerial discretion and the greatest potential for those with direct decision-making control to sacrifice general economic efficiency in order to obtain personal benefits. Typically the bureau's output is not priced, and so there is no direct connection between the value of the output it supplies and the revenue it receives. Even if there is a charge for the bureau's output, the resulting revenue is seldom returned to the bureau, and never returned as revenue that, once factor inputs have been paid, belongs to a residual claimant within the bureau. The bureau's budget, and the salaries of the public bureau's managers, come not from the sale of goods and services but from appropriations decided upon by a legislative body. This is not to suggest, however, that there is no connection between the amount of the output the bureau provides and the return received by bureau managers. Generally speaking, larger outputs justify larger budgets and larger budgets result in more prestige, perquisites, power, and salary for bureau managers.[1]

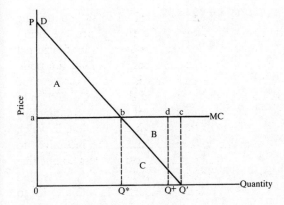

Figure 4.1 Niskanen's model of bureaucracy

These considerations led Niskanen (1971) to develop formal models of bureaucratic behaviour under the assumption that bureau managers are motivated by the desire to maximize their bureau's budget. This is obviously a simplifying assumption, although Niskanen provides reasons for believing that managers possess certain advantages over those in the legislature who determine the bureau's funding, and that these advantages make the budget-maximization assumption a reasonable one. Not surprisingly, however, since Niskanen's initial work, there have been refinements in his theory. Migue and Belanger (1974) argue that budget maximization may conflict with other objectives that bureau managers may have, and they develop a model of bureau behaviour around a more complicated objective function. Niskanen (1975) also develops a model around the assumption that bureaucrats maximize utility in a multiple objective utility function. Although these refinements are of theoretical interest, they leave intact Niskanen's insight that managers of government bureaucracies realize private advantages when the budgets of those bureaucracies are increased. And the results of the present paper are not materially affected by staying with the simple budget-maximizing assumption.

The basic Niskanen model is illustrated in Figure 4.1. The marginal benefit generated by the provision of the bureau's output is given by the demand curve D. Minimum marginal and average costs of providing the output are assumed equal, and therefore constant, and are given by the MC curve. The efficient level of output is given by Q^*, where marginal cost equals the marginal benefit, with the surplus being generated given by the area in triangle A. If the bureau provides output Q* at minimum cost and receives an appropriation equal to its cost, then it receives a budget given by abQ*O, with the sponsoring legislature (or the constituents of its members) capturing the maximum surplus, A. However, given Niskanen's assumption that the bureau managers possess information not possessed by the legislature and are in a bargaining position superior to that of the legislature, bureau managers will be able to capture some of the surplus for themselves by expanding bureau output beyond Q* and acquiring a bigger budget based on the greater costs of production. Indeed, at the limit the bureau can expand output as long as the marginal benefit from doing so is non-negative and the surplus generated by the output is non-negative. As Figure 4.1 is constructed, this means that output can be expanded to Q' since the loss in surplus from expanding output from Q* to Q', area B, is less than the surplus at Q*, given by area A. Assuming least cost production, at output Q' the bureau receives a budget given by the area bcQ'O. Since A > B in Figure 4.1 it is conceivable that the bureau can obtain an even larger budget by increasing the per-unit cost of output to the point where no surplus is left at Q'.

Implicit in this admittedly abbreviated and simplified discussion of the Niskanen model of bureaucracy is the assumption that the bureau's output is made available to consumers at no direct charge. When considering the output expansion from Q* to Q', for example, it was assumed that consumer benefits increased by an amount equal to area C in Figure 4.1, which implies that consumption of the output expands as long as the marginal benefits derived from this consumption is non-negative. There is no reason, of course, why a direct charge cannot be levied upon consumers of the bureau's service. And if such a charge is imposed it will reduce the range over which consumer demand provides a justification for output expansion. At first impression it may appear that, in this situation, a user charge will promote efficiency by limiting bureaucratic overexpansion. However, first impressions can be, and often are, deceiving. We next consider the efficiency implications of imposing a user charge on the output of a budget-maximizing bureaucracy such as the one described in this section.

2   THE IMPOTENCE OF USER CHARGES IN A BUREAUCRATIC SETTING

Commonly, services provided by government bureaux are made available to consumers at either no direct charge or at a greatly subsidized charge. Examples include airports, roads, medical facilities, and public transportation. Because of the absence of a charge that reflects the marginal cost of supplying the service, it follows that consumption will expand beyond the point where marginal benefit equals marginal cost. It is for this reason that economists typically support imposing a user charge that reflects the marginal cost of production on many bureaucratically provided services. For example, the standard argument would recommend a per-unit user charge equal to MC in Figure 4.1 since this would reduce consumption to Q^*, which is seen as the efficient output.

It is certainly the case that in a setting characterized by market prices and residual claimants, a per-unit charge, or price, of MC would generate an efficient outcome given the demand and cost conditions described in Figure 4.1. Not only would a price of MC motivate an amount consumed of Q^*, it would also motivate an amount supplied of Q^*. A private supplier obviously has no motivation to provide a product or service in excess of the amount for which consumers are willing to pay. Also, the private supplier as a residual claimant is motivated to provide the service in the least cost way. This may not be the case, however, when a user charge of MC is imposed on a service being provided by a government bureau.

Consider again Figure 4.1 with no charge being imposed, an amount Q' being supplied, and the supplying bureau extracting a budget of $abcQ'O$ from the legislature. Should a per-unit user charge of MC now be imposed, quantity consumed will decline from Q' to Q^*. If the bureau responds with an equivalent decline in the quantity supplied, the generated consumers' surplus will increase from A − B to A. But note that the increased surplus comes at the expense of the bureau's budget, which declines from $abcQ'O$ to abQ^*O.

A Niskanen bureau is in a position to prevent such a big decline in its budget by maintaining output above Q^*. Under conditions most favourable to the bureau, it could maintain output at a level that finds the surplus from the service being provided equal to zero. In the presence of the user charge, any expansion in output beyond Q^* reduces surplus by the entire cost of production.[2] If output remains at Q', for example, the surplus would equal A − (B + C) which, as Figure 4.1 is constructed, is slightly negative. Since the Niskanen bureau cannot expand output beyond the point which exhausts all surplus, the bureau would have to reduce output somewhat below Q' in response to the user charge of MC, say to Q^+ in Figure 4.1, where area A is equal to area Q^*bdQ^+.

In this case it is clear that imposing the user charge has not improved efficiency. Indeed, as presented, efficiency has actually been reduced.

66   Charging for government

Before the user charge the output of the bureau was in excess of the efficient output, Q*, by a greater amount than after the charge, but some positive surplus remained. After the user charge is imposed, output declines but no surplus remains, because the reduction in consumption resulting from the charge reduces the benefit received from the service by more than the reduction in output reduces the cost of providing it.

It can be argued that under the user charge the bureau will not be able to reduce the surplus below the amount generated in the absence of the charge. If true, then in response to the charge the bureau's output will decline below Q^+ in Figure 4.1 until the surplus is the same as it was before the charge: A – B. But even in this case there is no increase in efficiency as a result of the user charge. There is no doubt that a user charge will reduce the amount consumed. But unless there is some reason for believing that a user charge will reduce the ability of the bureau to enhance its budget at the expense of the economic surplus its output creates, there is no reason to believe that a user charge on that output will increase efficiency.

In the discussion so far, it has been assumed that the bureau was producing at the least per-unit cost, regardless of whether or not a user charge was imposed. However, it is possible for a bureau to augment its budget by operating at excessive cost as well as by operating at excessive output, and this possibility is relevant to the prospect for improving efficiency by imposing a user charge on the bureau's output.

Consider Figure 4.2 where, as before, D represents the demand curve, or marginal benefit curve, for the bureau's service and MC represents the minimum marginal and average cost of production, which is

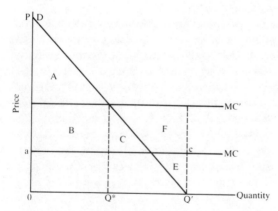

Figure 4.2 Inefficient bureau output

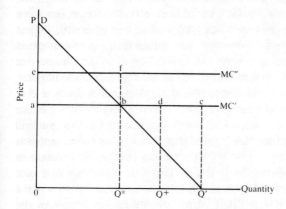

Figure 4.3 Bureau financed by a user charge

assumed to be lower than the MC in Figure 4.1. If, in the absence of a user charge, the budget-maximizing bureau produces at least cost it will produce an output of Q' and receive a budget given by the area OacQ' in Figure 4.2. But this budget leaves a large surplus (given by the combined areas ABC – E) unexploited by the bureau. The bureau can exploit this surplus to the full by operating less efficiently with marginal and average costs given by MC' in Figure 4.2, where MC' intersects D where price elasticity is unity. With this higher cost, output can remain at Q', exhausting all surplus (area A equals area F + E), with the bureau's budget increasing by an amount equal to the area B + C + F.

Assume now that a per-unit user charge equal to MC' is imposed on the bureau's output. In response, the amount demanded will decline to Q* from Q'. Turning attention to Figure 4.3, in which D and MC' are the same as in Figure 4.2, it is obvious that the bureau cannot continue operating at Q' with cost curve MC' since to do so would, with the reduced consumption, result in negative surplus (area Pab < area bQ*Q'c). If the bureau continued to operate with costs MC' it will have to reduce output to $Q^+ = 1/2 (Q^* + Q')$, since area Pab equals area bQ*Q+d in Figure 4.3. This will leave the bureau with a budget of adQ+O.

The bureau could expand output beyond Q^+ by operating more efficiently (operating along a lower marginal cost curve), but to do so would reduce expenditures (and therefore the budget) over the range where the lower marginal cost curve is below the demand curve by more than it increased the surplus that could be captured through a larger budget because of the extra output. On the other hand, increasing marginal costs above MC' (which would reduce the budget-maximizing output) would reduce the expenditure up to the point where the higher marginal cost intersected the demand, and reduce the surplus that could be captured by producing beyond that point. The most the bureau can capture is equal to its expenditure at the point where its marginal cost curve intersects the demand curve, plus the consumers' surplus at that point. And it is when the marginal cost curve intersects the demand curve at the point of unitary demand elasticity that this sum is maximized, and therefore the bureau can do no better than operate along this marginal cost curve.[3] Of course, to capture the consumer surplus that exists where the marginal cost intersects the demand, output has to be expanded beyond this intersection point. And when a user charge is being imposed that prevents consumption from expanding as output is expanded, the bureau's output can be expanded less than otherwise.

So if the bureau is operating inefficiently to maximize its budget before the user charge is imposed, the imposition of the charge will result in a smaller output. But there is still no gain generated by the charge. Both before and after the user charge is imposed, the surplus from the service being provided is entirely dissipated by a combination of excess cost and output.

It may seem that if, somehow, the legislature were able to impose a limit on the output of the bureau then it could generate an increase in efficiency with a user charge. For example, in the situation described by Figure 4.3, the legislature could impose a user charge of MC' on the bureau's output and then restrict the bureau's output level to Q*. However if we remain with the assumption that the bureau can enhance its budget through inefficient production this restriction on output will motivate the bureau to operate even less efficiently than it was when producing along marginal cost curve MC'. With output restricted to Q*, the bureau can improve its situation by increasing its marginal cost to MC'' in Figure 4.3. With marginal cost MC'', the bureau's budget when producing an output of Q* will be area OefQ* which exhausts all surplus resulting from the service and leaves the bureau's budget the same as it was with output Q+ and per-unit cost of MC' (area aefb equals area Q*bdQ+).[4] Even with the assumed increase in legislative control over the bureau, no efficiency gain results from imposing the user charge on the bureau's output.

It is true, of course, that if the legislature could, in addition to restricting output to the efficient level, restrict per-unit cost to a reasonable, if not the minimum, level, efficiency would increase with the imposition of a user charge. But if the legislature had the control necessary to force the bureau to reduce output below pre-user charge levels, while controlling per-unit costs, it would have sufficient control to increase bureau efficiency without imposing a user charge. Also, the type of legislative control just discussed is inconsistent with the assumption of a setting characterized by a Niskanen bureau. To the extent that bureaux are able to behave in the way Niskanen modelled them, there will be little, if any efficiency gain from imposing a user charge on the bureau's output, even when that charge is set equal to the marginal cost of production.

It is unlikely that the interplay of political pressures that are relevant to the setting of a user charge will result in the charge being set at the marginal cost of production. It is reasonable to believe that the bureau supplying a service will prefer a zero, or very low, user charge. Even though a bureau is able to resort to the practices just discussed in order to maintain its budget in the face of a decline in the amount demanded, it is undoubtedly the case that the budget-maximizing objectives are more easily achieved when the amount demanded is high. It has also been argued by Benson and Mitchell (1988) that private suppliers will typically supply complements to government services, and these private suppliers will apply political pressure in favour of keeping the government services uncharged, or charged at heavily subsidized levels. Obviously, when a user charge is set at a very low level there is little efficiency gain even if the bureau makes the appropriate supply response to the charge. And when the charge is extremely low (with the amount demanded remaining high) it is easier for the bureau to frustrate any efficiency gain with an inappropriate supply response.

Despite the political pressure favouring a low user charge, it is possible that offsetting pressure in favour of an inappropriately high user charge will prevail. This is particularly true when user charges are motivated by the desire for, and seen as an effective means to, more political revenue. If a user charge is set at the revenue-maximizing level it may reduce, or distort, consumption to such an extent that efficiency is reduced even if the bureau makes the appropriate supply response to the charge. According to an empirical study by Wilson (1986), road user charges were set so high in Singapore that commuters, and very likely the general society, were made worse off.

3 SOME QUALIFICATIONS

In cases where the government bureau produces a product like postage stamps, which if not consumed will visibly accumulate, the problems discussed in the previous section will be less likely to arise. If there is a decrease in the amount consumed in response to an increase in the per-unit charge it would be difficult for the bureau to justify producing the good, and accumulating it, in excess of the amount sold.

But for many services provided by government bureaux the provision of the service is tied to a facility, with the connection between the size of the facility and the amount of service consumed being very flexible. It is this flexibility that allows a bureau to maintain its expenditures, and therefore its budget, in the face of decreases in the consumption of the service it provides. Relevant examples are the services provided by roads, parks, airports, mass transit facilities, and medical facilities. In providing these services it is not difficult for a bureau to secure funding that will maintain a facility capable of providing an amount of service far in excess of the demands placed upon it. Empty buses are a common sight, many national parks are lightly visited, and many publicly supported hospitals contain a large amount of excess capacity.

In the cases just mentioned, the short-run marginal cost will typically be quite low once the facility is in place, with most of the cost being considered fixed. Over the long-run, however, the appropriate size of the facility depends on the use of the facility and the cost of maintaining, replacing, and possibly expanding the facility, and this cost can properly be attributed to the use of the service provided. Our analysis has been greatly simplified by considering the marginal cost of use to be the long-run marginal cost, which includes what in the short-run is considered the fixed cost associated with the facility.

The conclusion of the analysis holds, however, even if the short-run difference between fixed and marginal cost is considered, with the user charge taking the form of a two-part fee to accommodate efficiently the two costs involved. Assume that the user charge consists of a lump sum access fee to cover the facility cost and a per-unit user fee equal to the low marginal cost of use. With this two-part fee arranged efficiently, no one who finds the advantage in paying the fixed charge will be discouraged from expanding their consumption to the efficient level, and no one whose benefit from using the facility exceeds the costs (both long-run and short-run) of doing so will be discouraged from paying the access charge.[5]

The efficient two-part pricing scheme will, however, reduce consumption below the level which will occur when there is no charge, because the charge will eliminate altogether some people as consumers. The reduction in consumption will require a smaller facility as the efficient supply response. However, given the assumption of bureaucratic incentives and control made in this paper, the bureau will continue to receive the budget necessary to maintain a size of facility in excess of that which would efficiently serve the reduced demands placed upon it. If the legislature is able to respond to the reduction in consumption by requiring a smaller facility the bureau can still frustrate the desire for increased efficiency by increasing both the long-run cost of maintaining the smaller facility and the short-run marginal cost associated with use of the facility. So even when the analysis is extended to consider both fixed and marginal components of costs, and the necessity of a two-part pricing scheme to realize efficiency, it is still the case that efficiency can, and likely will, be frustrated by bureaucratic behaviour.

4 THE BUREAU'S IDEAL USER CHARGE

In general a government bureau producing a service would prefer that no charge be imposed on the use of that service. Although we have seen that the budget-maximizing bureau can often circumvent the efficiencies economists hope user charges will generate, the imposition of such a charge can, at the same time, reduce the size of the maximum bureau budget. But this does not mean that a budget-maximizing bureau will object to all user charges. It is possible to describe the characteristics of a user charge that such a bureau would consider ideal. This charge would do nothing to reduce the amount of the bureau's service that is demanded; it would focus public and political attention on the demands the public is placing on the bureau's services, and it would lead to an exaggerated view of those demands; and it would raise money that can be earmarked to the bureau to supplement, rather than substitute for, existing appropriations.

The reason a bureau would favour a user charge which had these three characteristics is obvious. What is not so obvious is how a genuine user charge could have these three characteristics. And, indeed, it is not clear that a genuine user charge can satisfy all three, particularly the one requiring that the charge should not reduce the amount demanded of the service being charged for. Yet there has been a tax proposal put forth, and justified as a user charge, which would do nothing to reduce the amount demanded of the service supposedly subject to the charge. Also, the proposed 'user charge' tax has been used to call attention to what are claimed to be tremendous demands on the medical profession and government funding of health care.[6] In addition, the revenue raised by the tax is typically seen as a source of additional funding for medical care.

The tax being discussed here is the excise tax on cigarettes, and the proposal is that of increasing this tax and earmarking the revenue for medical care. The justifying rationale for this proposal is that cigarette smokers supposedly make greater use of medical care services than non-smokers and, therefore, an increase in the cigarette excise tax can be thought of as a user charge.

The ability of the cigarette excise tax to raise money for the medical bureaucracy and to serve as a vehicle for calling attention to the demand for medical services is obvious. What may not be so obvious is the lack of any clear connection between an increase in the cigarette excise tax and the amount of health care demanded. The assertion that smoking is unhealthy and therefore if people smoke less they will demand less health care has been repeated so incessantly that it is widely accepted without question. If the cigarette tax is raised then the number of cigarettes demanded will decrease, and therefore it must be true that health care expenditures will also decrease, or so the argument goes.

In fact, there is no convincing evidence that increasing the cigarette tax will reduce the amount of health care demanded. First, while the demand curve for cigarettes is downward sloping, as are demand curves in general, the price elasticity of demand for cigarettes is quite low. This means that if the price of cigarettes is increased by 1 per cent the number of cigarettes demanded will decrease by far less than 1 per cent. But quite apart from the question of how much smoking will decrease if cigarette prices increase, there is no reason to expect that the amount people smoke has any effect on how much lifetime health care they demand.

Without getting into a discussion of the health consequences of smoking, it should be obvious that even if smoking is detrimental to one's health it does not follow that smoking increases the total demand for health care. If smoking is a health hazard, then the smoker's demand for medical services may peak at an earlier age than will the demand of the non-smoker, but this does not imply that lifetime health care demands will differ between smokers and non-smokers. On this point, there is evidence that smoking has no influence on the amount of lifetime health care demanded. Leu and Schaub (1983), for example, performed a simulation study of Switzerland under the assumption that, beginning in 1876, Switzerland became a smokeless nation. Given the assumption that smoking is a health hazard, Leu and Schaub concluded from their study that the medical expenses in the smokeless Switzerland would be roughly the same as in the real-world Switzerland with its many smokers.

So the claim that the cigarette excise tax is justified as a user charge for health care is fallacious. There is no connection between the amount of health care an individual consumes and the amount he will pay through the cigarette tax 'user charge'. But it is for this very reason that the user charge justification for the cigarette tax is so popular with those associated with the medical bureaucracy. It is a charge which can be used to increase their budgets without doing anything to reduce the demands which are used to justify budget increases.

5 CONCLUSION

Imposing a charge on a good or service equal to marginal production cost generates obvious efficiencies when that charge results from, or is accompanied by, the profit incentives found in private firms. It is for this reason that economists recommend imposing user charges on services provided by government bureaux.

Unfortunately, this recommendation implicitly assumes that government bureaux will respond to demand consequences of increasing the per-unit charge on their product in the same way a private firm does. This assumption is not warranted according to the standard analysis of bureaucratic behaviour as formulated by the Niskanen model of bureaucracy. Given the incentives and control that a bureau has in the Niskanen model, imposing a user charge on a bureau's output cannot be expected to increase efficiency. The bureau will respond to the decrease in consumption that results from the imposition of a user charge by some combination of failing adequately to reduce output and increasing per-unit cost. The motivation for this response is the desire to maximize the bureau's budget, and the result of this response is that there is no increase in the surplus provided by the bureau's output.

It may be the case, however, that by reducing the amount of the bureau's service demanded, a user charge on that service will reduce the maximum budget obtainable. In general, then, bureaux will oppose the imposition of a user charge on the service they provide. However, a bureau can be expected to embrace the standard justification for a user charge if that charge will raise money likely to be used to increase the bureau's budget while doing nothing to reduce the amount of the bureau's service demanded. The medical bureaucracy, for instance, has exactly this motivation behind its attempt to justify increases in the cigarette excise tax as a user charge for medical care. Such a tax increase would raise money that can be earmarked to public expenditures for health care without doing anything to dampen the demand for medical care.

NOTES

1 As will be discussed, budgets can also be increased within limits by increasing per unit costs as well as by increasing output.
2 It is assumed here that none of the output in excess of Q* is consumed, even though output in excess of Q* is available for consumption. As an example, imposing a higher bus fare reduces the use of the bus system even though the amount of bus service supplied remains unchanged.
3 This conclusion is based on the assumption of a horizontal marginal cost curve.
4 If the user charge were increased to MC' when the bureau increased its costs to MC', then the increase in cost would have reduced the size of the budget the bureau could capture.
5 For a discussion of the conditions necessary for efficiency in a two-part pricing scheme in the case of a public good, but which is completely applicable to this case, see Lee (1982).
6 Although medical care is not provided by a government bureau, narrowly defined, the medical establishment receives such a significant portion of its revenue through government programmes that in many respects it faces much the same cost-increasing, output-expanding, budget-maximizing incentives as Niskanen bureaux.

REFERENCES

Baumol, W.J. *Business Behavior. Value and Growth.* New York: Macmillan, 1959.
Benson, B.L. and Mitchell, J.M. 'Rent Seekers who Demand Government Production: Bureaucratic Output and the Price of Complements'. *Public Choice* 56, 1 (1988): 3–16.
Demsetz, H. 'The Structure of Ownership and the Theory of the Firm'. *Journal of Law and Economics* 26 (June 1983): 375–90.
Fama, E.F. and Jensen, M.C. 'Separation of Ownership and control'. *Journal of Law and Economics* 26 (June 1983): 301–25.
Fama, E.F. 'Agency Problems and Residual Claims'. *Journal of Law and Economics* 26 (June 1983): 327–49.
Lee, D.R. 'On the Pricing of Public Goods'. *Southern Economic Journal* 49 (July 1982): 99–105.
Leu, R.E., and Schaub, T. 'Does Smoking Increase Medical Care Expenditure?'. *Social Science and Medicine* 17 (1983): 1907–14.
Marris, R. *The Economic Theory of Managerial Capitalism*, New York: Free Press, 1964.
Migue, J.L. and Belanger, G. 'Towards a General Theory of Managerial Discretion'. *Public Choice* 18 (Spring 1974): 27–43.
Niskanen, W.A., Jr. *Bureaucracy and Presentative Government.* Chicago: Aldine-Atherton, 1971.
Niskanen, W.A., Jr. 'Bureaucrats and Politicians'. *Journal of Law and Economics* 24 (December 1975): 617–43.
Penrose, E. *The Theory of the Growth of the Firm.* Oxford: Oxford University Press, 1959.
Wilson, P.W. 'Welfare Effects of Congestion Pricing in Singapore'. Unpublished manuscript, Univesity of Georgia, 1986.

5 Subjective cost, property rights, and public pricing

Richard E. Wagner

By now a vast literature has developed on the welfare economics of public-enterprise pricing.[1] This literature seeks to specify rules for setting prices that public enterprises should follow if they are efficiently to promote consumer welfare. User charges are themselves a form of public-enterprise price, for they too represent prices charged by government for services it provides. A charge imposed on boat owners by the Coast Guard, and declared to be a fee for services rendered, is as much a public-enterprise price as is a charge imposed by a public electric company. Hence the literature on public-enterprise pricing is fully applicable to user charging, as are the controversies and problems associated with that literature.

User charges are commonly thought to be an instrument for promoting fiscal efficiency. On the surface they would seem to represent a practical way to implement the benefit principle of public finance, in that people pay for publicly provided services according to their usage of those services. In this context, there would seem to be two main lines of objection to user charges, one normative and the other positive. Normatively, even though it might be relatively easy to charge users of parks, it might also be objected that doing so is unfair to people with relatively low incomes. Positively, although the principle of charging beneficiaries might be acceptable, there might not exist any practical way of doing so. The provision of water and highways might both appear suitable in principle for user charges; however, user charges are surely easier to implement for water than for highways, because it is much less costly to meter usage and practise exclusion for water than for highways.[2] In this chapter I focus on that subset of cases for which user charges are generally considered appropriate and explore some of the conflicts between the normative principles that would seem to undergird user charges and the actual practice of user charging.

When it is applied to user charges, the literature on public choice explains why the mere articulation of normative statements about efficient pricing policies does nothing to assure that those polices will actually be implemented. The policies that are actually implemented will depend on incentives that are possessed, both by managers of the enterprises and by the legislative sponsors of those enterprises. Those pricing policies will also depend on knowledge that managers and sponsors possess about such things as methods of production and consumer demands, as well as on the incentives those people have to discover and use such knowledge. The actual practice of user charging may diverge substantially from the principles articulated in the normative literature.

A full consideration of the possible divergence between the theory and practice of user charges would consider both the choice to impose charges instead of taxes and the selection of a particular charge in those cases where charges are imposed. In other words, it would be necessary to consider both whether political processes can be expected to operate to impose charges where they are appropriate, and to consider whether the level of charge that is imposed will be appropriate, as this is defined by standard efficiency criteria. While I shall consider both topics, I will concentrate on the second one.

1   WHEN SHOULD USERS BE CHARGED?

What is the scope for user charges in a model where government is presumed to be driven by the dictates of economic efficiency, as these are articulated by the benefit principle of public finance? In the first instance, such a model would have private goods being provided through market processes while public goods were provided by government and financed by taxation. User charges would find themselves in some form of classificatory suspension. If users cannot be charged for their usage the theory of public goods asserts the normative case for tax finance, as represented by models of Lindahl pricing and the like. But if users can be charged for their usage, if the service is divisible among users and if exclusion can be practised, market provision would seem suitable, leaving no place for public provision. So it is necessary in any examination of user charges from an efficiency perspective to consider the circumstances under which user charging might be appropriate in the first place.

There would seem to be two primary ways to justify user charges for divisible services on efficiency grounds. One is that the service in question jointly supplies private and collective consumption services, or is otherwise subject to significant external effects. If this were so, efficiency in provision might require a combination of tax finance and user charge. For instance, education is often portrayed as supplying a divisible, private service, as represented by the formation of individual human capital, while at the same time providing a collective consumption service, as represented by assertions about the general value of living in a better-educated society. To be sure, this joint supply of private and collective consumption services does not, by itself, imply that efficiency requires collective provision. Market provision of the service in question is possible, with provision of the collective portion supported by a subsidy extracted in Lindahl fashion.

Moreover, the jointness in supply does not imply that inefficiency will characterize the provision of the collective consumption service. Rather, such jointness means only that inefficiency *might* result. It is certainly possible that the choices that people make within markets will simultaneously generate an efficient supply of the collective consumption component. The presence of external benefits from education does not mean that marginally significant externalities will remain after people have exercised their market choices. None the less, such external effects can provide a rationalization for collective provision, with some reliance being placed on user charges. In this case education, or any other similarly situated service, would be supplied collectively at below-market prices, with the subsidy being necessary to induce the output expansion required by the externality.

The other main efficiency argument for user charges is that they are preferable to tax finance for financing various public enterprises that are naturally monopolistic. Many governments supply airline and railroad services, many are involved in the supply of electricity and gas, and numerous other examples that correspond to notions of natural monopoly could be given. In these cases the justification for public provision is not so much that there is some jointness between collective and private attributes of the service being produced, as that market provision may be inefficient even if the service is essentially private in nature. User charges are seen as appropriate ways of financing such public enterprises because the alternative of provision through private enterprises would be inefficient. To be sure, in such cases it is possible to leave the activity in private hands and to regulate it instead. Whether public provision financed through user charges would be superior to provision by private but regulated firms is open to question, but at least this possibility offers a circumstance under which user charging can square with efficiency precepts.

2   A SIMPLE MODEL OF EFFICIENT PUBLIC PRICING

A vast literature, surveyed nicely in Bös (1986), has by now developed
on the economic theory of public enterprise pricing. And the principles
and problems of efficient user charging are fundamentally the same as
those that surround public-enterprise pricing. There is no essential
difference, normatively speaking, between the pricing policies of such
traditional public enterprises as electric companies, phone companies,
and post offices on the one hand, and fees imposed by governments for
usage of libraries, golf courses, garages, and parks on the other hand.

The primary part of the literature on public enterprise pricing is
concerned with complications arising out of the conflict between
average cost and marginal cost pricing, when average cost is declining
over the relevant range of output.[3] This conflict is illustrated by Figure
5.1. An enterprise that set price equal to average cost would produce Q_a
at a price of P_a per unit. But in doing so it would impose a welfare loss
on consumers of the service, because the value of a marginal unit of
output exceeds the cost of that marginal unit by *ab* at Q_a. This welfare
loss could be eliminated by marginal cost pricing, which would yield an
output of Q_m and a price of P_m. However, marginal cost pricing
generates a loss of *cd* per unit of output. Hence, a conflict results
between marginal cost pricing, which is efficient but inconsistent with
survival of the enterprise, and average cost pricing, which though
inefficient allows the enterprise to survive.

Much of the literature on public-enterprise pricing has explored,
often from a second best perspective, various approaches to resolving or
at least softening the conflict between these two pricing rules. One line

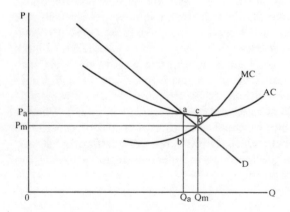

Figure 5.1 Marginal cost pricing dilemma

of approach involves a subsidy to the enterprise to cover the loss that marginal cost pricing would entail. But to provide the subsidy requires the imposition of taxes, and those taxes will inject new sources of excess burden into the economy, unless they are imposed in a lump-sum fashion, which is generally acknowledged to be impossible.[4] Another line of approach involves the use of multi-part pricing.[5] The loss of cd per unit of output in Figure 5.6 results because all units of output are priced identically with the marginal, Q_mth unit; when all units are priced at P_m, when average cost is $P_m + cd$, a loss of cd per unit must result. But marginal cost pricing does not require that all units of output be priced identically. It requires only that the marginal unit be priced at marginal cost; inframarginal units can carry higher prices. When multi-part pricing is allowed there will be many particular pricing plans that will both cover the cost of the enterprise and set the price of the marginal unit equal to marginal cost, resulting in a rate of output of Q_m. In such cases as these, the loss that would result from uniform pricing would not have to be covered by taxation, but actually would be contributed voluntarily by the consumers of the service, and with those contributions representing a kind of membership fee in a consumers' club, as Buchanan (1968) explains.

While these questions surrounding declining average cost are interesting in their own right, the complexities they introduce are not relevant to the types of issues I wish to raise here. For these issues are independent of whatever particular 'solution' may be adopted to the conflict between average cost and marginal cost pricing. In other words, whatever conclusion may be reached about efficient pricing under a condition of declining average cost, there are grounds for doubting that either the knowledge or the incentive exists to implement that pricing policy. To develop this argument in its simplest fashion I shall assume that average cost is constant over output. Admittedly, this assumption clashes with the common, natural monopoly justification for much public enterprise. But the essential features of this argument would not be changed by making the argument more complex, as through introducing multi-part pricing.

The main issues I wish to explore here can be examined with reference to Figure 5.2. With marginal cost assumed constant, the efficient public price would be P_c and the resulting public output would be Q_c. By contrast, the natural monopoly outcome would have a price of P_m and an output of Q_m. All this is in the form of instructions to a public enterprise: the enterprise is exhorted to charge a price of P_c, and if it does so people would consume Q_c if their demands were appropriately characterized by D.

But suppose we observe an actual public enterprise. Do we conclude

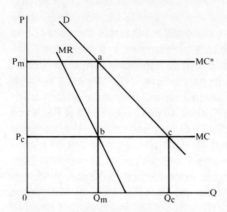

Figure 5.2 Monopoly pricing by public enterprise

that its price corresponds to the efficient price described in Figure 5.2, by virtue of the mere fact that the enterprise is a *public* enterprise? This is surely wishful thinking clouding reality. In light of the public choice revolution and related developments in economics, few people would observe a particular public price and conclude that this price *must* correspond to the efficient price characterized by such economic models as that represented by Figure 5.2. At the very least it would be necessary to give some argument as to why such an observed price is likely to correspond to the efficient price; or, alternatively, to explain why such a correspondence is unlikely to result. It is the latter approach that I will take here.

3   KNOWLEDGE AND RULES FOR PUBLIC PRICES

For actual user charges to correspond to efficient charges it is necessary for those who set charges either to have knowledge of the relevant demand and cost conditions or to operate within an institutional environment through which such knowledge emerges at the relevant margins of choice. The former condition is unlikely for any productive enterprise, public or private. Neither demand nor cost is some objective magnitude that is available for some enterprise manager either to compute or to solicit from someone else. There is no assured recipe for success as it were, which in turn means that there is no way, even with respect to the simple situation depicted by Figure 5.2, that some external observer can judge whether an enterprise manager would be following a rule or instruction to set price equal to marginal cost.[6]

While such knowledge is not available to business firms either, there are grounds for arguing that competitive market processes will tend to result in outcomes that correspond reasonably closely to P_c and Q_c in Figure 5.2. But when it comes to public enterprises there is surely less reason to associate the observed prices and quantities with the conceptual constructs represented by Figure 5.2. If the public enterprise were simply one firm among many in a competitively organized industry, all of which were playing by essentially the same rules of the game, it might be reasonable to assume that this tendency held as strongly for the public enterprise as for the various private enterprises that also participated in the market. After all, a cost function is just a conceptual construct and not some tangible entity. It is a boundary that separates the possible from the impossible: it is always possible to produce a particular output in a more costly manner, but it is impossible to produce that output at lower cost. While such a boundary cannot be located by some cartographical survey, there are strong grounds for suggesting that a competitive process in which people are rewarded for increased efficiency in production will be the best available guide to the location of that boundary.

But rarely if ever do public enterprises operate simply as one participant among many within the market process. To the extent public enterprises stand outside that process it becomes less likely that their observed prices will correspond to the idealized prices. This will be true even if the enterprise manager has a single-minded devotion to trying to achieve such an idealized price. For there is no recipe for optimal production that some optimality-seeking enterprise manager can follow.

Take one small component of cost: office supplies. Numerous individual choices will determine what those expenses will be. Memoranda can be printed on one side of the paper only, or on both sides. And they can be printed on 20-lb bond paper or on recycled paper. Whatever choice is made about the type of paper to be used, less of it will be used if printing takes place at twelve or even fifteen characters per inch than if it takes place at ten. Stationary can come in one generic format for all offices, or it can be individualized in varying degrees, with information about particular offices and phone numbers. Choices about the sizes of inventories to carry will likewise affect office expenses. There is no managerial cookbook that can be followed to determine the uniquely least-cost way for handling office expenses. And what holds for such a small component of cost as office expenses holds for all other components as well.

Different people, all of whom could be described as possessing a single-minded devotion to productive efficiency, will make different choices about office management, thereby producing different observed costs or expenses. One might use recycled paper while another uses bond paper, with the latter believing that the added expense is worthwhile in terms of the better image it presents to outsiders, and perhaps in terms of enhanced employee morale as well. While it might be possible to construct a conceptual experiment that would test these contrary beliefs in a particular setting, such a test would be valid only for that particular setting and could not be presumed to be valid for other office settings. And as a practical matter it is exceedingly unlikely that any such conceptual test could be implemented without allowing some considerable margin for error.

Production is not a matter of following recipes, for they do not exist. Hence, there is no uniquely determined cost of production that exists independently of human judgement and choice. Therefore, there is no way that public prices could be set equal to marginal cost, or to some fraction of marginal cost in those cases where it is presumed that external effects call for some degree of subsidization. This means, on the one hand, that a well-intentioned public manager who wanted to implement the dictates of welfare economics, as represented by notions of marginal cost pricing, could not do so by following any external authority. This absence of external authority also means that there is no 'rule' that can be used both as instructions for public managers to follow and as a standard against which to assess managerial performance.

4   INCENTIVES AND PUBLIC PRICES

A public manager possessed by a single-minded desire to implement a programme of economic efficiency could turn to no cookbook for guidance. And no external source would exist against which to check that manager's performance. Furthermore, such single-mindedness is surely rare. For public prices are established within an institutional arrangement in which there may be higher pay-offs to enterprise managers from adopting prices other than those that would be required by economic efficiency, recognizing all the while that there is no way such efficient prices can be computed by some external observer. Public enterprises would seem at best to have weak incentives to acquire the necessary information and to incorporate it into the enterprise's pricing policies.

In many such cases the very reason for public provision would seem to reside in some pattern of subsidization that public provision entails, and which would be rescinded should market provision be relied upon.

An important component of public provision is surely the cross subsidization that benefits some consumers at the expense of others, as Posner (1971) explains. Another important component is likely often to be the interests of input suppliers, who can capture quasi-rents under conditions of rising supply prices. In some cases public provision is a way of making good on legislative deals, as represented either by schemes of cross-subsidization or by expansions of output that particularly benefit owners of inputs in relatively inelastic supply.

For instance, it has often been observed that public enterprises have more uniform prices than private enterprises in situations with periods of peak demand.[7] This difference in the extent of peak-load pricing seems consistent with what is known about incentive differences between public and private enterprises. For a private enterprise that faces periods of peak demand, a shift away from uniform to peak-load pricing can increase the firm's profitability while reducing the size of the firm's plant at the same time.

That the enterprise is public rather than private does nothing to affect the possible social gain from peak-load pricing. Yet there are understandable reasons why public enterprises might make less use of peak-load pricing, thereby operating in a more costly fashion than would a private enterprise. The owners and managers of public enterprises cannot gain directly by increasing the profitability of their enterprises. But there can be indirect ways they can profit, and they do so more fully by failing to practise peak-load pricing.

Uniform pricing creates an excess demand during the peak period, and the congestion that results might be an effective way of creating a coalition in support of an expansion in the capacity of the enterprise. For one thing, so long as the expected excess of the peak price over the uniform price exceeds the extra taxes that peak demanders would expect to pay under uniform pricing, those people will support uniform pricing combined with higher appropriations to finance the larger plant necessary to serve the peak demands. Furthermore, and as already noted, the interests of enterprise managers and the suppliers of specialized inputs will be advanced by uniform pricing and plant expansion.

Beyond this, the creation of a public enterprise that produces divisible services, as most of them do produce, is a legislative choice. Those services could have been produced by private enterprises instead. To be sure, it is commonly taken for granted that when faced with naturally monopolistic conditions a private enterprise will price monopolistically. To offset this monopoly price, two approaches are possible: first, public regulation of the enterprise's price; and, second, public ownership of the enterprise. The main type of general-interest justification for public ownership would seem to run in terms of the greater knowledge about processes of production that enterprise managers possess relative to that possessed by outside regulators. With public regulation of private enterprises this type of differential knowledge might suggest an inability of regulators fully to control monopolistic practices. Direct public ownership, by contrast, is often presumed *ipso facto* to give competitive outcomes, despite the monopoly character of the enterprise.

This line of argument is surely an adventure in fantasy. It is based on one of two premises: either that people who work for government are morally superior to those who do not, or that the institutional arrangements within government operate more strongly to constrain people to act as if they were morally superior. While moral standards seem clearly to differ among people, it would seem difficult to sustain an argument that governing officials, as a class, are morally superior. And in the light of what is probably an inherently untestable proposition, a presumption of general moral equality would seem to be reasonable and, indeed, to be the only real option. As for the claim that governmental institutions constrain people to act more morally than market institutions, despite the moral equality of those involved, this, too, seems an incredible argument. The institutional arrangements that characterize the market process are represented by the principles of property and contract, in which people respect the rights of others and operate by getting the consent of those who own whatever it is they would like to use in their own productive activities. In contrast, political processes are not constrained by the principles of property and contact, for a great deal of political activity is directed to efforts to form winning coalitions to abridge other people's rights of property and contract through legislation—though such efforts also take place privately as well.

Hence there would seem to be nothing inherent in the establishment of a public enterprise that would serve any general-interest function. A monopoly would seem to act monopolistically regardless of whether it were private or governmental; all that might matter would be the identity of the owners whose interests were being advanced. To understand the creation of such enterprises and their pricing policies it would be necessary to look to the interests served by the legislation that creates and maintains such enterprises. The creation of public enterprises and the establishment of a particular pattern of enterprise prices would seem to be best understood as a means of subsidizing those particular, dominant interests that have been successful in the market for legislation.[8] The pattern of prices charged by public enterprises would thus be better seen as part of a process of taxing and transferring than as a process of securing efficiency in the face of natural monopoly.

So, too, would be the various restrictions that concomitantly are placed on competitive private enterprises. One type of restriction simply confers an advantage on the public enterprise. The award of subsidies through supplementing user charges with appropriations is one illustration. The exemption from taxation of public enterprises is another. Both of these features operate to make such public enterprises as the postal service seem less costly than they truly are. An alternative type of restriction is the outright prohibition on the establishment of competitive private enterprises. Private citizens are generally prohibited from carrying first-class mail in competition with the postal service, though the development of fax machines and the like clearly attest to the ability of technological progress to undermine monopoly positions, however those positions might have been grounded.[9]

5 USER FEES, FISCAL POLITICS, AND DISGUISED TAXATION

Financing governmental activities through user fees is commonly portrayed as an alternative to tax finance. But in many, and perhaps in most, cases they are probably more accurately seen as a disguised form of taxation. Whether a user fee is more accurately characterized as an alternative to tax finance or as a disguised form of taxation would seem to depend to a considerable extent on whether the fee is instituted to finance a new governmental activity or to finance an activity that previously had been financed through the general fund. If the latter is the case, the user fee would seem more accurately characterized as a disguised form of new taxation.

Consider the various proposals to shift a portion of the expenses of the Coast Guard on to users and away from taxpayers in general.[10] These proposals for user fees envision fee revenues that would generate about half the revenues that are now being provided through appropriations from the general fund. The types of fees advocated include annual registration fees for recreational boats, graduated by size of boat, and similar, though significantly heavier, charges on fishing vessels. Charges would also be imposed on commercial shipping.

These proposed charges are justified on the grounds that they are a means of getting boat users to pay for services that the Coast Guard renders to them in particular. The most prominent category of expense is for search-and-rescue operations, about three-quarters of which are attributed to recreational boating. The provision of navigational aids looms close behind in annual expense. A variety of safety and environmental regulations are also administered by the Coast Guard, and these too are justified as being expenses caused directly by boating and shipping, and so are presumed to be suitable for financing through user fees.

It is surely conceivable that boaters and shippers would be willing to pay for search-and-rescue services and navigational aids through ordinary market processes. Absent governmental involvement, those services would be supplied in one way or another through market arrangements, much as Coase (1974) describes how lighthouse services were provided through market arrangements in Great Britain. And user fees could be thought of, ideally, as some form of substitute method for providing those services, recognizing all the while that collective provision cannot truly duplicate the results of actual market processes, for reasons discussed above.

But it is different if user fees are inserted into a situation where the services had previously been provided by government and financed by general-fund appropriations. For recipients of the services now subject to user fees do not experience any reduction in their general tax liabilities. The user fees do not provide the means for beneficiaries to supply themselves with a service they previously were doing without. Rather, what the fees do is allow for expanded appropriations on other items. The user fee operates as a tax, with the revenues used to finance additional appropriations elsewhere in the budget – appropriations that otherwise would have been used to provide the services now financed by the user fee.

6 A FINAL WORD

The normative approach to public pricing aims to describe rules for optimal pricing. The structure of this approach has a deceptive simplicity about it, with the deception arising because of the subjective nature of cost. The cost of choosing one production option is the value of some alternative option that could have been chosen but was rejected in favour of the option actually chosen. The cost of such a comparatively simple activity as choosing how many cattle to add to a herd depends on judgements about such things as the future prices of beef and feed, among many other relevant considerations. A number of people all instructed by and sincerely interested in following such a rule as choosing a size of herd that maximizes profit can reasonably be expected to make different choices, with those choices reflecting different evaluations of such things as anticipated future prices of beef, feed, transportation, and the like. Hence, it is impossible to determine from the actual choices people make the degree to which they are faithful to a rule of maximizing profits. Although some people may make greater profits than others after the fact, they could all be described as attempting to maximize profits or as following a rule of setting price equal to marginal cost.

People who act within the same institutional setting, say one of residual claimacy or profit-and-loss, can choose different options in the light of the same data because, among other things, they vary in their assessment of the likelihood of different possibilities. Consequently, it is certainly reasonable to expect people to make different choices under different institutional settings, even though the data on which those choices are based may not differ. If a person in one setting shares in the profits and covers part of the loss, while in a second setting a person is paid through a fixed salary and has options for higher wealth in securing future employment with a present client, the cost of choosing one course of action over another is likely to differ between those settings. In the former setting, profit maximization is likely to be the dominant motivation, but in the latter setting some willingness to sacrifice profits to give business to a potential future employer has relatively stronger survival value. Any effort to understand the actual conduct of public enterprises, rather than simply describing norms for their desired conduct, takes on added interest once it is recognized that cost, and the degree to which pricing rules are adhered to, is not an objective fact but rather depends on the evaluation by some person of the options for choice. With respect to the articulation of norms for user charging, it is surely necessary to ask why such charges are imposed in the first place. If user charges are to finance water, electricity, refuse collection, sewerage, postal services, hospitals, and the like, why have those services provided by government in the first place? One possible answer is that this prevents monopoly pricing. To which a public choice response might be that monopolies will price monopolistically in any event, though public monopoly may lead to a different distribution of monopoly rents because of differing patterns of ownership.

There would seem to be substantial areas of divergence between the lines of justification that have been advanced for user charges and the actual practice of user charging. While it might be possible to point to cases where user charges serve as instruments of fiscal efficiency, this will not be a general characteristic of user charges under prevailing institutional or constitutional arrangements. To a considerable extent user charges will be an instrument of rent seeking, as represented by programmes of cross-subsidization. Moreover, this is unlikely to change within a constitutional environment where the returns to rent seeking are relatively high. While the principle of charging beneficiaries is an element of economic efficiency, that interest in efficiency must be constitutionally rooted if it is to be sustainable.

NOTES

1 A terse survey with references is presented in Atkinson and Stiglitz (1980: 457–81).
2 With a system of transmitters and receivers installed in cars and embedded in roads, it is now actually possible to charge people directly for their use of highways.
3 Exactly the same issues arise when optimal prices are presumed, because of the presence of external benefits, to be less than full marginal cost. For in such cases the relevant cost functions are fractions of those portrayed in Figure 5.6 and this fractional quality does nothing to disturb the argument developed here.
4 For further elaboration see Lee and Tollison (1985).
5 The classic treatment of multi-part pricing is Coase (1946).
6 On the impossibility of assessing objectively whether an enterprise is following a rule of setting price equal to marginal cost, see Thirlby (1946) and Wiseman (1953), both of which are reprinted, along with several other pertinent essays in Buchanan and Thirlby (1973). For a general treatment of the subjectivity of cost, see Buchanan (1969). For a careful examination of the significance of such subjectivity, see Vaughn (1980).
7 See, for instance, Peltzman (1971).
8 For a survey of the idea of a market for legislation, see Tollison (1988).
9 Indeed, the ability of private suppliers to be competitive despite the restrictions on what they can do, despite the tax-exempt status of public enterprises, and despite the subsidies that public enterprises often receive is strong evidence against the general-interest characterization of public enterprises.
10 For an examination of Coast Guard fees as one instance among several possibilities, see Congressional Budget Office (1983, pp. 47–60).

REFERENCES

Atkinson, A.B. and Stiglitz, J.E. *Lectures on Public Economics*. New York: McGraw-Hill, 1980.
Bös, D. *Public Enterprise Economics*. Amsterdam: North Holland, 1986.
Buchanan, J.M. 'A Public Choice Approach to Public Utility Pricing', *Public Choice* 5 (Fall 1968): 1–17.
Buchanan, J.M. *Cost and Choice*. Chicago: Markham, 1969.
Buchanan, J.M. and Thirlby, G.F. *L.S.E. Essays on Cost*. New York: New York University Press, 1973.
Coase, R.H. 'The Marginal Cost Controversy', *Economica* 13 (August 1946): 169–82.

Coase, R.H. 'The Lighthouse in Economics', *Journal of Law and Economics* 17 (October 1974): 357–76.

Congressional Budget Office. *Charging for Federal Services*. Washington, D.C.: US Government Printing Office, 1983.

Lee, D.R. and Tollison, R.D. 'There is No Such Thing as a Free Tax', *Finanzarchiv* 43, 3 (1985): 541–3.

Peltzman, S. 'Pricing in Public and Private Enterprises: Electric Utilities in the United States', *Journal of Law and Economics* 14 (April 1971): 109–47.

Posner, R.A. 'Taxation by Regulation', *Bell Journal of Economics* 2 (Spring 1971): 22–50.

Thirlby, G.F. 'The Ruler', *South African Journal of Economics* 14 (December 1946): 253–76.

Tollison, R.D. 'Public Choice and Legislation', *Virginia Law Review* 74 (March 1988): 339–71.

Vaughn, K.I. 'Does It Matter That Costs Are Subjective?' *Southern Economic Journal* 46 (January 1980): 702–15.

Wiseman, J. 'Uncertainty, Costs and Collectivist Economic Planning', *Economica* 20 (May 1953): 118–28.

6 The practice and politics of marginal cost pricing

The case of the French electric monopoly

Henri Lepage

This chapter is distilled from an Official Report I wrote for the French Ministry of Industry in response to a complaint by one of the Ministry secretaries that Electricité de France (EDF) violated its own announced principle of marginal cost pricing (Lepage 1988). The main charge was that EDF underpriced its service to residential customers in order to induce those customers to increase their investment in electric heating equipment. EDF claimed, to the contrary, that its 'all-nuclear' policy of the 1970s had led to a substantial amount of excess capacity, and in the light of this excess capacity lower prices were required if it were to adhere to its principle of marginal cost pricing. EDF argued that its prices were as consistent as possible with its official doctrine that utility prices for each category of customers should be set at the 'marginal cost' incurred for development of new plants needed to meet the demand forecast for that category.

In the light of these contradictory claims it would seem natural to look to empirical evidence about whether EDF prices reflect marginal costs. However, the success of any such endeavour would be exceedingly problematic. For to discover whether EDF violated its own rule of marginal cost pricing it must be presumed that 'optimal' prices can be discovered by an economic calculus. But, so long as the production and distribution of electricity is monopolized by one public company covering the whole country, such an economic calculus is impossible to apply. For there is no way of discovering the optimal price independently of the competitive process itself.[1] EDF's belief that it could provide its customers with the 'best' economic price by using marginal cost pricing as a calculational technique is just another case of scientistic pretence. Nobody can determine what would be the best price of electricity for the French market; such a price could be found only within a competitive economic process. It is only through allowing a competitive market process to operate that it is possible to conclude that efficiency is likely to characterize the production and distribution of electricity.

I will first give a quick story of 'marginal cost pricing' in France. Then I will explain how EDF computes its 'scientific' price structure. Subsequently, I will outline the specific complaints that the French Administration brought against EDF and will describe the defence that EDF advanced. Doing this will provide an understanding of the technical intricacies that are involved in such price management policies, and will show how a public monopoly can violate its own announced principles and instead pursue particular private interests. But to raise this alternative possibility is not to imply that this is what EDF is actually doing, for without a competitive process of economic organization there is simply no way to know the truth.

1   THE STORY OF MARGINAL COST PRICING IN FRANCE

Marginal cost pricing is a product of post-war welfare economics. It developed in response to the issue of how to run a public monopoly when there is no competitive market to set prices. Marginal cost pricing has been predominantly viewed as a pricing rule that, if followed by a state enterprise, will generate the same beneficial welfare properties that would result from a competitive market process.

The theory of perfect competition states that a condition for equilibrium is that goods and services be exchanged at prices that equal their marginal costs. When markets are imperfect a frequently advanced solution is to create a public monopoly and to instruct its managers to price at marginal cost.[2] When the company is able to insulate itself against political tinkering and governmental abuse such a policy will generate, it is argued, a structure of prices approximately similar to that which would prevail in a competitive process. Such a policy is thus 'liberal' in that it is supposed to deliver the same efficient economic outcome that a competitive market process would deliver.

EDF officially endorsed marginal cost pricing as its central doctrine in 1958. Public enterprise pricing is one of the rare fields in economics where the influence of French economists is worldwide. Marcel Boiteux and Maurice Allais, winner of the 1988 Nobel Prize, are the two best known. Marcel Boiteux ended his career as Chairman of EDF after serving as EDF's Director of Economic Studies, Research, and Development for most of his life. He had been a student of Maurice Allais at the famous Paris Ecole des Mines. As a professor in economic calculus, Maurice Allais taught the engineers who, after the war, developed the mathematical tools for 'optimal' management of public utilities.

Marginal cost pricing for a public monopoly is undeniably a French invention.[3] In terms of historical development, electricity in France was initially provided by private firms. But to provide electricity, producers must be able to lay power lines over private and public lands. As a condition for granting the necessary rights-of-way, local authorities usually extracted from the utility companies the right to fix maximum prices. To be sure, utility companies could set prices beneath the ceiling prices, but those ceilings were valid for the duration of utility contracts and could not be renegotiated.

Then came the First World War and inflation, with a threefold increase in consumer prices between 1914 and 1919. Most utilities would have gone bankrupt if a government decree had not created a new indexation scheme that allowed prices to rise. According to this scheme, maximum ceiling prices could be revised according to an index based on wages and the price of coal (the main source of energy at that time). This first government regulation (1919) was an unexpected boon for the electric industry. When the subsequent Depression of the 1930s arrived, electric prices and profits held up better than those of most other products. Between 1930 and 1935 the stocks of electric power companies fell by over 60 per cent, from 700 to 250 in index terms. But, by comparison, textile stocks collapsed by nearly 90 per cent, going from 1000 to 130 during the same period. In 1935 electric industry profits were 50 per cent higher than they were in 1929, while in other industries profits had been reduced on average by one half. The indexation scheme worked like a shelter for the electric industry.

But the industry subsequently paid a heavy price. For the many people heavily harmed by the Depression, the industry's financial prosperity was widely resented. At that time France was ruled by a popular front government, and the electric companies became the scapegoat of a union-directed campaign against capitalism. The federation of municipally owned electric utilities, managed by socialist leaders, asked for the nationalization of electricity. In 1935 the French government issued two orders that started the process that led to nationalization. First, it forced electric companies to reduce their rates by 10 per cent. Second, it established price controls. The economic policy of the Socialist-Communist government coalition was a general disaster, one aspect of which was a huge balance of payments deficit. At that time, coal, which had to be imported, was the main source of energy. The government promoted a policy of energy substitution. France had large hydroelectric resources located mostly in her southern part. Government called on the industry to hasten the pace of its hydroelectric projects and to cooperate in the development of a national grid. But the industry was short of cash, and its leaders were reluctant to enter into such a plan. In 1938, the government took a strong position: it would fulfil its plans even without voluntary cooperation from the electric companies.

Threatened by partial or even full nationalization, the companies gave up. They agreed to enter into a 'joint venture' with the government. The Ministry for Public Works was put in charge of devising the main investment plans. Private companies were granted subsidized government loans, for which, in return, they had to relinquish what was left of their freedom to set prices. The first national grid began to operate in 1940, a few weeks before the German invasion. At that time the electric industry was already operating under a state-mandated cartel arrangement, which needed very little change to be adapted to the needs of a war economy.

Nationalization of the electric industry was voted in 1946. Industrial assets of the private companies (Union d'Electricité, Energie Industrielle, Groupe Empain, Compagnie Generale d'Electricité, Compagnie Parisienne de Distribution Electrique) were consolidated into one large public monopoly, Electricité de France. But because of the 'corporatist' industrial institutions that emerged during the 1938–45 period, their staffs were already accustomed to working and thinking in terms of nationwide electric planning.

Marginal cost pricing became the official EDF doctrine ten years later. But the conceptual origin of that doctrine dates back to the 1930s. To a significant extent, the emergence of marginal cost pricing within EDF was a product of a French geographical peculiarity. As mentioned earlier, France is a country with large hydraulic resources, but they are mostly located in her southern part. By contrast, the main consumer markets are in Paris and in the north. At the end of the 1920s, Paris and the northern region were supplied by local coal-powered generators. Hydroelectric power plants involved very heavy initial investment, but once they were built, current production costs were relatively low. The reverse was true for coal power plants: depreciation costs were relatively low compared to current production costs. Looking for markets, the hydroelectric companies developed high-voltage power lines that converged towards Paris. Rapidly they discovered that large cost savings could be realized by coupling local coal-power generators with hydroelectric plants located several hundred miles away. This coupling required sophisticated decision making, so that lower-cost hydroelectric equipment would be used first, with the more expensive coal-generated equipment used only to cover peak periods. To accomplish this, new management tools were needed. It is during this period that engineers developed their first mathematical 'optimization' models.

In the middle of the 1930s, when demand plummeted, a destructive price war was widely expected, with it being presumed that hydroelectric companies would be able to outbid their rivals because their costs were lower. But this did not happen. Although it was first developed to optimize internal production programmes, the marginal calculus was actually used in the 1930s to promote cartel pricing among the utilities. The success of these cartels showed that it was possible to develop an integrated national network for the production and distribution of electricity, without having to nationalize the whole industry. But the success of this cartel also led many engineers and managers to envision a utopia of one large, nationalized company that would save on the large 'transaction costs' of private cartels, thereby making it possible to maximize 'national interests'.

When Electricité de France was formed it devoted substantial energy to the development of efficient models for optimizing investment strategies. Subsequently, EDF played a leading role in developing the ideology of planning in post-war France. Key planning committees were staffed by EDF people. Primary planning concepts (for example, the 'national depreciation rate') were forged by EDF economists. One of the leading figures of French Planning in the post-war period, Pierre Masse, had spent his entire career in the electric industry. After he retired from the Commissariat General du Plan, where he had been appointed by General de Gaulle, he became Chairman of EDF. After wrestling with the optimal regulation of a complex network of rivers and reservoirs, the regulation of complex systems of economic flows and stocks did not seem to involve any great conceptual difference. Management of the electric industry in a time of severe scarcity served as the prototype for economic planning in a mixed economy.

However, once investment choice is 'optimized' according to some planner's scheme, one substantial uncertainty still remains. Values are optimized only in so far as demand develops along the lines that have been forecast by the planner. His interest is to make sure that demand forecasts are actually achieved. If they are not, economic 'waste' will result, because capacities will no longer be optimal. To deal with this deficiency in its investment planning, EDF was led to develop a form of demand planning through 'optimized prices'. The function of price planners in this scheme is to fix rates at such a level that future demand conditions will not differ too much from what is required for the planned investments to operate in the optimal way. Welfare economics argues that this can be achieved through a policy of 'marginal cost pricing'.

EDF's management also discovered that marginal cost pricing had a quite commendable advantage quite apart from any consideration of social welfare or national interest. For it serves also as a device to preserve the autonomy of EDF management against interference from government and unions. In principle, prices are set by the government, acting upon a proposal advanced by EDF. In practice, the government has little choice but to agree to what EDF's management proposes. After all, how could a politician discuss a 'scientific' price? It is likewise with labour unions. The Nationalization Act had given unions one-third of the seats on the Board of EDF, and 1 per cent of annual sales is earmarked for unions to support their social activities. This is one of the major sources of funds for the Communist-led national union, CGT. The doctrine of marginal cost pricing, which is interpreted as 'scientific' price management, further neutralizes the possible influence of unions by forging a company-wide consensus about the impossibility of doing any better than EDF's scientific pricing.

Protected by its 'scientific' doctrine, EDF is now the biggest French industrial company. It is also the largest electric firm in the world. Moreover, it is one of the very rare companies in the world whose management is controlled by economists: its present Executive Director is a professional economist, as was the previous one.

2   PRICE DETERMINATION WITHIN EDF

Electricité de France employs several hundred people in its Economic Research Department. Economics forms the base culture of EDF and is central to its process of price determination. This process begins with forecasts of future consumption. Huge masses of statistics are compiled that essentially project past trends over the next five or ten years. EDF was the first French company to give so much weight to the accumulation of statistical data for medium-term and long-range planning.

Demand forecasts, curiously enough, are based upon a presumption that demand elasticity is zero, for no allowance is made for price variation to influence the amount of electricity people will use. Variations in future use are related only to variations in such macroeconomic data as the growth of income, the distribution of income, and regional and sectoral differences in projected growth rates.

One of the main tasks of these forecasts is to project the shape of seasonal and daily demands five and ten years into the future. Of particular interest is a projection of maximum power needs at peak hours on peak days, with these needs becoming a 'given' fact to which the supplier must adapt. Simultaneously, production functions are specified which tentatively incorporate everything that is known about technical and innovative developments and about trends in future costs.

A very large and sophisticated econometric model is then used to derive estimates of the new production capacities that will optimally be needed to meet the forecasted demand. Given the estimates of the evolution of investment costs, the price of fossil and nuclear fuels, financial needs, and other relevant variables, the model not only delivers an 'optimized' list of investments ranked by order of economic efficiency, but also delivers a matrix of 'marginal costs' that represent the cost of each new kilowatt produced at every time of the day. The data are then rearranged to give estimates of the 'marginal production cost' of every kwh produced for each class of customers. When crossed with another model that draws a national demand schedule from local meteorological information, the model estimates, by class of customers, what it will cost for production to increase in such a way as to meet maximum forecasted demand. These estimates of 'marginal development costs' guide price determination by EDF.

These 'marginal costs' have nothing to do with traditional business accounting. They are not 'production costs' as companies understand them. They are nothing more than 'prospective evaluations' of what EDF believes it will cost the company to develop the capacity to supply one more kwh in some place to different customers in five years' time. EDF often refers to two sorts of marginal costs: short term and long term. Both sorts refer to the same future year (for example, 1995). The first estimates what it would cost in 1995 to supply one more kwh needed by some category of customer by forcing more power on existing capacities (the main cost in this case being an increase in energy losses due to the overcharge of transportation power lines). The second estimates what it will cost in 1995 to supply the same increase in power by building a new plant or by developing a new transportation line.

According to EDF's theory of marginal cost pricing, 'optimality' obtains when, for the future base year, short-term marginal costs and long-term marginal costs are equal. Investment capacities are then allocated in such a way that one can do nothing to increase further the efficiency of the production system planned for that year. Ideally, it is these marginal costs, when capacities are efficiently 'adapted', that are used by company planners to determine future price schedules for each customer class. These projected price schedules are compared with present price schedules, and a path of price increase or decrease is worked out that will bring future base year prices into line with the 'efficient' prices computed by the model.

The modelling structure is such that final price estimates are mathematically determined by the initial investment equations. This implies that the theory has operational meaning only to the extent that it is the 'optimal' investment programme that is actually carried out. In the light of the foregoing discussion about the construction of this 'optimal' investment programme by EDF, this is surely an exceedingly strong limit on the ability of EDF actually to implement such a programme. None the less, the system gives EDF very strong, quasi-religious arguments to convince its public supervisors that they must not interfere with its investment plans.

Periodically, industrial tests are made to check that actual costs do not differ from estimated targets. When the parameters of the relevant equations are changed in response to some unforeseen event, cost estimates are recomputed. Investment plans are accordingly modified, and new price targets are proposed. This process of modification occurred twice, in 1974 and in 1981. The 1974 modification was a consequence of the unexpected oil price shock that produced an 80 per cent increase in fuel prices. Future cost estimates and price targets had become meaningless in the presence of such increases. In 1981 new price targets for 1990 were worked out and gradually introduced into the actual price structure.

But by 1985 these new targets had again become obsolete. Consumption did not increase as fast as had been expected. In 1972, EDF projected that demand would be between 370 and 430 TWH in 1985. Four years later, those consumption estimates were revised downward to between 355 and 385 TWH. Actual consumption in 1985 was only 303 TWH. In 1980, EDF planners projected that 1990 consumption would reach 450 TWH. Actual consumption in 1987 was only 325 TWH, and likely estimates for 1990 are only 347 TWH.

The structure of power demand also evolved in an unexpected manner: the industrial share in total consumption decreased and the demand for household heating increased faster than anticipated. On top of this, a new market developed that had never been planned: exports to such neighbouring countries as Germany, Italy, and England increased rapidly (30 TWH in 1987). Consequently, the estimates of long-term marginal cost that were computed in 1981 had to be revised downward by a margin of about 13 per cent. Accordingly, EDF, with government agreement, began to review the level of its prices. A first 1 per cent reduction was introduced in 1985, a second in 1986, and a third in 1987 (with a slightly different weighting for domestic, professional, and industrial consumers). At the time of the Official Report (Fall 1987), it was EDF's belief that these corrections accounted for about two-thirds of the difference between actual prices and the new, 'optimized' targets.

3   SYSTEMATIC BIAS IN EDF PRICES?

How reliable are these new price estimates? The head of the government department whose function is to monitor EDF's activities and to act as its formal stockholder argued that EDF's prices were systematically biased in favour of domestic consumers and against industrial users. Such a claim about EDF's prices must, of course, be grounded in some argument that those prices do not conform to 'actual' marginal costs. In support of this claim, the Administration pointed to the continuous and unexpected rise of household consumption of electricity. In consequence, EDF now faces very tight winter peak periods, even though it is generally thought that EDF has an overcapacity of about ten nuclear generators.

This change in circumstance is a consequence of EDF's commercial policy. For the last ten years it aggressively promoted the 'all electric' house. In 1979, 1 million domestic units used electric power for household heating. By 1987, 3.4 million units did so. As a result of its promotional success, EDF now has difficulty meeting its winter-time demand peaks. Much of this difficulty stems from EDF's pricing policies: French families are encouraged to use electric heating in the winter, when the demand for electricity is already high and the power company must use its least efficient plants.

An examination of the evolution of EDF's prices over the last fifteen years shows that residential rates declined slightly while industrial rates increased by as much as 50 per cent. The actual structure of electric rates is surely far from equilibrium; EDF can hardly be telling the truth when it justifies its present prices by invoking the doctrine of marginal cost pricing. In earlier years only 16 per cent of residential yearly consumption was supplied by expensive marginal plants. Now 24 per cent is so supplied. A larger proportion of production costs should now be charged to residential consumers if the doctrine of marginal cost pricing were being followed. Residential rates should have gone up and not down. But down they went.

There is a gap between rates actually charged by EDF and what those rates would be if EDF truly practised marginal cost pricing. The public monopoly has failed to adapt its rate structure to cost changes that have recently occurred. To some extent this failure seems to have resulted because it is more rewarding for EDF managers to increase sales rather than to pursue economic efficiency. Ten years ago EDF overinvested in nuclear power and has subsequently sought to cover this difference as fast as possible. Its professional reliability, and also its independence, are at stake. Its interest is not to tell the truth about actual costs but to maintain lower residential prices subsidized by higher industrial rates – a policy that also increases total consumption, provided that residential demand is more elastic than industrial demand. EDF uses its 'scientific' doctrine to ask government not to interfere with its management. But the truth is that it does not practise what it preaches; its pricing practices contradict its stated doctrine.

How is it possible for EDF's actual pricing practice to diverge from its announced principle of price determination? For the most part the answer resides in the absence of any competitive market process through which prices are determined. A state monopoly is just that – a monopoly. It possesses neither the knowledge nor the incentive necessary to simulate a competitive market. Optimization models work with data that are projections or estimates of future values. But there is no objective source to which someone might turn to get data on costs and demands. A set of people, all of whom could be described as having a single-minded devotion to practising marginal cost pricing, will select many different prices. There is no way that an external observer can declare that one of those prices conforms more closely to marginal cost pricing than another. What can be said, however, is that a competitive market process will tend to produce pressures for efficiency to replace inefficiency.[4]

It is hardly likely, however, that EDF officials could be described as having a single-minded devotion to marginal cost pricing. For there are surely plausible grounds for asserting that EDF economists bias their projections by retaining only numbers, forecasts, and error margins that fit best their own corporate interest. For example, estimates of marginal development costs are calculated on the hypothesis that demand for electric power will not reach 430 TWH before the end of the 1990s. The choice of such a long-range planning horizon entails one important consequence. The longer this horizon, the greater the economies of scale that are likely to appear in the distribution system. Residential rates are more sensitive to distribution costs than are industrial rates within EDF's calculational framework. Therefore, a longer planning horizon will give a rate structure with relatively lower residential prices than will a shorter planning horizon.

Investments for improving distribution networks are partly financed by allocations from local authorities. However this source of funds is becoming relatively less significant: the share of investment directly financed by EDF increased from 59 per cent in 1981 to 63 per cent in 1985. Present estimates are based on the unlikely hypothesis that EDF's share will remain constant. This unrealistic forecast lowers estimated cost for the coming ten years, and thus serves to justify lower residential rates.

EDF's projections regarding the failure rate of nuclear plants are also very conservative. While the actual failure rate for the last ten years was no higher than 5 per cent, EDF's projections assume a 15 per cent failure rate. This excess of projected over actual failures increases the projected production costs that are entered into EDF's computations of 'marginal cost'. The consequence of this is a justification for higher relative rates for industrial users, especially for very large industrial users.

EDF announced that it plans to increase its spending to improve the quality of its service. But its econometric time series are based on a simple extrapolation of past investment trends. Consequently, its actual cost estimates result from calculations that entail less investment in distribution networks than EDF actually expects to make in the future. On the other hand, a higher demand for household heating will force EDF to invest more to improve the quality and reliability of its service. In both cases, EDF's econometric models underestimate what will have to be spent for distribution lines and equipment. As a result, EDF proposes lower residential rates than marginal cost pricing would seem to require.

Critics of EDF argue that the use of more plausible figures and projections would create a significant shift in the structure of electricity prices. Some of these estimates suggest that industrial rates would fall by 8 per cent, and that rates for residential users without electric central heating would fall by 2.5 per cent. For industrial users, this would represent a reduction of 30 per cent from average accounting cost. In contrast, residential customers who use central heating would pay for their electricity at a rate 40 per cent above its average accounting cost. Such a revision would save industry about 6 billion francs, and would eliminate the price disequilibrium that explains the greater difficulties that EDF faces during its winter peak periods.

4   EDF'S JUSTIFICATORY ARGUMENT

To be sure, EDF does not admit to any systematic and substantial disparity between its announced principle of marginal cost pricing and its actual pricing policies. EDF denies that its price structure entails any significant transfer from industrial to residential consumers. To be sure, EDF does not claim perfection. It acknowledges that its forecasting technique is fraught with uncertainty and imprecision. Economic calculus is not flawless, and some degree of arbitrary decision making cannot be avoided. But, after forty years of experience, EDF argues, it has acquired the engineering sophistication and the capacity to compute marginal costs for different classes of consumers and with only minimal error to transform those costs into rate schedules.

Hence, EDF is able to argue that the relative increase in industrial rates stems from its pursuit of marginal cost pricing. EDF claims that it responded to the oil price shock in the mid–1970s by assuming that the increase in production cost would be shared equally across all units of production. But to assume production cost increased proportionately across all units of output does not imply that prices should also increase proportionately. For the production cost component is a greater share of the total cost for industrial consumers than it is for residential consumers. Distribution costs, on which the oil price increase had no effect, are relatively more significant for residential consumers. Thus marginal cost pricing would require industrial prices to increase relative to residential prices, which has been exactly the course of EDF prices.

This is not to say that actual rates are perfect illustrations of marginal cost pricing. Some customers undoubtedly pay more than they would pay under true marginal cost pricing, while others pay less. But this cannot be avoided if one wants to keep rate structures simple. Moreover, recent price options have sought to correct some of these discrepancies. Efficiency dictates that the cost of unpredictable events be borne by people for whom the cost of temporarily reducing their consumption is least. One new price option relates to industrial firms that agree to have a certain proportion of their power supplies temporarily cut off without notice at peak periods. The function of prices is not only to convey to entrepreneurs information about social costs that an increase in consumption entails, but is also to make them aware of what society would save if consumption were reduced.

As to the household heating issue, there is nothing mysterious here either. Heating implies that customers subscribe for more electric power than is usual for individual homes. This is paid for by a higher annual fee. But one must also pay attention to the existence of a 'spread effect'. Not everyone turns their lights on and off at the same time. Actual power needs are thus smaller than they would be if all lights and appliances were simultaneously turned on. The greater the population, the greater the spread effect. For residential customers the spread effect is very large. Even if individual heating users are growing rapidly, they account for an excess demand that is only a small proportion of total domestic consumption. The average individual cost effect is no higher than the supplementary price people pay by way of a higher annual subscription fee. If that cost effect were to become more important, a correction could be introduced by extending new price options to private customers. With modern electronic metering and monitoring devices, such a policy will soon become economically feasible.

EDF views its prices as being the 'right' prices. While no econometric technique is perfect, EDF claims that its calculation margins remain within acceptable norms. Nothing proves that present rate structures significantly differ from 'actual' long-term marginal costs. To be sure, no one would expect EDF to say anything else. Remember that the rate structure is mathematically determined by the structure of initial investment plans. To agree that rate structure truly needs to be revised would be to imply that EDF initially undertook an incorrect programme of investment. But to admit this would undermine the very core of EDF's social legitimacy. If doubts are raised about its ability to 'optimize' social investment EDF loses its very *raison d'être*. All of its achievements of the last forty years will have been lost.

Present overcapacity, none the less, is clearly a problem. There is a strong discrepancy between 'short-term' and 'long-term' marginal development costs. It is difficult to reconcile this discrepancy with EDF's claim that its prices are scientifically determined 'equilibrium' prices. As was mentioned before, using 'marginal development costs' as a technique for discovering 'optimal' prices makes sense only when production capacities are optimally 'adapted' – i.e., when short-term equals long-term marginal cost.

However, EDF reacts by emphasizing the need of customers for stable price signals. The function of price signals is to convey information that helps customers to plan their future investments efficiently and not to induce them to change their immediate consumption plans according to signals given by contingent prices. Electric power consumption is determined by past investment decisions. It is the amortization period for these investments that matters for optimal planning. This period is usually between five and ten years, a long enough period to assume that by the end of the planning period the structure of the electric system will be back to optimal capacity. Consequently, EDF argues that present capacity disequilibrium does not reduce the economic value of its price structure, because that structure is derived from 'long-term' marginal development costs.

5   WHO IS RIGHT?

The Administration has a case. But EDF's defence is not without weight. Whom should we believe? For its critics, EDF's marginal cost pricing policy is meaningful only so long as a quick return to optimal capacity is likely. Such quickness is doubtful. It used to take four years to build a new power plant. Now, with nuclear technology, it takes as long as eight years. Moreover, nuclear power plants have a longer life-span than conventional fuel generators. Consequently it will take much longer to correct past mistakes in investment planning. The hope of a quick return to an optimal investment structure is now less likely than it might have been in the past. EDF estimates are now fraught with a much wider margin of uncertainty. Even if it were thought that marginal cost pricing was once an appealing doctrine, much of that appeal has surely vanished in today's setting. Moreover, it is doubtful that such an appeal was ever warranted in the first place. This is not to deny that a company might consider marginal cost pricing to be a desirable technical or managerial tool. With investments of very long duration, and with variable demand over time, there might be reasons why electric power companies would practise some form of marginal cost pricing. However, these pragmatic considerations do not allow a public monopoly to claim that marginal cost pricing is the key to 'scientific' truth.

According to EDF's doctrine, sophisticated mathematical tools of economic calculus allow the corporate planner to discover an ideal price structure that meets the requirements of optimality and equity even when the company has no market competitor. This is an impossibility. Such an ideal price structure can exist only in the imaginary construction of mathematical models where agents are no more than programmed automatons choosing between utility levels that are unmeasurable by mere human beings. Such a theory has no connection with reality. It cannot be used as a guide in a concrete world with human beings whose minds cannot be reduced to mere physical and mechanical processes; human beings who think, and have to search for information on which to base their personal judgements.

When EDF argues that its pricing procedures result in prices close to what would be the product of a competitive market, it promises to deliver something that it cannot deliver, and which nobody will ever be able to deliver, whatever the sophistication of its mathematical and statistical techniques. EDF ignores the epistemological impossibility that results from the pretence of mimicking the market process, while at the same time social institutions deprive individuals of those very freedoms that are needed for market processes to facilitate this accomplishment.

As Mises, Hayek, Buchanan, and many others have already pointed out, the theory of perfect competition is an invaluable intellectual device for understanding the role of prices in a complex market order.[5] But one cannot derive from this theory any normative and operational statement. One can derive operational norms from basic welfare theorems only by posing a radical break between the concept of 'cost' and individual decision making. But doing this implies an epistemological jump that deprives the whole theoretical construction of its internal consistency, and puts us outside the realm of scientific discourse.

The Administration's criticisms of EDF pricing are correct but they miss the real point: EDF promises something that it cannot deliver. Its marginal cost theory, whatever its degree of mathematical sophistication, is just a trick to fool people. The Administration argues that EDF models systematically underestimate marginal costs to residential consumers and, thereby, penalize industrial users. While the existence of such a bias is surely plausible the demonstration of its existence is quite problematical. Might not the Administration's calculations be infected with an opposing bias? It is impossible for anyone to demonstrate that the Administration's calculations are closer to or farther from the 'truth'. Nobody knows, and it will be impossible for anyone ever to know. Statistics, data gathering, and the choice of econometric concepts remain a matter of subjective value judgement. Nobody can eliminate this human factor.

Econometrics as a discovery instrument has scientific value only so long as there are several rival firms that use it in a competitive way. One single model cannot tell the 'truth'. Only when competing models are used by competing firms is it possible systematically to acquire better knowledge of the real world. The debate between EDF and the Administration looks like a quarrel between two planners who rely on the same technique but who disagree on the numbers to feed into the computer. But basically they share the same erroneous epistemology.

What about cross-subsidization across customers? With present rates such transfers surely exist, for it would be miraculous if present rates fit the optimal economic pattern. But can we go further and explain which change in rates would be the most appropriate to eliminate cross-subsidization? Here again is a question on which the economist has nothing to offer. To be confident that some alternative rate structure would be socially more efficient, it is necessary to assert that the progress of scientific knowledge can, by itself, move us closer to competitive equilibrium – independently of the operation of any actual competitive process. But this is precisely the sort of knowledge that is non-existent. The only thing an outside expert can say is that a particular, proposed rate structure is 'better' than the present one because it better corresponds to the subjective view of the world held by the people the expert wants to satisfy. But how does he know that this 'optimum' is socially superior to the one EDF pretends to achieve through its actual pricing? There is no way to know this. There is no best solution existing in its own right that experts could discover with no help other than their scientific genius.

Think of the difficulty of trying to give estimates of the actual cross-transfers generated by EDF's present pricing structure. Even to start, it would be necessary to acquire some very detailed information, including monthly real accounting costs for every plant (or at least every type of power plant), detailed monthly supplies provided to every customer class, and the proportion of supplies provided for each customer class by each type of power plant. While EDF has a very detailed and precise accounting system it does not compute such data, though it could do so. Its managers are not interested in knowing their actual average costs by class of kwh or by customer categories. Consistent with its pursuit of its organizational interests, EDF's data gathering and processing is entirely focused on the computation of future 'economic' marginal costs.

Such a dearth of accounting data is a consequence of monopoly. If there were a competitive market, firms would be forced to keep a constant watch on the relative position of their actual production costs and revenue sources. But a public monopoly has no need for such information. Only 'economic costs' matter. Consequently, the monopoly is itself immunized against any quarrel about the value of its price information because there is no possible check on its calculations.

To be sure, the Administration used EDF figures to construct a set of 'reconstituted' data. These data were used to compare actual revenues in four markets – high power, medium power, low power without electric heating, and low power with home electric heating – and to estimate what revenues would have been if electricity sales had been undertaken at prices just covering average costs. The ratio of the latter to the former gives an order of the magnitude of financial transfers and rents that accrue to some customers to the detriment of others. These figures showed that residential customers with electric heating paid only 60 per cent of what they should have paid if they were not to benefit from any positive transfer. By contrast, heavy industrial users paid 30 per cent more than they should have paid – according to the Administration's alternative, though equally conjectural, calculation of what marginal cost pricing would have required. Medium-size industry was estimated to have paid 41 per cent more than it should have paid. And residential customers without electric heating were estimated to have paid 34 per cent more than they should have paid. These figures argue strongly that residential customers with household electric heating were heavily subsidized by other users.

But here again we must remain cautious as to the meaning of such computations. These figures cannot be used as proof that moving to the alternative rate structure would eliminate observed transfers and would necessarily bring the system closer to economic 'equilibrium'. In the absence of a genuine market process there is no scientific basis to choose between EDF's and the Administration's equally conjectural claims about pricing. Therefore, it cannot be denied that EDF's reply, that it is more important to focus on long-term price equilibrium than to play with contingent prices, has some merit.

6 STRATEGIES AND GROUP INTERESTS

The controversy between the Administration and EDF is now two years old. EDF's antagonist has been moved to another administrative position. Elections have been held, with a new majority resulting and with a new minister being appointed. Nobody in Paris thinks that electricity rates are really an issue. EDF managers and agents can once again enjoy the peace of their monopoly without being disturbed by queries from zealous bureaucrats.

We are, however, in a position to better understand the strategies and group interests that fuelled both sides of the argument. Let us first look at EDF. Its present rate structure leaves room for large transfers among customer classes. There remains a need to explain why EDF would accommodate such transfers. A 'positive' explanation might account for the apparent discrepancy between reality and EDF's descriptions to the contrary. EDF faces a structural overcapacity that is likely to last well towards the end of the 1990s. EDF's growth prospects are dim. Power demand has slowed down to such an extent that projections are constantly revised downward. EDF's productivity is deteriorating, and excess employment is thought to be in the order of 25,000 people. As a legacy of the nuclear dreams of the 1970s, EDF is heavily in debt. Furthermore, it now faces competition from alternative energy sources.

It should not be surprising that EDF behaves as it does. The rent provided by its monopoly position benefited its workers not so much through higher wages as through larger amenities and greater fringe benefits. EDF is well known for its stability of employment. To work with EDF means that one belongs to the aristocracy of the French working class. But to keep these benefits EDF must continually expand its sales. Its prices must therefore remain relatively low, especially on the domestic household market, where demand is relatively elastic.

For the first time in its forty years' life, EDF faces market price constraints. This makes it more difficult to maintain a strict principle of price neutrality. While EDF continues to articulate its traditional doctrine of marginal cost pricing, its actual practice of price determination is as murky as ever. As there is no 'objective' cost, biases must enter into the information-gathering system. EDF's private and collective interests tend to dominate decision making, to the detriment of a strict observance of its doctrine of marginal cost pricing. This process of dominance is not necessarily conscious. But conscious or not, what entrepreneur would not sacrifice some of his principles for the sake of social peace?

A discrepancy thus creeps in between official statements and actual EDF policy. Meanwhile, protected by the scientific complexity of its pricing procedure, EDF has no difficulty denying any charge that it countenances such a discrepancy. There is no lie involved here. The fuzziness of concepts, the fact that calculations are always approximate, the leeway it leaves for arbitrariness – all these factors make it easy for EDF to pretend sincerely to do what it cannot possibly do.

The Administration's side of this dispute is no less arbitrary. The basic principle of French Statute Law is that whenever there is a 'natural monopoly', it is the state's duty to monitor its investment and pricing policies. This is what happens for telecommunications and rail transportation. But for electricity it is a little different. EDF has become a 'state within a state'. In principle its activities are monitored by two ministries: Industry and Treasury. Long ago, the Ministry for Industry was 'captured' by EDF. 'Regulators' often come from the same *grandes écoles* as EDF officials. Past experience shows that many of them continue their careers by accepting positions within EDF. Its directors are among the very few who never wait to meet a minister.

As a consequence, EDF came to enjoy a very privileged position. The Ministry usually acted as its spokesman within the government, defending its policy choices against the more cautious attitude of Treasury agents, as well as endorsing its investment plans and prices without much argument. EDF had no commercial competititors and its supervisors were its surest allies. The efficiency of this lobby was demonstrated in 1981, when EDF circumvented socialist hostility to its all-nuclear plan. For years before, the Socialists had sided with the Greens and denounced its dangers. Within a few months they enthusiastically endorsed it.

In 1986, matters became more complex. It was difficult to deny that planners had been overly optimistic about the industry's future. Reality ratified the judgements of opponents to the nuclear plan. One of those opponents was appointed to oversee the regulation of EDF activities. This led EDF to change its allies. EDF now sided with Finance bureaucrats, who were opposed to any plan that might bring an increase in domestic household rates and have inflationary effects.

On the other side, Industry became openly critical of the way EDF was managed. It was backed by French multinational companies that were deeply involved in activities with very large energy needs.

Benefiting abroad from preferential rates for their foreign subsidiaries, those companies were hurt by the dogmatic attitude of EDF. They threatened to move their French plants abroad and used the Ministry as a spokesman for their demands.

This story shows the other side of the coin. Arguing about the right way to implement marginal cost pricing is not simply a matter of scientific knowledge. The real issue is to decide who truly owns the right to set prices for a monopolistic public company. Choosing one or the other side of the argument means deciding who has the right to allocate the dividends represented by the monopolistic 'rent'. Either one sided with EDF, its unions, its engineering bureaux, and its industrial suppliers, or one preferred to serve the interests of other industry groups. As there is no 'scientific' way to weigh the 'objective' benefits and costs of either solution, the choice could only be politically contingent. Prices of public monopolies are politically determined. There is no way to escape this fact. Marginal cost pricing is just an artifact used to make gullible people believe that it may be different. It is the last remnant of post-war planning ideology.

NOTES

1 For a valuable collection of essays on this theme, see Hayek (1935). For related contemporary scholarship, see Sowell (1980) and Lavoie (1985).
2 For a thorough survey of the welfare economics of public enterprise pricing, see Bös (1986).
3 On the theory of marginal cost pricing and its application in France, see the collection of essays in EDF (1987). This collection includes papers by such intellectual leaders of marginal cost pricing as M. Boiteux, G. Dessus, M. Francony, P. Penz, J. Bergougnout, J.J. Mosconi, and P. Bernard.
4 The subjective nature of cost is spelled out in a set of essays written by scholars associated with the London School of Economics in the 1930s and collected in Buchanan and Thirlby (1973). Further amplification is provided in Buchanan (1969).
5 Besides the works cited in Notes 1 and 3, see Hayek (1949).

REFERENCES

Bös, D. *Public Enterprise Economics*. Amsterdam: North-Holland, 1986.
Buchanan, J.M. *Cost and Choice*. Chicago: Markham, 1969.
Buchanan, J.M. and Thirlby, G.F., eds. *LSE Essays on Cost*. London: Weidenfeld & Nicolson, 1973.
Electricité de France (EDF). *Le Principe de Tarification d'Electricité de France*. Paris, EDF, 1987.
Hayek, F.A., ed. *Collectivist Economic Planning*. London: Routledge & Kegan Paul, 1935.

Hayek, F.A. *Individualism and Economic Order*. London: Routledge & Kegan Paul, 1949.

Lavoie, D. *Rivalry and Central Planning: The Socialist Calculation Debate Reconsidered*. New York: Cambridge University Press, 1985.

Lepage, H. *EDF et la Tarification au Coût Marginal: Rapport au Ministre de l'Industrie*. Paris: Documentation Française, February 1988.

Mises, L. *Socialism*. New Haven: Yale University Press, 1951.

Sowell, T. *Knowledge and Decisions*. New York: Basic Books, 1980.

7 The political economy of tax earmarking

Dwight R. Lee and Richard E. Wagner

Tax earmarking is a far more common practice than the sparcity of literature about it would seem to suggest. Although the extent of earmarking varies from government to government, earmarked revenues probably typically account for between one-third and two-thirds of governmental expenditures in the United States. For instance, in a study cited by McMahon and Sprenkle (1970), 41 per cent of state tax revenues were found to be earmarked. In cases where it is considered politically inappropriate or economically impractical to charge directly for governmentally provided services, tax earmarking is commonly argued to be a useful way to impose such a charge indirectly. By imposing a tax on a product that is complementary in consumption with the governmentally provided service, and earmarking the revenue to financing the supply of that service, a type of quasi-pricing of the governmental service results.

The earmarking of revenues from the taxation of gasoline for the support of highway construction and maintenance is perhaps the most prominent illustration of such quasi-pricing. Barring direct charges for the use of highways, earmarking gasoline taxes to highway construction and maintenance is widely accepted as a reasonably fair and efficient method of highway finance. The correlation between gasoline consumption and highway use is strongly positive, even if not perfect. There is also a positive correlation between the efficiency with which highway departments use their revenues in accommodating the demands of travellers and the amount of revenues those departments have available to them by virtue of the gasoline tax.

At the state-and-local level of government, much earmarking takes place through the use of special districts whose activities are financed by earmarked taxes or otherwise dedicated revenues. Public education is financed in this manner in most American states. And so are numerous other services, covering such things as mosquito control, libraries, flood control, and agricultural subsidies. Earmarking is also prominent at the federal level of government: the social security programmes, in which revenues from the payroll tax are earmarked for expenditure on retirement and Medicare, is by far the largest instance of tax earmarking in the United States.

Perhaps inspired by the apparent success of tax earmarking for highway finance, other candidates for earmarking are continually being placed upon the public agenda. For instance, the National Association of Railroad Passengers has proposed a 4-cent per gallon increase in the federal gasoline tax, with 1 cent earmarked for Amtrak and 3 cents earmarked for mass transit. At the level of state government, California enacted by referendum in 1988 a 25-cent per pack increase in the cigarette tax, with the revenues earmarked for a variety of programmes that include state aid to public libraries, health education, and care for the indigent.

Despite the substantial fiscal significance of tax earmarking, the literature on public finance has given relatively little explicit attention to earmarking as an alternative to general-fund financing. What little literature exists mostly views earmarking negatively as impeding budgetary efficiency. In this chapter we shall first review some of the main lines of argument that have been advanced with respect to tax earmarking. Not surprisingly, different perspectives on the character of political and budgetary processes lead to different assessments of earmarking. Generally, traditional civics-type presumptions about budgetary processes lead to negative assessments of earmarking, whereas presumptions about those processes that have been inspired by public-choice scholarship have generated more favourable assessments of earmarking.

In this respect it is especially notable that a comprehensive earmarking is a central feature of Knut Wicksell's (1896) celebrated contribution to the public-choice perspective on budgetary processes.[1] However, to advance a case for earmarking as potentially offering improvements over general-fund budgetary processes is not to foreclose the possibility that earmarking may none the less deserve a negative evaluation. As we shall explain in the closing part of this chapter, the assessment of earmarking depends ultimately on the constitutional framework within which budgetary processes operate. While it is possible to conceptualize budgetary settings in which earmarking represents an improvement over general-fund financing, it is also possible to conceptualize settings in which it does not.

1   TAX EARMARKING, USER CHARGING, AND BUDGETARY PROCESSES

Most discussions of budgetary process, which in turn typically have been framed within an administrative perspective of good government or benevolent despotism, see little scope for tax earmarking.[2] Within this perspective, the collection of revenues is seen as properly divorced from the expenditure of those revenues, because the overall budget is seen as an instrument for promoting social welfare. Revenues are collected and expenditures made so as to maximize some social welfare function, and no questions arise concerning either the incentives possessed by public officials and administrators to do so or the knowledge that would be required for them to be able to do so.

General-fund financing is the norm, in that a single, unified authority makes a set of choices regarding the raising of revenues and the authorization of appropriations that best promote the social welfare. Within such a framework tax earmarking would seem at best to be redundant, in that whatever might be accomplished through earmarking could be accomplished through general-fund financing. It is more likely, however, that earmarking would be regarded as inferior, because, to the extent it could actually modify budgetary outcomes, it would do so by injecting obstacles and rigidities into the budgetary process, thereby impeding the activities of the budgetary authorities in their efforts to promote social welfare.

At best, the case for earmarking would have to be carried by the case for user charging as an alternative to general-fund financing; earmarked taxation would be a form of quasi-user charge, as it were. Moreover, the case for user charges requires at least partial acceptance of the benefit principle of public finance, in contrast to the welfare principle that informs the administrative approach and the optimal tax literature.[3] In this case the budget comes to be seen normatively not as an instrument for the maximization of some social welfare function but as some means for reflecting individual evaluations in collective outcomes.

Direct user charging is clearly superior to the indirect, quasi-charging that tax earmarking represents. But there can be many cases where direct charging is prohibitively expensive to implement. In this case tax earmarking must be compared with general-fund financing. It is not obvious that such a comparison would show that earmarking is superior. The same revenue can be raised at a much lower rate than that of an excise tax through a broad-based tax that provides a general fund, so the use of the earmarked excise tax will entail a greater excess burden than will the use of general fund financing. But the quasi-charge that earmarking represents promotes greater efficiency in public expenditure, both by rationing existing output and by providing sharper signals about the valuations consumers place on additional output. Hence, it is impossible to determine on *a priori* grounds whether tax earmarking or general fund financing is more efficient.

Furthermore, to assert a normative case for user charges is not, of course, to ensure that actual user charges conform to such a normative case. But keeping within the normative framework of user charging, tax earmarking may serve as a sensible substitute for user charges in some instances, even if no universal statement can be made. In cases where user charges might be impossible, or perhaps only subject to high transaction costs, a tax on a complementary service earmarked for provision of the service for which direct charging is impossible might be a reasonable substitute for the user charge. A tax on gasoline used to finance highways once provided the classic illustration of this case, though perhaps it no longer does, because the technology now exists for the direct pricing of highway services without the use of toll booths, through a system of transmitters and receivers embedded in roads and installed in cars. But such technology aside, a tax on gasoline, with the proceeds earmarked to finance highways, would seem to be an approximate substitute for the direct pricing of highways.[4]

To be sure, earmarking in this case would not be able to establish any form of peak-load pricing, because the amount people pay would depend only on the amount of gasoline they buy and not at all on when they use it. Moreover, the general reluctance of governments to use peak-load pricing in such settings where it could be applied, as illustrated by electricity and mass transit among others, seems itself to be evidence that considerations of social efficiency are to some degree downgraded in the service of political and bureaucratic self-interest. Peak-load pricing makes it possible to provide the same output with a smaller physical plant and labour force. The widespread reluctance within the public-sector to use peak-load pricing seems explainable in terms of the ability of uniform pricing to accommodate the expansionary interests of politicians and bureaucrats by inducing a larger demand for plant and labour than would result under peak-load pricing.

Much of the standard criticism of earmarking involves not a rejection of the ability of earmarking to serve to some extent as a substitute for user charges but a belief that earmarking creates fiscal inflexibility, the cost of which exceeds whatever gains the price-like qualities of earmarking might offer. Setting aside questions of peak-load pricing, suppose initially the revenues from a gasoline tax were sufficient to provide a highway network of the size that would be provided through user charges. This relationship is unlikely to hold through time. Highway expenditures are determined within the market for gasoline and not within the (non-existent) market for highway services. It will be purely accidental if the growth of highway expenditures financed through the gasoline tax will duplicate the growth pattern of those expenditures that would have emerged had there been a market for highway services. Revenues may grow too slowly or they may grow too rapidly, but in either event earmarking will come to serve less well as a substitute for user charging with the passing of time, at least as compared with the adjustments in expenditures that a 'well-working' legislature would enact within a system of general-fund financing.[5]

2   TAX EARMARKING, FISCAL POLITICS, AND BUDGETARY PROCESSES

Such a presumption of a 'well-working' legislature does, of course, clash with the emerging literature on public-choice processes. Once it is acknowledged that budgetary processes are not driven by omniscient beings with single-minded devotion to maximizing some social welfare function, but rather are driven by ordinary, self-interested beings with limited knowledge, many fiscal practices and institutions come to be seen in a different light. Tax earmarking is one of these, and it becomes important to assess earmarking, along with general-fund financing, in terms of the incentives it injects into fiscal processes.

Whereas a presumption of benevolent despotism leads naturally to a focus on how earmarking impedes budgetary fine tuning by the legislature and its delegated budgetary authorities, a presumption that the people who participate in budgetary processes are essentially the same as those who participate in other economic processes has led to generally more favourable views on earmarking by such scholars as Buchanan (1963), Goetz (1968), and Browning (1975). These scholars all examined earmarking within a context of actual budgetary institutions and processes, and generally rendered more positive assessments of earmarking than were rendered by those who, by their very neglect of questions concerning public-choice processes, accepted the framework of benevolent despotism.

Buchanan, and subsequently Browning, recognized that earmarking entails a very different process of budgetary choice than does general-fund financing, and that with this difference in process different budgetary outcomes are likely to emerge. Earmarking calls for a simultaneous choice on a level of taxation and expenditure on an item-by-item basis. Within the framework of the median voter model used by Browning, the aggregate budget under tax earmarking would simply be the sum of the amounts desired by the median voters for the individual services that constitute the budget.

But this is not so with general-fund financing, as Browning also explained. General-fund financing separates choices about taxation from choices about expenditure, and conceptually creates a two-step decision process, in which the aggregate level of taxation is chosen first and the distribution of those revenues among expenditure programmes chosen afterwards. Buchanan emphasizes how general-fund financing creates a tie-in sale within the budgetary process, which favours consumers and suppliers of services in relatively elastic demand through a shift in budgetary composition in their favour. Browning notes that general-fund financing destroys the uniqueness in outcomes that results, within the context of a median voter model. As compared with earmarking, general-fund financing could lead to either increased or decreased aggregate spending, as well as to changes in the composition of the budget. Moreover, this conclusion that general-fund financing makes anything possible was developed independently of considerations of logrolling, considerations that would only serve to increase still further the range of uncertainty over what would result under tax earmarking.

These works emphasize how earmarking might be better able to reflect personal preferences in collective choices than would be likely under actual processes of general-fund financing. Earmarking can also be seen as a way of changing the incentives of politicians as they operate within budgetary processes. This approach is taken by Brennan and Buchanan (1978; 1980: 135–52), who argue that earmarking can be a means of channelling the incentives of politicians in socially useful directions. Suppose politicians have little desire to provide public services, preferring instead to spend the revenues on their own account. There are, of course, various rules and institutions designed to curb this desire. But tax earmarking can create incentives in this direction independently of such rules and institutions. When politicians have the gasoline tax as a revenue source they will be induced to some degree to provide highways, independently of either any beneficence on their part or any external restrictions on their use of revenues. For it is only through providing highway services that people value that politicians will be able to generate revenues via the gasoline tax.

In view of the way in which the assessment of earmarking by different scholars varies with the presumptions about the nature of budgetary processes they bring to their work, it is notable that Knut Wicksell's (1896) contribution to budgetary processes advocated an extensive system of tax earmarking. In addition to his suggestion that budgetary choices require high degrees of consent – somewhere in the order of three-quarters to nine-tenths consent – within a legislature selected according to principles of proportional representation, Wicksell suggested that any proposal for public expenditure would have to be accompanied by a proposal for taxation to finance the expenditure.

Wicksell explicitly rejected any approach based on benevolent despotism, noting in particular that 'the traditional theory of public finance ... still rests on the now outdated political philosophy of absolutism. The theory seems to have retained the assumptions of its infancy, in the seventeenth and eighteenth centuries, when absolute power ruled almost all Europe' (1958: 82). Along with his rejection of benevolent despotism, Wicksell embraced the normative presumption that governmental outcomes should reflect the consent of the governed, and sought to set forth actual fiscal institutions that would be consistent with such a normative presumption. There was no omniscient and benevolent despot to whom the generation of such outcomes could be trusted. Rather, such outcomes could emerge only within an appropriate framework for making budgetary choices.

The earmarking of taxes was essential, Wicksell recognized, to the evaluation of proposed programmes of public expenditure. Without such earmarking it would be difficult for people to make rational choices on whether to support particular programmes of public expenditure. With general-fund financing, the personal cost from supporting a particular programme, or from an increase in spending on that programme, involves making some projection or inference about either what decreases in other items of expenditure the legislature will make or what types of tax increase the legislature will enact. But with Wicksell's proposal for tax earmarking, a direct link would be established between increased expenditure and the increased taxation necessary to finance that expenditure. Since a choice of whether to support an expenditure programme, or an increase or decrease in that programme, cannot be made rationally without knowledge of the personal costs of such choices, earmarking is an essential ingredient in any budgetary process that seeks to reflect personal preferences in collective outcomes.

3   EARMARKING AND MAJORITARIAN POLITICS

To show that the case for tax earmarking strengthens when benevolently despotic models of budgetary process are replaced by realistic models does not, however, imply that earmarking represents an improvement by those normative standards. To say that earmarking may represent an improvement over general-fund budgetary processes is not to say that it does represent an improvement. It is one thing to give a normative argument in support of earmarked taxation. It is a quite different thing to explain actual taxation as something that accomplishes what those normative arguments envision, even if only reasonably well and not perfectly. To go from normative argument to positive explanation, there must be some institutional or constitutional process that shapes and constrains political outcomes so that those outcomes conform to the postulated norms. This will not happen automatically, but rather is something that will happen only to the extent that it is the rational outcome of a particular constitutional order.

Although earmarking can be a way of constraining fiscal outcomes in generally desirable ways, the injection of such constraints into fiscal processes does not represent the only way that earmarking can be characterized. Earmarking may also emerge as part of a process of rent seeking and income redistribution. People interested in expanding spending on particular programmes may advocate earmarking as a way of getting larger appropriations than they could get through general-fund financing. Decisions concerning earmarking, as well as taxation generally, emerge from within in-period political processes, and as such are essentially no different from other political outcomes. Although it is possible to describe circumstances under which tax earmarking will be socially beneficial, it does not follow that the actual implementation of tax earmarking will be a means of securing those benefits. Earmarking can also serve as a means by which spending on particular items is expanded beyond what could have been obtained through general-fund financing.

Some cases of earmarking correspond relatively closely to the classic illustration of taxing something that is highly complementary to the public service being provided. The earmarking of the gasoline tax for highway construction is perhaps the paradigmatic case of this use of earmarked taxation. But there are also many cases of earmarking where the degree of complementarity is low or even non-existent. The earmarking of tobacco tax revenues to finance such services as education, sewer construction, or pollution control illustrate such an alternative use of earmarking that does not conform to the normative case for earmarking. And it is possible for the service being provided with the tax revenues to be a substitute for the service that is taxed. The use of gasoline tax revenues to finance mass transit and Amtrak would illustrate this situation. The presence of earmarked taxation in settings that are clearly unjustified by standard normative arguments is strong evidence that earmarking involves more than just an increase in economic efficiency from what would have been possible under general-fund financing.

The earmarking of tobacco taxes to finance health education or the earmarking of gasoline taxes to support mass transit clearly represent an alternative to the efficiency characterization of earmarking that is rooted in notions of quasi-user pricing. In these situations earmarking represents not a quasi-price on a service consumed by drivers or smokers, but rather represents a particular tax imposed on those activities, with the proceeds transferred to others. While a large share of the gasoline tax may be looked upon as a quasi-price for highway services, this would seem unlikely should part of the gasoline tax be earmarked for mass transit, for this portion would almost surely be more plausibly seen as a tax imposed on users of highway services, with the proceeds used to subsidize non-users. Such earmarking would represent, in other words, an ordinary rent-seeking process through which politically dominant groups enrich themselves at the expense of others. It is the same with an earmarked cigarette tax used to finance health education, and with numerous other cases, actual and proposed, of tax earmarking.

In cases where it is not possible or feasible to charge directly for a publicly provided service, a reasonable, though not compelling, case can be made for tax earmarking, if the conditions suitable for tax earmarking are satisfied. These conditions require, first, that a strongly positive correlation exist between the consumption of the taxed good and the consumption of the good being financed by the earmarked tax revenues; second, a high degree of uniformity in the preceding relationship over individuals, in that everyone who benefits from the earmarked good should use the taxed good; and, third, the amount of revenues that agencies financed by the earmarked taxes have to spend should depend directly on the ability of those agencies to provide the earmarked service efficiently, as opposed to, say, their ability to incite political hostility towards a particular group or to take advantage of existing hostility towards such a group by imposing a greater tax burden on its members.

Within majoritarian political regimes it is possible for political pressure for tax earmarking to exist in situations that fail to satisfy the above conditions. To illustrate, consider the political pressure that currently exists to increase excise taxes on cigarettes and to earmark the revenues to help finance medical care. The justificatory argument is grounded on the same efficiency and equity arguments as those used to justify earmarking gasoline tax revenues to highways: it is argued that there is a strongly positive correlation between the number of cigarettes people smoke and the use they make of health care services. Earmarking cigarette tax revenues for medical care, therefore, assertedly would promote efficiency and equity by the system of quasi-charging that would be created.

But are the conditions suitable for tax earmarking satisfied in the case where revenues from a cigarette tax are earmarked for the support of health care? The most fundamental difficulty arises because, despite constant assertions to the contrary, there is no evidence that smokers make greater use of health care services than non-smokers. Assuming negative correlation between smoking and health, that assumption does not imply a positive correlation between smoking and medical expenses. A positive association between smoking and illness (and lower life expectancy) may affect the timing of the health care people receive without affecting the amount they receive over their lifetimes. Indeed, should smokers die earlier, on average, than non-smokers, it is quite possible they incur lower medical expenses over their lifetimes.

In the absence of any such positive correlation between cigarette smoking and lifetime medical expenses, the case for earmarking cigarette taxes to fund medical care and research collapses on both efficiency and equity grounds. There is no firmer foundation for imposing a special tax on smokers to help finance health care than there is, for example, for imposing a special tax on health care workers to help finance the highway system. And even if it were established that smokers placed greater lifetime demands on health care services than non-smokers, the use of an earmarked tax on cigarettes to help provide that care would be inconsistent with the underlying rationale for publicly provided medical care. For that rationale is simply that everyone, regardless of circumstances, is entitled to an 'adequate' level of care whenever the need for that care arises. This rationale cannot be reconciled with a requirement that smokers must make a special payment to support health care. For there is no equitable basis for singling out one group, whether they be smokers, beef lovers, egg eaters, rock climbers, or motorcycle riders, and requiring that the members of this group make a differential contribution to such governmental programmes as Medicaid and Medicare.

Neither is there an efficiency case for earmarking a cigarette excise tax to help finance health care, even if we continue with the unsubstantiated assumption that there exists a positive relationship between smoking and lifetime expenditures on health care. There are no obstacles to the direct pricing of health care; indeed, much health care is priced directly through private market arrangements. The only reason for substituting public financing for market charges in the provision of a significant portion of health care is that, for reasons already mentioned, it is considered inappropriate at times to charge directly for health care. If, however, it is deemed appropriate to back away from the reluctance to charge for health care, as seems to be suggested by proposals to earmark cigarette taxes to publicly provided health care, it would be better to resort to true market pricing than to take the half-way step of imposing tax earmarking.

A direct charge is a more efficient way of allocating a service than is tax earmarking, even under conditions ideally suited to efficient tax earmarking. So it would be more efficient to impose a differential charge on smokers directly for the use of heath care, instead of attempting to do so indirectly with an earmarked tax on cigarettes. Another advantage of requiring that any differential charge on a particular group of health care users be made directly through market prices is that this would make the discriminatory aspects of singling out such a group fully visible. It would highlight the inconsistency between an attempt to impose a differential charge on smokers for their use of publicly provided health care and the underlying rationale for that health care in the first place.

Finally, earmarking cigarette tax revenues for the support of publicly provided health care does not satisfy the condition that the desire for the earmarked tax revenue be correlated strongly and positively with performance in providing the earmarked service rather than with some indicator of hostility to the group being taxed. It is clearly the case that an important, and probably the primary, reason that earmarking cigarette taxes is on the political agenda is because of a perceived increase in public hostility towards smoking and smokers. There is no doubt that this hostility has been cultivated by groups which want cigarettes taxed more heavily, and which also want the resulting revenue earmarked to health care projects they support and from which they benefit. There is no reason to question the general benefits from such health care projects, or the sincerity of those who support them. But neither is there any reason to believe that earmarking cigarette tax revenues to health care programmes establishes any connection whatsoever between how efficiently more revenue can be utilized by these programmes and the amount of revenue directed to them. In an earmarked environment, revenue recipients would find, at least with respect to the earmarked portion, their budgets influenced more by their ability to foment political hostility against smokers than by the efficiency with which they utilized their budgets.

The disapproval that those who would benefit from earmarked cigarette tax revenue feel towards smoking and smokers could be the source of a yet undiscussed inefficiency. The recipients of any revenues raised from increases in the cigarette tax can be expected to value an increase in that tax quite apart from the value they place on the extra revenue received: the penalty that increasing the tax imposes on smokers and smoking will be valued in and of itself. This implies that even if somehow the tax revenue recipients were, under general-fund financing, motivated to request the socially efficient budget, under tax earmarking they would request a higher budget because of the pleasure they derive from imposing higher tax burdens on smokers.

This assumes, of course, that a higher cigarette tax results in greater tax revenue. If the political power of the tax revenue recipients is sufficient to push the cigarette tax beyond revenue-maximizing limits they will do so at the certain cost of inefficiency. Because of the independent value the tax revenue recipients place on penalizing smokers and smoking, they will be willing to sacrifice revenue up to a point in order to have a higher cigarette tax. There is a limit to this willingness to sacrifice revenue in order to penalize smokers, and a group earmarked to receive cigarette tax revenue will almost surely be opposed to a prohibitive tax on cigarettes, no matter how much they claim to disapprove of smoking.[6] But any time a tax is increased above the revenue-maximizing rate an inefficiency results. In the case of an earmarked cigarette tax such an increase would result in less revenue for health care services (with no greater revenue for other services) and a greater excess burden imposed by the tax on cigarettes.

4 EARMARKING IN CONSTITUTIONAL PERSPECTIVE

The generally strong opposition to tax earmarking and support instead for general-fund financing is grounded in the presumption that benevolent despotism rules budgetary processes. The case for a comprehensive use of tax earmarking is a strong one; as Knut Wicksell (1896) recognized, earmarking is a *sine qua non* for rationality and efficiency in fiscal affairs. But to say this is not to say that particular forms of earmarking that emerge within existing budgetary processes represent improvements over general-fund financing. It is possible to accept the reasoning behind the arguments showing the potential advantages of tax earmarking while rejecting the presumption that earmarking as it actually operates achieves that potential.

For instance, Browning's (1975) comparison of earmarking and general-fund financing is based explicitly on the median voter model of collective choice. It is also based implicitly on a presumption of generality or non-discrimination in fiscal processes; although people are allowed to have different evaluations for publicly supplied goods, Browning's illustrations are none the less ones in which everyone consumes the service and has some positive evaluation of it. Similarly, although people may pay different amounts of tax they all face a non-discriminatory tax system. Stated differently, the comparison of earmarking and general-fund financing takes place implicitly within a setting of what Buchanan and Tullock (1962: 167–8) refer to as a 'general taxation–general benefit' model.

But actual fiscal processes are not limited in this way. General-fund financing involves heavy doses of special, rather than general, taxation, as excise taxes illustrate. It also involves a good deal of special, rather than general-benefit, spending. But earmarking, too, gives vent to such fiscal discrimination. The standard illustration of earmarking based on high complementarity between the activity being taxed and the service being financed, as represented by earmarking the gasoline tax for highway construction, is an illustration of non-discrimination or generality in taxation and expenditure. True, those who don't ride in cars don't benefit, at least directly, from highway expenditures, but neither do they pay taxes to finance the highways. Only users of the service pay, and in at least some rough proportion to their usage.

In contrast, the earmarking of gasoline tax revenues for mass-transit expenditures represents a discriminatory form of special taxation – on drivers of cars – and special benefit – for non-drivers. The ability of earmarking to perform as characterized by Browning, Buchanan, and other defenders of earmarking would seem to depend ultimately on the ability of constitutional rules to preclude fiscal discrimination, as Hutt (1966) noted in his review article on Buchanan and Tullock's *The Calculus of Consent* (1962). But in the absence of such constitutional constraints on fiscal processes and outcomes, there would seem to be little in general that could be said by way of a relative assessment of earmarking and general-fund financing. This is perhaps still one more illustration of the nihilism of second-best considerations: the Wicksellian system with its thoroughgoing earmarking, along with its other constitutional features, is superior to a rent-seeking system of majoritarian democracy with general-fund financing; but it does not follow that the instances of earmarking that arise within a rent-seeking budgetary process represent improvements over the outcomes that emerge through general-fund financing within those same rent-seeking budgetary processes.

5 CONCLUDING REMARKS

Tax earmarking may, under certain rather restrictive conditions, be an efficient way of financing some publicly provided services, in comparison with general-fund financing. Tax earmarking, because it imposes a differentially high tax on a particular product, will create a greater excess burden per dollar raised than will general taxation; however, when appropriately targeted, tax earmarking can serve to ration a publicly provided, though divisible, or at least congestible, service over competing users. But even under the most suitable conditions the efficiency case for tax earmarking is an ambiguous one. A necessary, though not sufficient, condition for tax earmarking to be an efficient and equitable alternative to general-fund financing is that there exists a positive correlation between the consumption of the taxed good and the earmarked good. Without this correlation, the greater excess burden imposed by tax earmarking is not offset by the benefit from rationing.

The most significant tax earmarking arrangement is that of imposing an excise tax on gasoline to finance highways. In this case, the conditions suitable for earmarking are clearly satisfied. However, political pressures exist to use excise taxes to help finance publicly provided services, the consumption of which is unrelated to the consumption of the product being taxed. An example is the current pressure to earmark the cigarette excise tax to publicly financed health care programmes. The argument is that such an earmarked programme is justified because smokers allegedly make more use of health care services than do non-smokers. Even if this were true, the case for earmarking the cigarette tax as a means of imposing a health care user charge on smokers is inconsistent with the equity rationale for publicly financed health care. But despite the common impression, there is no evidence that smokers do make greater lifetime use of health care services than do non-smokers. And unless it can be established that there is a positive relationship between smoking and lifetime health care use there is no efficiency case to be made for earmarking cigarette taxes to public health care programmes.

NOTES

1 An assessment of Wicksell's contribution in the light of the subsequent scholarship on public-choice and constitutional economics is rendered in Wagner (1988).
2 For a comparison of this administrative perspective with the alternative that has come to be associated with public-choice, see Ostrom (1973).
3 User charging would be redundant within a framework of benevolent despotism if omniscience were also added. But without omniscience, a benevolently despotic budgetary authority may prefer user charges over general-fund financing because of the superior information about consumer demands that user charging generates.
4 A problem may arise if the taxed good, gasoline in this case, is incapable of generating adequate revenue because it is used by only a fraction of those

who use the service financed by the earmarked tax. In this case, principles of efficiency and equity might both be violated. With respect to highways, this situation could arise if electric-powered cars came into any significant usage.
5 This common administrative perspective is set forth clearly by McMahon and Sprenkle (1970).
6 For a more detailed discussion and analytical development of this point, see Chapter 8.

REFERENCES

Brennan, G. and Buchanan, J.M. 'Tax Instruments as Constraints on the Disposition of Public Revenues'. *Journal of Public Economics* 9 (June 1978): 301–18.

Brennan, G. and Buchanan, J.M. *The Power to Tax*. Cambridge: Cambridge University Press, 1980.

Browning, E.K. 'Collective Choice and General Fund Financing'. *Journal of Political Economy* 83 (April 1975): 377–90.

Buchanan, J.M. 'The Economics of Earmarked Taxes'. *Journal of Political Economy* 71 (October 1963): 457–69.

Buchanan, J.M. and Tullock, G. *The Calculus of Consent*. Ann Arbor University of Michigan Press, 1962.

Goetz, C.J. 'Earmarked Taxes and Majority Rule Budgetary Processes'. *American Economic Review* 58 (March 1968): 128–36.

Hutt, W.H. 'Unanimity Versus Non-Discrimination (as Criteria for Constitutional Validity)'. *South African Journal of Economics* 34 (June 1966): 133–47.

McMahon, W.W. and Sprenkle, C.M. 'A Theory of Earmarking'. *National Tax Journal* 23 (September 1970): 255–61.

Ostrom, V. *The Intellectual Crisis in American Public Administration*. Tuscaloosa: University of Alabama Press, 1973.

Wagner, R.E. 'The *Calculus of Consent*: A Wicksellian Retrospective'. *Public Choice* 56 (1988): 153–66.

Wicksell, K. *Finanztheoretische Untersuchungen*. Jena: Gustav Fischer, 1896.

Wicksell, K. 'A New Principle of Just Taxation'. In R.A. Musgrave and A.T. Peacock (eds) *Classics in the Theory of Public Finance*. London: Macmillan, 1958.

8   Rent seeking and tax earmarking

Dwight R. Lee and Robert D. Tollison

The modern literature on tax earmarking has focused on the question of efficiency in government expenditures. Until Buchanan's 1963 paper, public finance theorists generally opposed earmarking tax revenues on the grounds that it imposed an unnecessary constraint on government. The preferences of taxpayer-consumers change over time, as does the technology available to respond to these preferences. By locking in an expenditure pattern based on a revenue pattern that may not be related in any meaningful way to changes in the efficient expenditure pattern, earmarking was seen to reduce the ability of government to accommodate changes in the desired composition of public services over time.

This criticism of tax earmarking is clearly based on a public-interest view of political behaviour. If government is an entity with both the motivation and the information to assess the social costs and benefits of alternative spending patterns and to implement that pattern which maximizes the general well-being, then surely it is the case that the fewer constraints on government the better. But this public-interest view of government is completely contrary to the public-choice view of government that Buchanan was so instrumental in developing. Buchanan's argument in support of the efficiency of tax earmarking is based on the argument that citizens as taxpayer-consumers have little control over the allocation of general revenues among public services. Instead, politicians with broad discretion over expenditures are more responsive to the demands of those groups that are organized around narrowly focused interests than to the diverse preferences of the unorganized general public. The earmarking of tax revenues, then, can serve as a quasi-constitutional constraint on the discretionary authority of politicians, which protects the general taxpayer against special-interest influence and increases the congruence between the actual and the efficient pattern of expenditures on public services. Subsequent discussions of tax earmarking have had to recognize the influence of competing special-interest groups on the allocation of government revenues.[1]

The motivation for the present paper comes from recognizing that decisions on taxes, and the resulting revenues, remain subject to special-interest influence even under tax earmarking. By directing revenues to a particular purpose, earmarking a tax creates a proprietary interest in the resulting tax revenues by organized interest groups. This is true even though the revenues are earmarked entirely for general-interest programmes. Such programmes are typically a major, often the primary, source of income for suppliers and workers who are in positions to capture rents from the programmes, and who are organized for the purpose of ensuring that they do. This fact has implications for the decision on how high the earmarked tax rate is set, the amount of rent-seeking costs associated with the tax rate decision, and the traditional deadweight loss imposed by the tax. Furthermore, it is also often the case that the organized interest benefiting from the revenue generated by an earmarked tax is concerned with the effect the tax has on the consumption of the product, or activity, being taxed. For example, there have been proposals to earmark excise taxes on cigarettes and alcoholic beverages for expenditures on medical care and research. In this case, those groups which, as suppliers of medical care and research, would receive the earmarked revenues are also interested in using the tax to discourage the use of products which they believe are harmful. Similarly, if some of the gasoline tax revenues were earmarked for the funding of mass-transit, those whose interests are tied to the viability of mass-transit systems would see advantage in discouraging use of private automobiles through a higher gasoline tax. On the other hand, those whose interests are tied to highway construction are recipients of earmarked gasoline taxes, but their desire for more revenue through higher gasoline taxes is tempered by their desire not to discourage use of the highways.

The purpose of this paper is to examine some of the economic implications of tax earmarking from the perspective of interest-group politics. In particular we are concerned with those situations in which those who are recipients of earmarked tax revenues have an interest in the amount of the taxed product that is consumed quite apart from the revenue the tax raises.[2] In the first section a simple model of an interest-group recipient of earmarked tax revenue is developed. This model recognizes that different degrees of earmarking are possible; i.e., all of the revenue can be earmarked, or less than all, with varying portions of the amount that is earmarked going to finance different functions. In the second section the model is utilized to consider the question of the socially efficient degree of earmarking to a particular recipient group. The third section makes use of the results obtained in the first section to consider tax earmarking from the perspective of those who are being taxed. The final section offers concluding remarks.

1 CHOICE OF THE TAX RATE BY AN INTEREST GROUP

We begin our analysis by considering an interest group that is the beneficiary of some positive percentage of the revenue generated by a tax imposed on a product. This earmarked revenue enters as a positively valued argument in the interest group's utility function.[3] In addition, it is assumed that the interest group attaches a direct value to the effect the tax has on the consumption of the product being taxed. This value is captured by entering the tax rate, T, into the interest group's utility function, as either a positive- or negative-valued argument. The relationship between T and the total revenue generated, R, is given by the function $R(T)$, where R increases in T up to some maximum value and then declines in T. The proportion of the revenue that goes to the interest group is given by α, where $0 \le \alpha \le 1$. The parameter α can be thought of as measuring the degree to which the tax is earmarked, with $\alpha = 1$ indicating full earmarking and $\alpha = 0$ indicating no earmarking. It is assumed in the present paper that α is a policy variable which is considered to be exogenous by affected interest groups. In a more complete model α would be subject to interest-group influence.

If the interest group could, at no cost, have the tax rate of its choice imposed its problem would be that of maximizing the utility function, $U(T, \alpha R(T))$ with respect to T. But any influence the interest group has over T can be exerted only through rent-seeking activity, which is costly both to the interest group and to society. Let T_0 be the tax rate that would exist in the absence of any political activity on the part of the interest group. Assume that by engaging in rent-seeking activity the tax rate can be increased above T_0 at a rent-seeking cost of $C(T-T_0)$, where $C(0) = 0$, $C' > 0$, and $C'' > 0$.[4] From the perspective of the interest group, this cost has to be deducted from the earmarked revenue in the above utility function. It is now possible to represent the problem faced by the interest group as that of maximizing

$$U(T, \alpha R(T) - C(T-T_0)) \tag{1}$$

with respect to T, subject to the constraint $T \ge T_0$.

The solution to the above maximization, which we represent as T^*, necessarily satisfies the condition

$$U_1 + U_2[\alpha R' - C'] \leq 0, \tag{2}$$

where the subscripts represent partial derivatives with respect to the indicated variable, the primes represent derivatives, and the strict inequality holds only if the constraint is active and $T^* = T_0$. Rewriting condition 2, we obtain

$$-U_1/U_2 \geq \alpha R' - C'. \tag{3}$$

The intuition behind condition 3 is subject to a straightforward interpretation. The left-hand side of the inequality in condition 3 is the slope of the interest group's indifference curve with respect to the tax revenue it receives, net of rent-seeking cost, and the tax rate. So this side of condition 3 tells us how much revenue the interest group is willing to sacrifice (if U_1 is negative this sacrifice is negative) in order to obtain a marginal increase in the tax rate. The right hand side of condition 3 is the slope of the curve giving the net revenue received with respect to the tax rate, and so it tells us how much revenue the interest group has to sacrifice in order to obtain a marginal increase in the tax rate. If we have an interior solution the interest group will push for a higher tax rate until the equality holds in condition 3 and the amount of revenue sacrificed in order to increase the tax equals the amount of revenue the interest group is willing to sacrifice in order to realize that increase. On the other hand, if a corner solution is called for, then condition 3 holds as an inequality, and the amount of revenue that has to be sacrificed in order to increase the tax above T_0 is greater than, or equal to, the amount the interest group is willing to sacrifice in order to achieve the increase.

The several possibilities suggested by condition 3 can be usefully illustrated graphically. We do this by considering, first, the situation in which $U_1 > 0$; i.e., the interest group attaches a positive value to discouraging the consumption of the product being taxed. In Figure 8.1 the revenue received from the earmarked tax by the interest group is given by $\alpha R(T)$. The function $R(T)$ is, of course, nothing more than the Laffer curve for the earmarked tax, and reflects the fact that no revenue is raised at either a tax rate of zero or a tax rate so high that it discourages completely the taxed activity (given by T_c in Figure 8.1). The curve $\alpha R(T) - C(T-T_0)$, which corresponds to $\alpha R(T)$ until $T > T_0$, gives the revenue received by the interest group net of its rent-seeking cost. And the curve given by I is an indifference curve of the interest group. Since we are considering the case where the interest group places a positive value on both the tax rate and the revenue it receives, its indifference curves are downward sloping over all $T < T_c$.[5] As Figure 8.1 is constructed, the slope of the net revenue curve is more negative than the

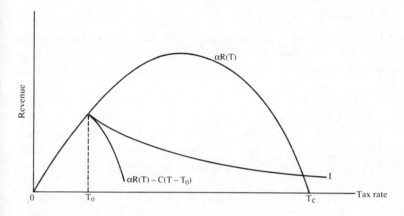

Figure 8.1 Tax earmarking with hostile interest group, I

slope of the indifference curve at tax rate T_0. Therefore, any attempt on the part of the interest group to increase the tax rate above T_0 requires the sacrifice of more net revenue than the interest group is willing to make. In this case the interest group will be content with the tax rate T_0; it does not pay the interest group to lobby for a higher rate. Note that this corner solution result can only apply, given the negatively sloped indifference curves, when the net revenue curve is negatively sloped at T_0. This can be the result of either a very high marginal rent-seeking cost or a T_0 that is positioned near that rate which maximizes total tax revenue. If T_0 is higher than this maximizing rate the net revenue curve is negatively sloped for any positive marginal rent-seeking cost.

Of course, a net revenue curve with a negative slope over the entire range $T_0 < T < T_c$ does not imply a corner solution. In Figure 8.2 the net revenue curve is, as in Figure 8.1, downward sloping over all $T > T_0$. In this case, however, the net revenue is not as negatively sloped at T_0 as is the relevant indifference curve. Therefore, the interest group finds it advantageous to engage in some positive amount of rent seeking for the purpose of increasing T above T_0. As shown in Figure 8.2, the optimal amount of rent seeking from the perspective of the interest group results in a tax of $T^* > T_0$.

In Figure 8.3, the net revenue curve rises to the right of T_0 before reaching a maximum and then declining. Since the indifference curves are negatively sloped, the maximizing T occurs on the declining segment of the net revenue curve and, in this case, it is necessarily true that $T^* > T_0$. As shown in Figure 8.3, T^* occurs where the curve $\alpha R(T)$ and

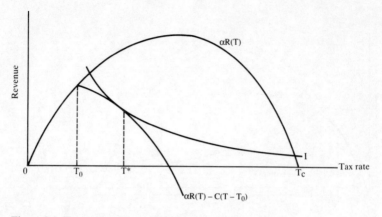

Figure 8.2 Tax earmarking with hostile interest group, II

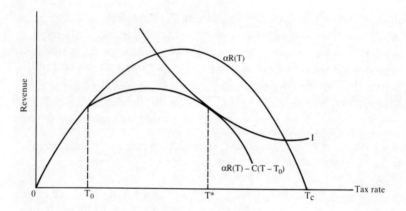

Figure 8.3 Tax earmarking with hostile interest group, III

therefore R(T) is also negatively sloped. This is only a possibility, of course, but it is a possibility that has significance when we consider tax earmarking from the perspective of those being taxed.

So far all of the cases considered have assumed that the interest group receiving the earmarked revenue realizes a direct utility benefit from discouraging the taxed activity. The interest group is willing to sacrifice some revenue for the pleasure of reducing the consumption of, say, alcoholic beverages, cigarettes, games of chance, abortions, private transportation, etc. We consider now the case where the interest group

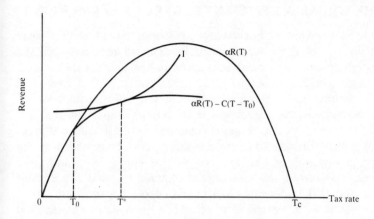

Figure 8.4 Tax earmarking with favourable interest group

receiving the earmarked revenue suffers a direct utility cost from discouraging the taxed activity. Examples here are more difficult to come by since it seems to be more natural for people to receive enjoyment, rather than displeasure, from knowing that others are being deprived from engaging in activities of their choice. The case of those who are involved in highway construction and maintenance receiving disutility from discouraging people from owning and operating private automobiles is probably a reasonable example.

In Figure 8.4 the revenue situation is the same as that described in Figure 8.3. The difference in Figure 8.4 is that the indifference curves are upward sloping to reflect the fact that the interest group requires additional revenue in order to compensate for the reduced consumption resulting from a increase in the tax rate. As constructed in Figure 8.4, the interest group maximizes its utility by engaging in an amount of rent seeking in support of a higher tax sufficient to achieve a tax rate T^*. A positive level of rent seeking is only forthcoming, however, when the net revenue curve is upward sloping over some initial range (rent seeking in support of a tax rate greater than T_0 would not occur with the net revenue curves in Figures 8.1 and 8.2). It is also clear that it will never be to the advantage of the interest group represented in Figure 8.4 to push for a tax rate in excess of that which maximizes total revenue. On the other hand, it is possible, even with an upward-sloping net revenue curve, that the corner solution $T^* = T_0$ obtains, and the interest group makes no effort to increase the tax above T_0.

2   THE SOCIALLY EFFICIENT DEGREE OF EARMARKING

We have analysed how an interest group responds to the receipt of some proportion, α, of the revenue raised by taxing a product when the interest group has a non-monetary interest in how much of the product is consumed. In this section we make use of results of that analysis in order to address the question: What is the socially efficient value for α?[6] The considerations that are relevant in answering this question are, first, the effect of α on the value of output generated by transferring resources (net of rent-seeking costs) to finance those activities provided by the interest group; and, second, the cost of that output in terms of the resources transferred, the rent seeking required to effect the transfer (increase the tax), and the deadweight loss imposed by the tax.

To proceed, we first examine the effect of an increase in α on the level of T*. Considered as an equality, and assuming that the sufficiency condition is satisfied, condition 2 defines T* as a function of α. Differentiating condition 2 with respect to α and solving for $dT^*/d\alpha$ yields

$$dT^*/d\alpha = -[(\alpha R' - C')U_{22}R + U_{12}R + U_2R']/ |D| \qquad (4)$$

where $|D|$ is negative by virtue of the sufficiency condition being satisfied. Therefore, the sign of condition 4 is the same as the sign of the expression within brackets which, in general, is indeterminate. There are, however, some things that can be said about condition 4. In order to keep the discussion as uncomplicated as possible, we consider only the situation where the interest group is hostile to the consumption of the good being taxed. In this situation, the first term in condition 4 is unequivocally positive, since $(\alpha R' - C') < 0$ at T* and $U_{22} < 0$ everywhere. On the other hand, assuming as we will that the slope of the indifference curves, given by $-U_1/U_2$, either remains the same or becomes less negative as we move up along a vertical line, then it follows that $U_{12} < 0$, and therefore $U_{12} R < 0$ also.[7] Finally, as established by the cases considered in Figures 8.2 and 8.3, R', and therefore U_2R', can be either positive or negative. Comparing Figures 8.2 and 8.3, it is easily seen that, everything else being equal, the smaller the rent-seeking cost, or the more value the interest group places on a high T relative to additional revenue (i.e., the steeper the indifference curves) the more likely it is that $R' < 0$. Therefore, if the indifference curves are vertically parallel (or become less negative as we move up in the vertical direction) and steeply negative, and the rent-seeking cost is relatively small, then it is possible that $dT^*/d\alpha < 0$.

We are now in a position to consider the efficiency implications of the choice of α. The choice of a value for α will affect the net revenue allocated to activities that the interest group under consideration favours; such activities that are potentially productive as providing public transportation or engaging in medical research. The value created by earmarking tax revenue to such an activity can be expressed, then, as a function of α, which we represent as

$$V(\alpha R(T^*(\alpha)) - C(T^*(\alpha) - T_0)) \tag{5}$$

It is assumed that the function V increases in net revenues at a decreasing rate, or $V' > 0$ and $V'' < 0$. Against the value represented in condition 5 we have to deduct, first, the opportunity cost of the total amount of the revenue transferred to the interest group, which equals that revenue, $\alpha R(T^*(\alpha))$; second, the rent-seeking cost associated with the transfer, $C(T^*(\alpha) - T_0)$; and, third, the deadweight loss imposed by the tax which is given by $D(T^*(\alpha))$, where $D' > 0$ and $D'' > 0$. Therefore the socially efficient α is that which maximizes

$$V(\alpha R(T^*(\alpha)) - C(T^*(\alpha) - T_0) - [\alpha R(T^*) + C(T^*(\alpha) - T_0) + D(T^*(\alpha))] \tag{6}$$

subject to the constraint $\alpha \geq 0$.

The maximizing α, which we denote α^*, necessarily satisfies the condition

$$V'[(\alpha R' - C')dT^*/d\alpha] + V'R - (\alpha R' + C' + D') dT^*/d\alpha - R \leq 0 \tag{7}$$

where the strict inequality holds only if $\alpha^* = 0$. The interpretation of condition 7 is the straightforward one that α should be increased as long as the marginal value from so doing exceeds the marginal cost, with the strict inequality holding only if the marginal value of an increase in α is less than the marginal cost for all non-negative α. In this latter case, the corner solution holds with $\alpha^* = 0$.

It is useful to rewrite condition 7 as

$$[V'(\alpha R' - C') - (\alpha R' + C' + D')]dT^*/d\alpha + R(V' - 1) \leq 0 \tag{7'}$$

Since we are assuming an interior solution to condition 2, or $T^* > T_0$, it follows that $\alpha R' - C' < 0$. If $R' > 0$ at the tax that exists when $\alpha = 0$, $T^*(0)$, which is likely to be the case, then the bracketed coefficient to $dT^*/d\alpha$ in condition 7 is unequivocally negative. Therefore unless $dT^*/d\alpha < 0$, or V' is large at the expenditure level for the interest group's output that exists in the absence of earmarking tax revenues to that group, then condition 7' holds as a strict inequality at $\alpha = 0$ and the efficient solution calls for no earmarking.

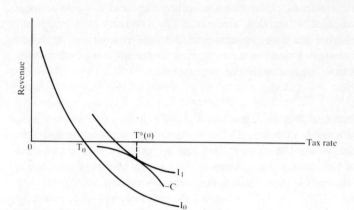

Figure 8.5 Efficient rate of tax earmarking

This case is depicted in Figure 8.5 where the interest group is motivated to devote some resources to pushing for a higher tax rate even though it receives no revenue from the tax. As shown, the indifference curve that intersects the horizontal axis at T_o is more negatively sloped than is the relevant net revenue curve, $-C(T-T_o)$ at T_o, and so the equilibrium tax rate is $T^*(0) > T_o$. In this case the rent-seeking activity of the interest group in favour of a higher tax rate is motivated entirely by its desire to reduce the consumption of the taxed product.

It is possible, of course, for condition 7' to hold as an equality because, say, at $\alpha = 0$ the marginal value of the activity engaged in by the interest group is large relative to the cost, including the rent-seeking cost, of financing it through tax earmarking. Increasing α can, and almost surely will over some initial range, encourage the interest group to act on its preference for a reduction in the consumption of the taxed product (as long as $R' > 0$, increasing α reduces the marginal net revenue loss the interest group suffers when rent seeking in favour of a higher T). If the preference for a reduction in the consumption of the taxed product is sufficiently intense (as reflected in steeply downward-sloped indifference curves), then, as analysed earlier, the interest group will push the tax rate into the region where $R' < 0$, and $dT^*/d\alpha < 0$. Under these circumstances some of the efficiency advantage realized from increasing α is that doing so increases the marginal cost of rent seeking for a higher tax (when $R' < 0$ an increase in α increases the negativity of $\alpha R' - C'$) and therefore moderates the distortions motivated by the interest group's hostility to the consumption choices of others.

There are many possibilities for particular solutions, including the possibility that $\alpha^* = 1$, in which case the inequality in condition 7' is reversed.[8] We could also expand the discussion by considering in detail the situation in which the interest group receives direct disutility from discouraging consumption of the taxed product. These additional possibilities will not concern us here, however, since the main point of the analysis is clear. Tax earmarking is not an all-or-none proposition, but rather a matter of degree, with there being a continuum of possibilities for the proportion of the revenue from a particular tax that is earmarked. And the degree to which a tax is earmarked can have important efficiency implications that go beyond the standard concern of how tax earmarking affects public expenditures.

3   FROM THE PERSPECTIVE OF THOSE BEING TAXED

In the formal model developed in the first two sections we considered only the motivations of the interest group in receipt (or potential receipt) of revenue from an earmarked tax. In this section we consider, although not within the context of a formal model, the concerns of those who are producing and consuming the activity, or product, being taxed.

Those whose interests are tied to either low prices or a large quantity demanded of a product prefer that any tax on that product be as low as possible. In general this preference for a low tax translates into a preference for preventing any tax that does exist from being earmarked for a specific purpose, and therefore to a specific interest group. As long as the revenue from a tax on a product goes into the general fund no organized interest has a strong motivation to exert political pressure in favour of increasing the tax. Although many different groups benefit from increasing the revenue available through the general fund, each will receive that benefit whether or not the general fund is 'enriched' by its efforts. In essence, the general fund is seen as a common property resource which many interest groups are interested in exploiting, but few, if any, are interested in replenishing. Once the tax on a product is earmarked, the revenue on that tax becomes treated as proprietary by a politically organized interest group. Such a group clearly is strongly motivated to incur costs in order to increase the tax and the resulting revenue.

If those who want to keep the tax on a product low find that there is no way of preventing the tax on that product from being earmarked, they can be expected to prefer that the revenue be earmarked to a group which receives benefit, either directly or indirectly, from the consumption of the taxed product.[9] As suggested by Figure 8.4 and the attendant discussion, in this case the motivation of the revenue-receiving group to lobby for a higher tax is moderated by its interest in maintaining the consumption of the taxed product. Those paying the tax can be sure that the recipients of the earmarked revenue are not interested in a tax as high as that which maximizes the total tax revenue. If the group receiving the earmarked revenue is neutral with respect to the consumption of the taxed product (neutral except for the revenue generated), then those paying the tax can still be confident that, assuming marginal rent-seeking costs are positive, the tax will remain below the revenue-maximizing rate.

In stark contrast, however, the revenue-recipient group could be hostile to the product being taxed. This situation surely characterizes the tobacco industry, which is continually confronted with suggestions that cigarette tax revenues be earmarked to help finance health care and research. The tobacco industry has opposed earmarking the cigarette tax, perhaps in part because it recognizes that the health care industry is the most likely recipient and that the health care industry is politically powerful and hostile to smoking. The fear is that earmarking the revenue to the health care industry would provide this influential interest group with an even stronger motivation to increase the tax on cigarettes. Our analysis suggests, however, that this reason for opposing earmarking may be misplaced. For there may well be circumstances under which the tobacco industry might fare better should cigarette tax revenues be earmarked for the health care industry. If, for example, the health care industry's political influence increases to the point where it is able to push the cigarette tax above the revenue-maximizing level, the tobacco industry might gain by having the cigarette tax revenues ear- marked. From the cigarette industry's perspective, the first choice for a recipient group would be one with no hostility (or better yet, negative hostility) towards smoking, and with sufficient political influence to neutralize that of the health care industry. Such an arrangement would result in a reduction in the cigarette tax, as the recipient group now uses its influence to secure a tax on cigarettes that maximizes cigarette tax revenues.

Suppose, however, that no group exists which has both no hostility to smoking and the political power to oppose successfully the health care industry on the issue of cigarette taxes. And if such a group does exist there is no guarantee that the tobacco industry could secure it as the recipient of the earmarked cigarette tax revenues. In this situation, the tobacco industry might gain by going along with the proposal to earmark the revenues from the cigarette tax to the health care industry. A proprietary interest in the revenues raised by the cigarette tax on the part of the health care industry would create a powerful restraint on its desire for a prohibitive cigarette tax. As recipients of the revenues from the cigarette tax, a health care industry with the political influence to obtain an extremely high tax may still use its political influence to push the tax beyond the revenue-maximizing rate, but it will not push the tax as high as it would without a proprietary interest in the cigarette tax revenues. Indeed, it is possible that it is to the tobacco industry's advantage to have the cigarette tax earmarked to a hostile and politically powerful health care industry, even if a feasible alternative is to earmark the tax to a neutral interest group with the political influence to choose the cigarette tax it prefers (which is obviously the one which maximizes revenue). It may be the case that with the cigarette tax earmarked to the neutral interest the health care industry has less interest in, and influence over, the tax rate, so that the rate is lower than if the tax were earmarked for health care. But, at the same time, the health care industry may be able to reduce smoking by exerting its political influence in favour of non-tax restrictions on smoking. There are a large number of ways that government can discourage smoking other than taxing tobacco products. Draconian restrictions can be imposed on where smoking is allowed, publicly financed advertising against smoking can be expanded, agricultural allotments to domestic tobacco growers can be reduced, and quotas on tobacco imports can be tightened. When the health care industry receives no tax revenue from the sale of cigarettes it has a strong motive to push non-tax political restrictions on smoking as far as it can. Therefore, it may be in the interest of the tobacco industry to have cigarette tax revenues earmarked to the health care industry even if this results in a higher tax, in order to reduce the political support for other policies that restrict smoking.

The situation just described is illustrated in Figure 8.6. With the cigarette tax earmarked to a neutral interest group the tax may be T_1 rather than T_2, which would be the case if it is earmarked to the health care industry. However, the relevant revenue curve with tax T_1 is given by R_1, which reflects the stringent non-tax restrictions against smoking obtained by the health care industry. With the tax revenue earmarked to the health care industry, the political support for the non-tax restrictions on smoking are less, and the relevant revenue curve is given by R_2. Clearly, the tobacco industry is better off with a cigarette tax of T_2, which raises R_h in revenue, than with a lower tax of T_1, which raises only R_n in revenue.[10]

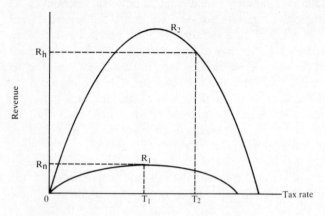

Figure 8.6 Interest group pressures on tax earmarking

4 CONCLUSION

Tax earmarking can be seen as a means of committing government to a set pattern of expenditures, and in so doing reducing the influence of organized interest groups. If tax earmarking were an all-or-none decision it might have the effect of reducing interest-group influence once the earmarking decision has been made. But tax earmarking is not an all-or-none decision. There is a continuum of possibilities for fixing the proportion of the revenues from a tax that is earmarked to a particular purpose. Also, once an earmarking proportion has been fixed for a particular purpose, the funding devoted to the purpose can be increased or decreased by changes in the tax rate.

We have concentrated attention on the effect tax earmarking has on the tax rate decision. Once a tax has been earmarked to a particular expenditure programme, an interest group has a strong interest in increasing the amount of revenue raised by the tax. In addition, it is often the case that the interest group is motivated by the desire to discourage, or to encourage, the consumption of the product being taxed quite apart from the revenue it receives. Coupling the interest group's desire for revenue, and in affecting the consumption of the taxed product, with a rent-seeking cost to the interest group of obtaining an increase in the tax rate, it is possible to develop a model in which the tax rate depends on the proportion of the tax revenue that is earmarked to the interest group (or to the expenditure programme to which the interest group is attached). This suggests that the efficiency of a tax-earmarking proposal depends on the proportion of the resulting revenues that are earmarked to particular programmes and the political influence and objectives of the interest groups associated with those programmes.

In the absence of tax earmarking, political competition among interest groups will be motivated by the desire on the part of each to obtain a larger share of what is considered a common pool of revenue. In this setting, however, no interest group has a strong incentive to take political action for the purpose of increasing the size of the revenue pool. In a setting characterized by tax earmarking the direct competition among interest groups may be reduced as each now has a claim on a particular revenue source. But the political influence of organized interests is not reduced by tax earmarking. Instead, the influence is simply redirected from efforts to obtain a larger share of a large common pool of revenue to efforts aimed at increasing the size of a smaller, but dedicated, pool of revenue.

NOTES

1 Goetz (1968) established that earmarking can be justified along the lines suggested by Buchanan, but under less restrictive assumptions than Buchanan incorporated into his analysis. Also see Deran (1965), McMahon and Sprenkle (1970), Goetz and McKnew (1972), and Browning (1975) for discussions of the influence of earmarking on spending.

2 In the case of those who receive earmarked gasoline tax revenues to supply mass transit, we are assuming that they believe it is important to discourage the use of private automobiles, and receive satisfaction from so doing, quite apart from revenue considerations. Similarly, those providing medical services are assumed to receive direct satisfaction from discouraging smoking, and those whose profession is to construct and maintain highways derive direct dissatisfaction from discouraging the use of highways.

3 Although it is convenient to refer to the interest group's utility function, and later to the interest group's indifference curves, we recognize that such a concept is theoretically vacuous unless all members of the group have identical preferences. In the discussion that follows references to the group's utility function or indifference curves can be thought of as being derived from the preferences of the group's median voter.

4 It is assumed that C represents both the cost to the interest group and to society. This is an assumption that simplifies the analysis but which may not be completely accurate. Some of what the interest group considers to be a cost may be a transfer which has no social cost. However, even in the case of what may be seen as a pure transfer (for example, a bribe) there will be competition among potential recipients of such transfers which diverts real resources away from wealth-producing activities. So even if there is a difference between the rent-seeking cost to the interest group and to society at large, this difference is likely to be small. The function C is not defined over negative values.

5 Since demand for the product is choked off at T_c, the interest group perceives no additional gain, in terms of reduced consumption, from a higher tax rate. The marginal utility of T, U_1, therefore equals zero at $T = T_c$ and all indifference curves become horizontal at that point.

6 As indicated earlier, we assume that α is a policy variable over which the interest group has no direct or indirect control. In a more complete model the interest group would engage in rent seeking over the value of α as well as the level of T.

7 If $-U_1/U_2$ is differentiated with respect to the second argument, with the result assumed non-negative, then $U_2U_{12} - U_1U_{22} \leq 0$. This implies $U_{12} \leq (U_1/U_2)U_{22} < 0$ The slope of the indifference curves could, of course, become increasingly negative as we move up a vertical line, and it could still be true that $U_{12} < 0$.

8 This assumes the constraint $\alpha \leq 1$. Such a constraint could be eliminated, of course, by transferring more than 100 per cent of the tax revenues to the interest group. Similarly, the constraint $\alpha \geq 0$ could be eliminated by imposing a penalty on the interest group equal to some percentage of the tax revenues. Such possibilities are ignored here.

9 A possible exception to this expectation is discussed later in this section.

10 This assumes that the return per pack of cigarettes sold is not significantly lower in the former case than in the latter.

REFERENCES

Browning, E.K. 'Collective Choice and General Fund Financing'. *Journal of Political Economy* 83 (April 1975): 377–90.

Buchanan, J.M. 'The Economies of Earmarked Taxes'. *Journal of Political Economy* 71 (October 1963): 457–69.

Deran, E. 'Earmarking and Expenditures: A Survey and a New Test'. *National Tax Journal* 18 (December 1965): 354–61.

Goetz, C.J. 'Earmarked Taxes and Majority Rule Budgetary Processes'. *American Economic Review* 58 (March 1968): 128–36.

Goetz, C.J., and McKnew, C.R. Jr. 'Paradoxical Results in a Public Choice Model of Alternative Government Grant Forms'. In J.M. Buchanan and R.D. Tollison (eds) *The Theory of Public Choice*, Ann Arbor: University of Michigan Press, 1972.

McMahon, W.W. and Sprenkle, C.M. 'A Theory of Earmarking'. *National Tax Journal* 23 (September 1970): 255–61.

9 Tax earmarking and the optimal lobbying strategy *

Mwangi S. Kimenyi, Dwight R. Lee, and Robert D. Tollison

What are the economic effects of earmarking the revenues from a tax to a particular expenditure programme? More precisely, is economic efficiency enhanced or diminished by dedicating a tax to a specified government purpose, such as education, highway construction, or medical research? Any attempt to determine the efficiency implications of tax earmarking requires some model, either implicit or explicit, of the political process. By imposing an additional constraint on government, tax earmarking can affect government decisions on not only how to spend tax revenues, but on how much tax revenue to raise.

A common argument is based on the assumption that the political process is responsive to broad public preferences. This is invariably an implicit assumption which is ungrounded in any clear model of government decision-making. It is simply accepted without question that government is an entity with both the ability and desire to provide efficiently to the public those goods or services that cannot be provided efficiently through private exchange in the market place. If such a capable and benevolent government were at the service of the public it would clearly be inadvisable to impose an unnecessary constraint on government. Why would anyone entangle a dutiful agent with constraints that can be avoided? By precommitting government to a particular expenditure programme, and therefore reducing its discretion, tax earmarking is seen as nothing more than an unnecessary constraint on government that can only reduce economic efficiency.

It is not surprising that it was one of the founders of the economic theory of government (or public choice) who attacked the unnecessary constraint argument against tax earmarking. Buchanan (1963) explicitly challenged the benevolent government assumption implicitly accepted by those opposed to tax earmarking. He argued instead that politicians can often realize political advantage by presenting voters with all-or-none taxation-expenditure packages that capture much of the voter's surplus in a way that is analogous to businessmen capturing consumers' surplus in the private sector with tie-in sales. Buchanan established the possibility that earmarking could increase efficiency by allowing taxpayers to constrain government expenditures in a way that brings them more in conformity with taxpayer preferences.

Goetz (1968) supported Buchanan by arguing that earmarking could provide a means whereby compromises among contending political factions could be enforced. This argument allowed Goetz to establish that earmarking can increase efficiency under less restrictive assumptions about political behaviour than Buchanan incorporated into his model.

The model of government employed by Buchanan, Goetz, and other public-choice economists, whether analysing the effect of earmarking tax revenues or any other public policy, recognizes the importance of the lobbying efforts of organized interest groups on political decisions. Government policies that create benefits which are widely dispersed over the general public typically fail to motivate organized support for the simple reason that the benefits to any one individual or organized group are too small to make such support worthwhile. It is those government policies that concentrate benefits on organized groups that it pays these groups actively to support through the exercise of their political influence. So when considering the likely results of any particular policy it is important to consider the effects the policy will have on different interest groups and the relative ability and motivation of those interest groups to respond to these effects.

Obviously, the effect of tax earmarking will depend on the political response earmarking generates. In particular, it has to be realized that tax earmarking does more than generate funds for specific government activities. By dedicating tax revenues to a particular purpose, earmarking creates a proprietary interest in the tax and the revenue it generates on the part of organized recipient groups. The focus of the present paper is not primarily on the efficiency comparison between earmarked and general-fund financing of public services. Our objective is to investigate the effect of lobbying on tax revenues when revenues are earmarked, as opposed to the situation in which revenues are allocated among various functions through the general fund.

Our basic argument is that under general-fund budgeting, individual interest groups are more concerned with competing for larger shares of the existing level of tax revenue than with lobbying for tax rates that increase the revenue pool. In contrast, under an institutional arrangement where tax revenues are earmarked each recipient group is interested in increasing revenue from a given source and therefore will lobby for revenue-increasing changes in the tax rate. We predict that changing from general-fund financing to earmarked financing of a particular government function will lead to an increase in the revenue generated by the tax that has been earmarked.

The paper is organized as follows: Section 1 briefly outlines interest-group behaviour under institutions of earmarking and general fund financing; Section 2 provides some empirical tests and results; Section 3 contains some concluding remarks.

1 TAX INSTITUTIONS AND LOBBYING

In the case of general-fund financing, each interest group can increase its benefits by pursuing either one of two different objectives: first, lobbying the legislature to increase the share of the total budget that the lobbying group gets relative to others; or, second, lobbying the legislature to adopt a tax structure that increases total revenues. The important difference between these two pursuits is that it is a relatively small organized group which receives the bulk of the benefits from the first pursuit and a relatively large, diverse, and unorganized group which receives the bulk of the benefits from the second pursuit. Therefore, if one group invests resources in lobbying for revenue-increasing tax rates there is no guarantee that the particular group doing the lobbying will benefit any more than others. In fact, if the other groups concentrate their resources in lobbying for larger shares of the budget, they may benefit more than the group that lobbies for the revenue-increasing tax rate. In the general fund setting, therefore, gains to each group are maximized if resources are invested in influencing the legislature for a larger share of the total 'pie'. The result is a situation where interest groups compete for budget shares rather than for changes in the fiscal structure. If a particular group decides to invest resources in influencing the legislature to adopt revenue-increasing tax rates, such behaviour would generate a positive externality to all other groups. Where there are many revenue-sharing interest groups a classical prisoner's dilemma arises, for a collusive outcome, which would increase total tax revenues, becomes difficult to achieve. The consequence is that no interest group is likely to lobby effectively for revenue-increasing tax changes, but rather all groups will compete for the available revenues.

It is important to enter a cautionary note at this point to be clear that we are not misunderstood. We are not arguing, or intending to imply, that under general-fund financing tax rates will be fixed. Lobbying activity on the part of individual groups aimed at securing a larger share of a common revenue pool puts pressure on politicians to satisfy a host of competing demands. One way to respond to this pressure is to increase effective, if not nominal, tax rates and to impose more cost on the general public in order to expand programmes favoured by organized interest groups. At least up to some point the political cost of spreading an additional tax burden over the dispersed, diverse, and unorganized public is less than denying the demands of an organized group for concentrated benefits. So the competing demands for larger shares of the revenue pool does exert upward pressure on the size of that pool. But it has to be recognized that when the demands are for a common revenue pool they are directly competing demands. The demands of one organized interest group are directly affected by the demands of others, and politicians will respond to the relative strengths of different interest groups by giving more to some by taking from (or giving less to) others.

With an increase in the number of programmes (and therefore attached interest groups) that are funded by the revenues from an earmarked tax, there will be an increase in the degree to which the demands of one group are insulated from the demands of other groups. We recognize, of course, that this insulation is, and can never be, complete, and that there is always some connection between the demands of different interest groups. But turning to the case where all revenues are earmarked, it is evident that an interest group can gain little, if any, by arguing that the programme it favours is more important, or deserving, than other political programmes. The gains obtained by an interest group from investing resources in lobbying the legislature for budget shares are nil. The way a particular interest group best expends its political influence in a world of tax earmarking is by lobbying the legislature to push for tax rates that increase the earmarked revenue. All of the gains realized from such lobbying activity are captured by the group doing the lobbying. No other group benefits as a free rider. We would expect then that tax earmarking, by internalizing the benefits from pushing for increases in tax revenues, would mobilize increased political activity in favour of increasing tax revenues.

In summary, the foregoing analysis suggests that rent-seeking groups will direct their lobbying activities either to increase total revenues or to obtain larger shares of the budget, based on the expected benefit from such lobbying. In the case of earmarking, lobbying for revenue-increasing taxes has the highest returns. Consequently, we would expect revenues from a particular tax to be greater if such revenues are earmarked for a particular function, *ceteris paribus*.

2 EMPIRICAL MODEL AND RESULTS

In order to subject the conclusion reached in the previous section to an empirical test we turn our attention to a tax which, though one that earmarking now brings immediately to mind, has not always been earmarked. The federal motor fuel tax provides a convenient and direct way to assess the level of revenues under general-fund and earmarked financing. Although a federal motor fuel tax was first imposed in 1931, revenues from the tax were not earmarked until 1956, following the enactment of the Highway Revenue Act of that year. Thus, between 1931 and 1956 revenues from the federal motor fuel tax were subject to competition by all interest groups, with no one group having proprietary claim on any portion of that revenue. Following our previous analysis we would expect that interest groups would have concentrated their resources in competing for the allocation of such revenues rather than lobbying for increases in fuel tax revenues. After 1956 a large share of the federal fuel tax was earmarked for highways. Our analysis suggests that under these circumstances the highway lobby would concentrate more resources in lobbying for fuel tax increases rather than lobbying for larger shares of the total budget. We would thus expect earmarking of motor fuel taxes to be associated with increases in highway tax revenues.

To test this hypothesis we constructed the following empirical models:

$$LRFEDR = a_0 + a_1 LRGNP + a_2 LMVR + a_3 DUMMY + a_4T + a_5T^2 + u \tag{1}$$

and

$$LPRFEDR = b_0 + b_1 LPY + b_2 LMVR + b_3 DUMMY + b_4T + b_5T^2 + u; \tag{2}$$

where,

LRFEDR	= natural logarithm of real federal fuel tax revenues;
LRGNP	= natural logarithm of real gross national product;
LMVR	= natural logarithm of motor vehicles registered;
DUMMY	= 0 before the fuel tax revenues were earmarked, and = 1 afterwards;
T	= linear time trend;
T^2	= non-linear time trend;
LPRFEDR	= natural logarithm of per capita real federal fuel tax revenues;
LPY	= natural logarithm of per capita income; and
u	= regression error term.

Increases in real income are expected to increase tax revenues. Given that increased economic activity is normally associated with increased demand for transportation, we expect fuel consumption to increase as income increases, and therefore fuel tax revenues to increase as well. The more motor vehicles registered, the higher the demand for fuel; therefore, we expect a positive relationship between fuel tax collections and the number of motor vehicles registered. In recent years, however, there has been an increase in the number of small, fuel-efficient cars in the United States. This implies that the level of fuel consumption may have increased at a lower rate compared with the increase in the number of vehicles registered. Such as effect would mitigate the impact of motor vehicles registered on tax revenues.

The focus of the paper is on the relationship between tax revenues and the binary variable, which takes on the value 0 when the fuel tax revenues were not earmarked and the value 1 when those tax revenues were earmarked. If our theoretical framework on the behaviour of interest groups is correct we would expect a positive relationship between the binary variable and tax collections. Over the earmarked period the interest group(s) benefiting from highway revenues would be expected to lobby more effectively for federal fuel tax increases than over the period before earmarking. This would lead to larger fuel tax revenues, *ceteris paribus*.[1] Finally, we included the linear time trend T to account for secular increases in fuel tax revenues accounted for by factors other than the demand variables included in the model. A non-linear time trend T^2, is included to capture such effects as changes in the composition of the population. The signs of the coefficients of T and T^2 are indeterminate, *a priori*.

Using data for the United States for the period 1933 to 1982, we estimated the empirical models using an autoregressive procedure.[2] The results of estimating various specifications of the models are shown in Tables 9.1 and 9.2. The coefficients of the income variable are positive and significant in all specifications. As income increases, fuel tax revenues also increase. The coefficients on the variable for motor vehicles registered are positive in three of the four specifications that this variable included, but are not statistically significant. This may be explained by the registration of an increased number of fuel-efficient cars in the last few years. No consistent results are obtained for the linear time-trend variable; however, the coefficient on the non-linear time-trend variable is negative and statistically significant.

The coefficients we are primarily interested in, of course, are those on the binary variables which indicate the effect earmarking the fuel tax has on the amount of revenue that tax raised. According to those coefficients the effect of earmarking on the level of fuel tax revenues is

Table 9.1 Regression results for the determinants of LRFEDR (1933–82)

| | Models | | | |
	1	2	3	4
Intercept	1.61	2.41	69.43	–2011.06
	(2.31)**	(1.62)	(2.46)**	(–2.01)**
LRGNP	0.87	0.94	1.23	0.72
	(7.43)***	(4.39)***	(5.19)***	(2.17)*
LMVR		–0.113	0.33	0.24
		(–0.50)	(1.10)	(0.80)
DUMMY	0.32	0.38	0.60	0.55
	(2.38)**	(2.68)***	(4.78)***	(4.45)***
T	–	–	–0.03	2.06
			(–2.34)**	(2.04)**
T^2	–	–	–	–0.005
				(–2.08)**
R^2	0.80	0.82	0.90	0.91

Notes: t-statistics in parentheses. R^2 is the adjusted coefficient of multiple determination. Asterisks denote significance at the 1 per cent (***), 5 per cent (**), and 10 per cent (*) levels. An autoregressive procedure was used to correct for serial correlation in all specifications.

positive and significant in all specifications. This is consistent with our theoretical argument that earmarking changes lobbying activities from competition for revenue shares to that of increasing revenue totals.

Although the number of registered vehicles is a useful proxy for the demand for gasoline, there are other candidates in this regard. In particular, as the quality of roads has increased over time, the number of vehicle miles driven, and hence the demand for gasoline, has increased. The improvements in road quality have been largely due to increased and continued federal funding of road systems. Federal financing for highway construction has greatly reduced the cost of highway travel and has resulted in significant increases in the number of motor vehicle miles driven.

To account for these changes we used motor vehicle mileage as an independent variable in the above models. Because the number of motor vehicles miles is likely to be dependent on the level of income, we regressed motor vehicle miles against the income variables and used the predicted values as instruments.[3]

Table 9.2   Regression results for the determinants of LPRPEDR (1933–82)

	Models			
	1	*2*	*3*	*4*
Intercept	21.24	−2684.93	48.98	−2493.92
	(2.21)**	(−3.16)***	(2.23)**	(−3.12)***
LPY	0.90	0.75	0.92	0.76
	(10.57)***	(8.40)***	(5.19)***	(2.17)*
LMVR			0.34	0.25
			(1.13)	(0.92)
DUMMY	0.54	0.48	0.59	0.52
	(4.01)***	(3.92)***	(4.57)***	(4.36)***
T	−0.01	2.75	−0.02	2.56
	(−2.11)**	(3.18)***	(2.07)**	(3.15)***
T^2		−0.0007		−0.0006
		(−3.19)***		(−3.18)***
R^2	0.81	0.84	0.84	0.87

Notes: See Table 9.1.

The regression results for these estimations are reported in Table 9.3. The variable for mileage is positive and significant in all specifications. The coefficients on the dummy variable are also positive and significant, suggesting again that earmarking of federal gasoline tax revenues resulted in an increase in such revenues.

3   CONCLUSION

Most analyses of tax earmarking have been concerned with the efficiency of this fiscal arrangement, which dedicates the revenue from a tax to a particular purpose, in comparison with the fiscal arrangement in which the revenue from a tax goes into a general fund. In this paper we do not claim to offer a normative judgement as to the superiority of either earmarking or general-fund financing in terms of economic efficiency. The purpose of this paper is, however, to consider, and empirically test a response to tax earmarking that is relevant to questions regarding the efficiency of earmarking.

The primary concern when considering the efficiency of tax

Table 9.3 Regression results for the determinants of LRFEDR and LPRPEDR (1933–82)

	Dependent variables			
	LRFEDR	LRFEDR	LPRFEDR	LPRFEDR
Intercept	40.02 (1.84)*	−2136.07 (−2.13)*	21.61 (2.25)**	−2684. 62 (−3.16)***
LMVM	1.34 (4.65)***	0.78 (2.12)*		
LMVMP			0.50 (10.51)***	0.41 (8.40)***
DUMMY	0.53 (3.93)***	0.54 (4.26)***	0.54 (4.01)***	0.48 (3.92)**
T	−0.02 (1.76)*	2.18 (2.15)*	−0.0104 (−2.11)*	2.75 (3.28)**
T^2		−0.0005 (−2.18)*		−0.0007 (−3.19)**
R^2	0.86	0.90	0.81	0.85

Notes: See Table 1. LMVM and LMVMP are the predicted values of motor vehicle miles

earmarking has been with the effect earmarking is likely to have on the allocation of revenues over competing expenditure alternatives. Is it is better, for example, to 'lock in' precommitted expenditures on different programmes or to maintain maximum flexibility in order to alter expenditure patterns in response to changing political influences? As important as the allocation of a given amount of revenue is to the objective of efficiency, it is only one consideration. Efficiency also requires that the correct amount of revenue, in total, be allocated.[4]

The point of this paper has been that tax earmarking can be expected to have a positive impact on the amount of money raised, and spent, by changing the incentives faced by organized interest groups. Having presented the argument upon which this expectation is based, our task has been to test the hypothesis that interest groups exert more upward pressures on tax revenues when those revenues are earmarked than when they are not. Using the example of federal fuel tax revenues, it has been demonstrated that earmarking leads to increased tax revenue in contrast with general-fund financing. The empirical results are consistent with our argument that tax earmarking shifts special-interest incentives away from lobbying over shares of a given revenue pie and towards lobbying for more revenue.

We recognize the partial, and incomplete, nature of our investigation. We have presented no model, or even discussion, that would allow a judgement to be made regarding the efficiency implications of more government spending. Therefore, even if our conclusion on the effect of tax earmarking is correct, it tells us nothing by itself about the efficiency of tax earmarking. Furthermore, by considering the effect of earmarking one tax alone we cannot be sure that the positive revenue of earmarking a particular tax is not offset by negative tax revenue effects elsewhere. Would earmarking all taxes result in an increase in aggregate tax revenue? We believe it would, based on our general argument of special-interest behaviour, but our empirical work is silent on this question.

Much work remains to be done if a definitive judgement is to be reached regarding the efficiency of tax earmarking. Any contribution this paper may have made in this regard comes from pointing to the importance of taking special-interest motivation into consideration when considering positive questions about the effect of tax earmarking.

NOTES

* This paper makes use of the empirical analysis contained in our 1990 paper. We appreciate the helpful comments of William Shugart.

1 Because the revenue effects of earmarking operate through the tax structure, we have omitted tax rates in the models presented here. It is important to note that federal gasoline tax rates changed before and after 1956. Expressed in real or percentage terms, the federal gasoline tax remained fairly constant from 1932 through the 1950s. It increased in the 1960s, and consistently declined over the remainder of the period studied. Our contention, however, is that whatever tax rates are chosen under earmarking will be revenue enhancing relative to rates chosen under general-fund financing.

2 All the data in this study are from *United States Historical Statistics, Colonial Times to 1970* (vols 1 and 2); and *US Statistical Abstract* (various issues).

3 The fitted values were obtained from the following regressions:

$$\text{LMVM} = \begin{array}{l} 0.53 + 0.90 \text{ LRGNP} \\ (0.48) \quad (5.03)^{***} \ R2 = 0.28 \end{array}$$

$$\text{LMVMP} = \begin{array}{l} -0.74 + 1.81 \text{ LPY} \\ (-3.01)^{***} \ (7.50)^{***} \ R2 = 0.47 \end{array}$$

where

LMVM   = natural logarithm of motor vehicle miles;
LMVMP = natural logarithm of motor vehicle miles per capita;

and where

LRGNP and LPY are as previously defined.

4 It should be recognized that the efficient allocation of government expenditures and the efficient level of those expenditures have to be determined simultaneously. For a discussion of the efficiency of limits on government expenditures which takes into consideration both the effect such limits can have on the allocation of expenditures and the effect the allocation can have on the level of expenditures which is efficient, see Lee (1989).

REFERENCES

Aronson, J.R. and Hilley, J.L. *Financing State and Local Governments.* Washington, D.C. : Brookings Institution, 1986.

Buchanan, J.M. 'The Economics of Earmarked Taxes'. *Journal of Political Economy* 71 (October 1963): 457–69.

Goetz, C. 'Earmarked Taxes and Majority Rule Budgetary Processes'. *American Economic Review* 58 (March 1968): 128–36.

Kimenyi, M.S., Lee, D.R., and Tollison, R.D. 'Efficient Lobbying and Earmarked Taxes'. *Public Finance Quarterly* 18 (January 1990): 104–13.

Lee, D.R. 'Special Interest Inefficiency: A Case For or Against Government Spending Limits?'. *Social Science Quarterly* 70 (September 1989): 765–71.

US Department of Commerce. *United States Historical Statistics, Colonial Times to 1970,* vols 1 and 2. Washington, D.C.

US Department of Commerce. *US Statistical Abstract, various issues.* Washington, D.C.

10 The constitutional economics of earmarking

James M. Buchanan

During the first half of this century, the conventional wisdom in normative public-finance theory was highly critical of the earmarking of tax revenues. Any restriction on the budgetary flexibility of the fiscal authority was adjudged to be undesirable, almost by definition. Such normative condemnation of earmarking was a consequence of the implicit acceptance of a political model that excluded all elements of democracy. The introduction of electoral feedbacks generates categorically different understandings of the fiscal process, which may lead to quite different evaluations of revenue earmarking. In one limiting case the taxing–spending operation can be modelled as an idealized exchange. In this analytical setting, sectoral budgeting, a form of earmarking, emerges as a necessity in any fiscal process that meets standard efficiency norms. A somewhat less restricted, but still limiting, model may incorporate pure majoritarianism. Such a model departs from that of pure fiscal exchange and allows for politically coerced transfers. In its idealized form, however, this majoritarian model does not introduce the independent existence of the 'fisc', as such. The normative implications for the desirability of earmarking institutions are far from clear.

Finally, effective electoral constraints on fiscal outcomes may again be removed from consideration, but with categorically different presumptions concerning the motivations of political agents than those which were implicitly embodied in the first model noted, that which informed the conventional wisdom early in this century. Political agents may be largely, if not wholly, exempted from direct electoral controls, but these agents may be modelled as independent utility maximizers on their own account.

The first four sections examine the four separate models of fiscal process: those of (1) the benevolent fisc, (2) fiscal exchange, (3) fiscal transfer, and (4) revenue-maximizing Leviathan. The examination and analysis is concentrated on the normative evaluation of earmarking institutions, as potential *constitutional* variables, in each of the models. The fifth section shifts analysis towards fiscal-political reality, in which there exists explanatory potential in each of the four models. Relatively robust conclusions may be reached with reference to the earmarking of tax revenues for spending on programmes that embody no complementarity with the generation of tax bases. Such earmarking is not supportable on normative grounds upon acceptance of any mix among the fiscal models. Earmarking that does relate tax-base generation to complementary publicly supplied services (for example, motor fuels tax revenues earmarked to finance roads) may be included in a normatively acceptable fiscal constitution, especially as a means of checking the potential overreaching of the transfer process and, at the same time, a means of introducing an incentive for political agents to provide desired levels of public goods and services.

1 THE BENEVOLENT FISC

Intellectual development has been so rapid since mid-century that it seems difficult in the 1990s to recapture the image or model of governmental fiscal authority that informed and dominated the thinking of the economists of the whole reform era, roughly between the 1880s and the 1960s, an era that I have extended a little and sometimes called 'the socialist century'. Perhaps a more descriptive term would be 'the Hegelian century', since this attribution would directly call attention to the philosopher whose influence on ideas was so great. The romantic mind-set was such that the model of government as potentially omniscient and benevolent went unchallenged for decades, and this despite the wholly contrasting set of attitudes towards the state that was dominant in the eighteenth and early nineteenth centuries. During the whole of the reform era, social scientists concerned themselves almost exclusively with alternative policy options that a benevolent authority might face and among which selection would be made.

The argument can be clarified if the model of government or the state within this paradigm is presented in its extreme, or idealized, form. In such presentation, the collectivity has an independent, organic existence and possesses a consciousness, a will, and an ability to choose, as A.C. Pigou (1947) explicitly suggested in his inquiry in normative public finance, a 'fiscal brain'. In its utilitarian variant, this decision-making authority organizes its taxing and spending activities so as to maximize total utility in the political community, total utility as represented by the summation of the utilities of the separate persons in the collectivity. In this idealized construction, government has no difficulty in securing the requisite knowledge concerning the utility schedules of persons, and it faces no barriers in being able to add utilities over persons. The simplistic logic of maximization dictates equalization of utility increments, negative and positive, over all margins of adjustment. Taxes are to be levied so as to ensure equi-marginal sacrifices in utility; benefits are to be allocated so as to generate equi-marginal utility gains; and, finally, marginal sacrifices in utility due to taxes are equated with marginal increments to utility due to benefits and/or transfers.

In this idealized construction there is clearly no basis for *any* constitutional limits on the authority of government, whether we restrict attention to fiscal activities or extend attention more widely. And, in one sense of course, the earmarking of tax revenues is always effectively a constitutional limit, whether or not it is explicitly discussed as such. Earmarking involves a prior dedication of revenue collections from specified taxes. And any such dedication necessarily reduces the discretionary authority of the spending agent or agency. Since this agent or agency aims to (and does) maximize total utility by equalizing utility per dollar's worth in all uses, any shift from the unique utility-maximizing allocation that may be induced by earmarking constraints must impose loss in total utility. Earmarking, as a fiscal institution, shifts the community to a position inside its utility possibility frontier.

When the model of the omniscient and benevolent state is presented in the idealized manner just outlined, its absurdities become apparent. But features of this model continue to exert normative influence even when the descriptive properties of the model are largely discarded. Governments, as they are observed to operate, may be acknowledged to lack omniscience, and, further, claims that governments act mono-lithically to further some abstractly imagined public interest may be dropped. But those persons who do assume roles as political agents, charged with making decisions on the part of the collectivity, may still be modelled to behave, even if quite imperfectly, so as to promote their own best interpretations of some generalized interest. This vision of politics and governance is a substantially watered-down model of benevolent authority, and its proponents may also acknowledge explicitly that utility, as such, is neither cardinally measurable nor interpersonally comparable in any objective or agreed-on basis.

In this more widely held conceptualization of the state and, specifically, fiscal authority, earmarking, as an effective constitutional constraint on the budgetary usage of tax revenues, may still be judged to be normatively undesirable. Despite epistemological limits, political agents charged with making decisions on outlays are seeking to promote citizens' well-being, as best that well-being can be ascertained and estimated. And any overtly imposed constraint on the ability of such agents to choose freely among spending options, in the large or in the small, must reduce the efficiency of the overall fiscal process. Earmarking, as an institution, remains categorically 'bad' in a fundamental, normative sense.

2 FISCAL EXCHANGE

In all variants of the benevolent fisc model, the decision-making authority of the collectivity is separated from the persons *for whom* choices are made, those persons who qualify for membership in the polity, and upon whom taxes are imposed and to whom governmental benefits are offered. The 'for the people' leg of the Lincoln triad receives exclusive attention; there is no room for any direct 'by the people' emendation.

The idealized model of fiscal exchange lies at the opposing end of the imagined analytical spectrum from the benevolent fisc. In the exchange model, considered in its pure form, the 'by the people' leg of the triad takes on a central role, and both the 'for' and the 'of the people' criteria are necessarily satisfied. The state, or government, exists only as a structure or process through which citizens (taxpayers–beneficiaries) make decisions collectively (publicly) rather than separately (privately), with the idealized division between individualized and collectivized choices being determined by choices also made by citizens themselves.

In this model, individuals effectively 'purchase' the goods and services that are supplied jointly to all members of the community by the payment of 'tax-prices' that are analogous to the prices paid for ordinary goods that are supplied separately to purchasers in markets. As distinct from market prices, tax-prices are differentiated among separate persons, but the structure of tax-prices is settled in a process of bargaining and ultimate contractual agreement, which also includes determination of the level or quantity of the collective goods or service to be purchased. In the idealized solution (sometimes called the Lindahl [1919] equilibrium), the marginal tax-price confronting each person equals the marginal evaluation of that person for the good or service at the quantity purchased, and, of course, the summed marginal evaluations over all persons equals the marginal cost of supplying the good or service (sometimes called the Samuelson [1954] conditions). In this idealized model of fiscal exchange, note that government, as such, does not exist.

Note that taxes, as such, are not *imposed* on citizens. Tax-prices emerge as voluntarily agreed-on elements in the many-person exchange contract. The operative rule for making collective decisions is that of unanimity or general consensus. As Knut Wicksell (1896) recognized, only the existence of such a rule would guarantee that collective fiscal action precludes the coercion of some members of the political community. In a seminal article, R.A. Musgrave (1938) labelled this model the 'voluntary exchange theory of public finance'.

The conditions outlined above must be met separately for each good or service that is 'purchased' jointly by the members of a collectivity. If there is more than one good or service, a conceptually separate evaluation-agreement process must take place for each good. Any arbitrary bundling of several goods and services that would then require collective purchase of 'baskets' rather than item-by-item adjustment would clearly reduce the efficiency of the whole fiscal operation.

The analogy with the market purchase of private goods is straightforward. The individual buyer-consumer makes purchase decisions separately for each good. Confronted with a market price, the individual selects an optimally preferred quantity. Any single good may, of course, be a complement or substitute for other goods, but such interdependencies are effectively incorporated in the independent adjustments made as each good is purchased. Any introduction of a tie-in sale of two or more goods necessarily reduces buyers' satisfaction. The endowment of the purchaser, summarized in a budget constraint, provides the revenue source for potential outlay on all goods in the market. But rational purchasing choice dictates that this common source be separately drawn on for the purchases of each good.

In fiscal exchange, the analogy to efficient decision processes in private goods markets is *earmarking*, at least of a sort. To allow for the separate consideration of each spending item, the collective contracting–bargaining process must involve examination and comparison of revenue requirements and preferred outlays simultaneously, but along each single dimension. If this idealized norm is translated into institutional reality, even to some first approximation, we should observe sectoral rather than general-fund budgeting. While the tax or revenue source for specified items of outlay would not be earmarked in advance of fiscal decision, there would exist a direct relationship between the structure of tax-prices incorporated in any proposed outlay and citizen evaluations of those outlays. In this fiscal exchange model, there is no flexibility allowed to any decision taker, whether this be the whole citizenry or some agent, to use revenues for other than spending on the good or service under consideration in isolation.

As we shift attention away from the idealized normative construction and move more towards feasible political–institutional arrangements, we may retain a generalized interpretation of the fiscal process as one involving imperfect fiscal exchange. And, in this framework, the relevance and importance of structural features akin to earmarking and sectoral budgeting become more apparent, even than in the idealized construction. Each proposed spending programme must be matched up against its projected tax costs in order for any semblance of a rational fiscal calculus to be present. So long as the overall fiscal process is conceived in the exchange paradigm there is no normative argument to be advanced for a unified budget, from which several programmes of public outlay are to be financed and into which revenues flow from separate tax sources.

As the discussion suggests, sectoral budgeting, which allows separate proposals for spending to be considered separately and in relation to alternative tax-financing sources, emerges in any institutional approximation of a fiscal exchange process. Note, however, that the emergence of an institutional similarity to earmarking does not imply that, in the fiscal exchange model, constitutionally directed dedication of revenues is efficiency enhancing. Any prior constraint on the potential sources for financing a spending programme might inhibit the reaching of agreement, as Wicksell emphasized. Separate tax financing for each and every programme is a necessary feature of fiscal exchange, but a constitutional linkage between specific taxes and designated spending programmes may not be desirable.

3   FISCAL TRANSFER

As noted, an operative decision rule of unanimity is a necessary element in the idealized model of fiscal exchange. Only the presence of such a rule, or its equivalent, can ensure that those members of the community who pay for the jointly demanded and collectively supplied goods are those who actually secure the benefits provided by these goods. Only in this setting can the fiscal process be conceptually modelled as voluntary exchange. And, as a corollary, only in the matching of the two sides of the fiscal account can there be any meaningful guarantee that the exchange increases value (Wicksell 1896; Buchanan 1976).

If the effective unanimity rule is dropped, as it must be in any approach to political reality, the model of the fiscal process dramatically changes, even if we retain the electoral democratic feature and continue to presume that an independently motivated 'fisc' does not exist at all. Consider, then, a model in which taxing and outlay decisions are made strictly by the operation of a majority voting rule, either in a direct democracy or in a representative democracy setting. In this political framework, a dominant majority coalition will tend to form, and members of this coalition will aim to use the fiscal process to impose coerced tax charges on non-members of the opposing minority, with the proceeds of these taxes used to finance benefits enjoyed by members of the majority. The limiting case of this model becomes the pure fiscal transfer, in which members of the minority, and only these persons, pay taxes that finance cash transfers to members of the majority coalition, and to no one else, in the polity. It is evident that any semblance of an exchange disappears in this transfer operation, and that any modelling of fiscal institutions in the exchange paradigm would generate misleading results.

The proclivity of majoritarian political competition to degenerate towards the pure transfer process should be noted. Members of successful political majorities may, initially, limit their fiscal demands to the financing of collective-consumption goods and services while imposing all costs of these goods and services on members of the unsuccessful minority. It will become clear, however, that the benefits from direct transfers will dominate those expected from collective-consumption goods and services. The transfer elements in the majoritarian political game will emerge to swamp the public-goods elements (Flowers and Danzon 1984).

Constitutional limits on the direction and magnitude of pure fiscal transfers would seem clearly to be desirable in majoritarian settings, limits that may take the form of requiring *generality* in both taxing and spending. Taxes that discriminate among separately classified members of the polity would be constitutionally prohibited, along with spending programmes that offer benefits or direct transfers only to designated groups of the citizenry. Note that we have observed such constitutional limits on the taxing side, but not on the spending side of the budget in the United States (Tuerck 1967). These inclusive constitutional limits are not, however, my primary concern here. I want to concentrate attention on the possible efficiency of revenue earmarking in the pure fiscal-transfer model.

Assume that there are no general-taxation–general-benefit constitutional constraints in existence. Would a constitutional restriction on revenue earmarking reduce or increase the potential for fiscal exploitation? In this setting, and absent constitutional attention, the dominant majority would use any available means of imposing taxes on members of the minority while absolving themselves from tax burdens. Revenue earmarking or dedication might well be descriptive of the workings of the transfer process. The successful imposition of taxes on specifically classified groups in the population might be accompanied by dedication of revenues from these taxes to programmes that concentrate benefits on members of the majority. Both sides of the account may be institutionally manipulated to ensure some approximation to the ultimately desired pure transfer. When such prospects are viewed constitutionally, as if behind some veil of ignorance or uncertainty as to membership in majority or minority coalitions, constitutional specification as to the directed use of tax sources might offer one means of constraining fiscal exploitation. If majority coalitions are prohibited, constitutionally, from the imposition of taxes on designated sources other than for the purpose of raising revenues for outlays on publicly provided goods and services that are either general in nature or are *complementary* to the activities that generate the source of the tax, the ever-present temptation to tax for transfer spending is inhibited.

Examples come readily to mind. If a majority coalition is not allowed access to, say, a motor fuels (gasoline) tax except for spending on roads, the usage of the revenues to finance cash transfers is simply out of bounds. In this setting, the pure tax-transfer process can be boxed in, so to speak, and limited to the exploitation of those general tax sources that ensure the presence of some tax costs on majority members.

4 CONSTRAINED LEVIATHAN

In both the fiscal exchange and the pure fiscal transfer models discussed in Sections 2 and 3, there is no independently existing 'fisc' or fiscal authority that has an interest in and exerts an influence on fiscal outcomes. Both of these models, in sharp contrast to that model of the benevolent fisc discussed in Section 1, embody the workings of idealized democracy, even if in dramatically differing forms. The model of fiscal exchange is, of course, one of idealized cooperation, whereas the model of fiscal transfer is one of idealized majoritarian conflict. The first model is positive sum, for all players; the second is negative, zero, or positive sum in the aggregate, but is necessarily negative sum for some players.

Any move towards recognition of fiscal-political reality will surely involve some departure from these idealized constructions. In its fiscal as well as in its other activities, government operates only through choices made by political agents, who are able, within limits, to pursue objectives that may not correspond directly to those of citizens, either those in the all-inclusive coalition or in the limited coalition of a political majority. In the benevolent fisc model treated in Section 1 these objectives were postulated to be defined by the agents' perceptions of some 'general' or 'public' interest. By contrast, in this section I propose to examine a model in which agents are postulated to act in furtherance of their own separately defined interests – that is, to behave as ordinary utility maximizers.

It is useful, initially, to assume that the political agents acting as the fiscal authority are not subject to electoral constraints at all. They are simply empowered to act on behalf of the collectivity in fiscal matters, bound only by whatever constitutional constraints may exist. It is clear that, under these conditions, the agents possessing such authority will seek to *maximize* revenue collections from any and all tax sources they are authorized to exploit and, at the same time, will seek to *minimize* outlays devoted to the supply of goods and services and transfers to others than members of their own preferred set of recipients, again within the constitutionally allowable limits (Brennan and Buchanan 1980).

In dramatic contrast to the benevolent fisc model of Section 1, where *any* constitutional limits are undesirable, the Leviathan model suggests that constitutional constraints are necessary if any semblance of an exchange relationship between citizens as taxpayers and as beneficiaries is to be preserved. Such constraints must be directed towards ensuring against overextension of the taxing authority and towards ensuring that tax revenues, once collected, are expended in providing benefits to citizens over and beyond those in the agents' preferred sets. The first objective can be secured, in some degree, by careful constitutional limits on tax bases or tax sources. The second objective can be achieved, in part, by constitutionally earmarking revenues for specific spending programmes that are designed to exploit the incentive structure offered in the complementarity between the generation of the tax base and the utilization of publicly provided goods and services.

The example introduced earlier remains applicable here. If the fiscal authority is constitutionally permitted to impose a motor fuels tax only if the revenues are dedicated to spending on roads, there is an incentive for the authority, even if it seeks to maximize revenues, to provide reasonably efficient levels of road services. Suppose, however, that the fiscal authority is empowered to levy a motor fuels tax without the required dedicated spending on complementary road services. For instance, the revenues from this tax might be dedicated to spending on toxic-waste clean-up. In this case, Leviathan will, of course, maximize expected revenue collections as before, but the share of these revenues expended on the designated outlay will be minimized, since there is no economic relationship between such spending and the revenue generation. The earmarking of revenues will not constrain the excesses of Leviathan unless the potential complementarity between tax sources and spending programmes is constitutionally exploited.

5 TOWARDS FISCAL REALITY

As we observe the fiscal process to operate in modern political democracy (the United States *c.* 1990) there are, of course, elements of each of the four models at work. To an extent, political agents who are responsible for making choices among taxing and spending options do, indeed, try to further the 'public interest', as best they can define and interpret this vaguest of objectives. But these agents are always sensitive both to actual and potential pressures from electoral constituencies, who seek to ensure that the taxes paid to government are exchanged for governmental goods and services that are broadly worth their costs. At the same time, much effort is devoted to attempts to secure differentially advantageous fiscal treatment, either via exemptions from taxes or via special benefits and/or transfers. And, finally, the natural proclivities of political agents are surely directed towards maximizing the size of the fiscal sector, which implies revenue collection beyond either plausible 'public interest' or potentially expressed exchange limits.

Given the mix of descriptive models that seems to characterize the fiscal activity that is observed, what normative conclusions may be drawn with reference to the institutions of earmarking revenues for specific programmes of outlay? Note that the possible constitution-alization of earmarking imposes directionally different effects in the first two models and in the last two models. Under either a benevolent fisc or a fiscal exchange model, earmarking, when imposed as a prior constitutional constraint, restricts budgetary flexibility, and, because it does so, tends to be efficiency reducing. This result is evident in the benevolent fisc model, but it is less obvious in the fiscal exchange model due to the emergence of something like sectoral budgeting in the idealized agreement process. Only in the third and fourth model of fiscal process, that is only under the fiscal transfer model and the Leviathan model, does the constitutionalization of earmarking offer efficiency-enhancing potentiality. It does so, in both cases, because revenue dedication may offer one among several instruments designed to keep fiscal exactions within the limits that would be constitutionally preferred.

To the extent that either or both of the last two models is considered descriptive of fiscal reality, revenue earmarking may be one component of an effectively operating fiscal constitution, provided that the institution is used to exploit the complementarity between the generation of tax bases and the utilization of publicly provided services. On the other hand and by contrast, we can reach more robust conclusions concerning the possible earmarking of tax revenues for outlay programmes that are not complementary with the generation of tax bases. Such non-complementary dedication of tax revenues does not, and cannot, serve efficiency-enhancing purposes, and should be constitutionally prohibited, in any and all models of fiscal process.

REFERENCES

Brennan, G., and Buchanan, J. *The Power to Tax*. Cambridge: Cambridge University Press, 1980.
Buchanan, James M. 'Taxation in Fiscal Exchange'. *Journal of Public Economics* 6 (Fall 1976): 17–29. Reprinted in J. M. Buchanan. *Freedom in Constitutional Contract*. College Station: Texas A & M Press, 1977.
Flowers, M. and Danzon, P. 'Separation of Redistributive and Allocative Functions of Government'. *Journal of Public Economics* 24 (August 1984): 373–80.
Lindahl, E. *Die Gerechtigkeit der Besteuerung*. Lund: Gleerupska, 1919.
Musgrave, R.A. 'The Voluntary Exchange Theory of Public Economy'. *Quarterly Journal of Economics* 53 (February 1938): 213–37.
Pigou, A.C. *A Study in Public Finance*, 3rd ed. London: Macmillan, 1947.
Samuelson, P. 'The Pure Theory of Public Expenditure'. *Review of Economics and Statistics* 36 (November 1954): 387–9.
Tuerck, D. 'Constitutional Asymmetry', *Papers on Non-Market Decision-Making* 2 (1967): 27–44.
Wicksell, K. *Finanztheorietische Untersuchungen*. Jena: Gustav Fischer, 1896.

11 Excises, earmarked taxes, and government user charges in a rent-seeking model

*Fred S. McChesney**

It is conventionally accepted that various forms of government intervention (i.e., intervention by government employees) into private markets are acceptable, even desirable. The most prominent examples of such 'legitimate' government intervention involve control of externalities and government production of certain goods and services. For both, the rationale for government intervention is often lower costs, particularly transaction costs. Excise taxes are, in theory, often a cheaper alternative to individual contracts or legal actions to control externalities; government production in some markets (roads, for example) can lower the transaction costs associated with hold-outs, free riding and revelation of demand. Maximizing social welfare in either case requires that government impose prices, either in the form of taxes or as user charges. Taxes and charges are often earmarked for particular purposes.

The economic case for various forms of excises and government user charges (whether or not earmarked) seems ironclad, as will be discussed in Section 1. However, the standard discussion of these charges makes several assumptions of questionable validity. Most fundamentally, the orthodox model of user charges depends on government actors behaving as would non-government producers in well-functioning private markets. This assumption, it is now agreed, is generally inappropriate for predicting government behaviour.

Once politicians and bureaucrats are treated, like everyone else, as maximizers of their own welfare, certain other assumptions in the orthodox model of user charges are seen to be unwarranted as well. As will be discussed in Section 2, much real-world government pricing behaviour is manifestly inconsistent with the textbook discussion of excises and other user charges. Prices are not set according to cost, as in private markets, but in accordance with predictable political processes.

It is seen that when actual government pricing, rather than the textbook model, is taken into account, there can be no necessary inference that a system of government production with user charges increases societal welfare.

Two other sources of welfare loss from user charges are also investigated in Section 2. First, the very power to levy excises and other user charges creates an incentive for politicians to threaten to impose them, but to forbear (for a price) from actually so doing. This sort of political extortion has several predictable consequences for overall economic performance. Second, one observes a different extortion problem arising with earmarked taxes. Earmarked taxes typically create a fund for subsequent, not current, expenditures. Once created, however, the fund becomes a hostage of politicians, who have the power to divert the fund to other purposes or to force intended beneficiaries to pay a second time for release of the escrowed funds. Several examples of both types of political opportunism are observed.

1   THEORY AND PRACTICE OF USER CHARGES AND EXCISES

The standard model

The welfare economics of user charges is well understood and needs no general explanation here (Atkinson and Stiglitz 1980: 457–518; Due and Friedlander 1973: 90–115). Certain goods (for example, highways, airports) supposedly can be produced more cheaply by government than by private suppliers. Most often, the advantage claimed for government production is government's ability to use its eminent domain power to amass large holdings of land at lower transaction costs, thus avoiding problems of demand revelation, holding out, and free riding. Highway construction, for example, requires assembly of large plots of land, and the transaction costs of inducing hundreds or thousands of sellers to convey their land may exceed the potential profit of the project. User charges substitute for private prices in rationing the use of governmentally produced goods and services for which exclusion is possible. Like prices in private markets, governmental prices optimally would be set according to marginal cost.[1] Often, user charges are earmarked for special funds that are held for periodic replacement of capital assets that depreciate over time (Buchanan 1963). For example, the highway trust fund (financed by gasoline taxes) disburses funds for road construction. The Airport and Airway Trust Fund, financed by the tax on air flight tickets, was created to finance airport and related construction.

The orthodox theory of excise taxation is similar. In principle, excise taxes are supposed to force private producers to internalize costs that would otherwise be external, and so not taken into account.[2] But, fundamentally, they are just a form of user charge. A pollution tax forces private producers to pay for the air or water they use, although the compensation is paid to the government rather than to the owner of the resources used. Government's task in the orthodox model is exactly the same as if it owned the air or water itself: to impose the correct user's fee. Excise taxes are justified by the same rationale offered for direct government production of goods and services: the transaction costs of excises taxes are supposedly cheaper than individual contracts or lawsuits by private owners seeking compensation for the use of their resources. Like user fees, excise taxes are to be set according to marginal (external) cost. One therefore can speak generally, therefore, of 'user fees' as referring both to excises and charges for governmentally produced goods and services.

While the general model of user fees (charges or excises) is well understood, two points merit emphasis. First, the welfare case for such fees depends on government setting the optimal price. This is illustrated by Figure 11.1. Suppose that private producers' marginal cost of constructing some good like highways is prohibitive: at MC_1, no highways are profitable, since demand D, at every point is less than the cost of construction. No highways will be built privately. If government can produce more cheaply, say at MC_G, and charges P for access to the roads, societal welfare increases by the area of consumer surplus, ABP.

However, if government underprices the public good, it is not

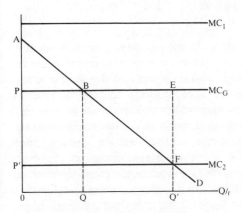

Figure 11.1 User charges and social welfare

necessarily true that public provision increases social welfare. Suppose that, although true resource costs of government production are MC_G, the good is actually priced at P'. Users will purchase Q' of the item, paying only $OP'FQ'$ for resources that actually are worth $OPEQ'$. The welfare loss of BEF from underpricing is greater than the gain, ABP, available when government prices correctly. It would be better not to have the good produced at all, despite consumer willingness to pay a price that would cover the true costs of government producing it.

In other words, even if government production costs are lower, one cannot know whether government provision of goods and services not produced by private markets is desirable, without knowing whether the prices charged are allocatively correct. In fact, many government user fees are apparently sub-optimal. Goods and services for which government could charge fees are provided 'free' and funded instead out of general revenues. This is notably true of local government services, like libraries and city parks.[3] Exclusion is possible, yet no price is charged at all. Entry to many national parks, likewise, is free, although admission fees could easily be charged. Even when fees are charged they often are conspicuously sub-optimal.

> Granted, goods produced from the forests and Yellowstone National Park already entail user fees, ranging from livestock grazing rights to campground and park entrance charges. But these fees are very low compared to similar activities in the private domain. People are willing to spend $15.00 to $27.50 for a daily ski lift ticket, yet the entrance fee to Yellowstone is now $10.00 for one vehicle for a seven-day stay at the park, raised in 1988 from $5.00. The fee charged for livestock grazing on federal land was recently raised from $1.35 to $1.54 for an animal unit month, still only about one-third of that charged on comparable private land (Leal 1990: 41).

Other examples of sub-optimal pricing abound. The existence of limited-access toll roads in several states (as well as similar highways in other countries like France and Italy) indicates that a system of direct highway user fees is workable. Yet access to federal highways does not require payment of a fee. Meat and poultry producers are not charged for federal grading and inspection, although a fee could easily be levied.

There are at least three important sorts of welfare loss associated with such undercharging. The first, as noted above, is the over-consumption of valuable resources. As Leal notes of national parks, 'underpricing goods on our public lands encourages overconsumption of resources. Hunting pressure on public lands during the deer and elk seasons grows steadily, as more hunters pursue dwindling numbers of animals' (Leal 1990: 41). The second welfare loss stems from the queuing and related deadweight losses entailed in getting access to the underpriced goods and services. 'Arbitrarily low user fees force people to compete for goods through means other than prices. In public campgrounds, this means waiting in long lines or making reservations months in advance' (Leal 1990: 41). And, third, making up revenue shortfalls from general revenues necessarily produces welfare losses in the excess burdens from the additional taxes required.

The standard model of user charges fails to account for the repeated instances of under-pricing observed. The few accounts that recognize incorrect prices charged by government typically ascribe the problem to human error due to a lack of information about the 'true' price as it would be registered in private markets.[4] This seems an unlikely explanation, however: in many markets government production competes directly with privately produced goods and services, and continues to underprice them. In education, for example, government underprices public schools and funds the revenue shortfalls out of general property taxes (West 1967). Likewise, government takeover of services provided privately, like fire protection and municipal transportation, results in prices being charged that are insufficient to cover costs, with deficits being funded out of general revenues (Ahlbrandt 1973; McChesney 1986; Pashigan 1976).

User fees and political gains

The inability of the orthodox model of user fees to explain these phenomena lies in its treatment of political incentives. In the private-market paradigm, it is producers' desire to maximize their profits or utility that drives them to produce the appropriate quantity and sell it at the optimal price. Individual gain – Adam Smith's invisible hand – guides producers' personal rewards into alignment with social welfare. Producers likewise bear the costs of their incorrect price and output decisions.

But once government enterprise replaces private ownership, producers who price efficiently (i.e., so as to maximize collective welfare) are no longer rewarded; those who operate inefficiently do not bear the costs of so doing. The orthodox model of user fees fails to take this distinction into account. Standard analyses maintain that, in intervening in or replacing private markets, government 'seeks to ensure that firms produce at socially desirable levels', as opposed to private firms, 'which seek to produce at their profit-maximizing levels' (Due and Friedlander 1976: 97). But there is little incentive for public producers to strive for efficiency or greater social welfare. The politician or bureaucrat who sells Q units at price P cannot keep the profits or social gains he creates; nor does he pay the losses caused by producing too many units, Q', at too low a price, P'. With no personal incentives to be efficient, politicians and bureaucrats should not be expected to produce and price optimally.[5]

It is inconsistent, in other words, to treat economic actors as public-spirited while in government but as self-interested in private firms. A more consistent and more persuasive model would view economic actors in both situations as motivated by their own welfare. And in fact, the self-interest of government actors helps to explain the frequent under-pricing of governmentally-produced goods and services noted above. One item of benefit to politicians is votes. Voters will favour those politicians who deliver more benefits to them. Again referring to Figure 1, consider two candidates with opposing stands on the operation of a public enterprise. Candidate A, the incumbent, has favoured a policy of pricing at P, thus selling Q of the item produced and leaving net consumer benefits of ABP. Candidate B instead promises to lower prices to P', increasing output to Q'. The benefits to consumers of the product rise to AFP'. Thus, intensely interested users of the product will vote for Candidate B. Taxpayers as a whole, including non-users, must make up the revenue shortfall PEFP', so the politician must design the system so that there will be more consumer-users who vote for the politician than there are general taxpayers who vote against him. This means that many government goods and services will be systematically underpriced. As Peltzman explains,

> [T]he government enterprise manager must select a set of prices such that the number of net gainers exceeds the number of net losers. One obvious conclusion that follows . . . is that there will be a downward bias in government enterprise prices. Higher than profit maximizing prices result in losses to voters both as consumers and taxpayers.
>
> (Peltzman 1971: 113)

Empirically, Peltzman finds that, in fact, government prices are systematically too low. Electricity and alcoholic beverages (in states where liquor prices are government-controlled) are systematically less than prices charged by private enterprises.[6]

The role of politics in underpricing government services can also be seen in the different prices charged voters in different jurisdictions. As Peltzman states,

> [G]overnment enterprises may sell to non-voters. If these enterprises benefit voters to secure political support, there is no reason to expect

them to benefit non-voters. Therefore, prices should generally be higher to non-voters than to voters.

(Peltzman 1971: 114).

This prediction, too, is borne out empirically. Maloney, McCormick, and Tollison (1984) have examined public-utility prices for electricity and find that prices are higher to customers outside the political jurisdictions in which the utilities are located.

Underpricing of governmentally produced goods and services is useful not just to politicians but also to bureaucrats responsible for administering or selling government production. Low prices mean 'too much' of the product, Q' rather than Q, will be produced and sold, necessitating greater bureaucratic budgets and more personnel. Controlling queuing and allocating output in non-price ways also require greater manpower and therefore larger budgets. So does the need for new taxes in other markets to make up revenue shortfalls when user fees for a particular good or service are too low. Thus, one observes frequently that civil servants are among the most ardent supporters of government, rather than private, production.[7]

In short, there are two necessary conditions for government enterprise financed by user charges to be optimal. First, government must be a lower-cost producer than a private enterprise would be. Second, user charges must be set optimally. But there is good reason *a priori* to expect that the second necessary condition will not be fulfilled. Politicians face predictable incentives to underprice the goods and services produced by government; examples of sub-optimal user charges are ubiquitous. The result is overconsumption of valuable physical resources, waste of valuable consumer time, and deadweight excess-burden losses from the additional taxes needed to compensate for underpricing. Even assuming that government is in some cases a lower-cost producer, the inefficiency of its user charge policies negates any necessary inference that, overall, society is better off when government produces and prices by user fees.

2 POTENTIAL FOR POLITICAL EXTORTION

The likelihood that fees will be set at sub-optimal levels means that government enterprise may have costs (BEF in Figure 11.1) exceeding benefits. But underpricing is not the only predictable source of welfare loss stemming from government user charges. Once a sub-optimal price like P' has been set, two other avenues of political gain for politicians arise. Both of these involve extortion of some of the consumer gains that sub-optimal prices initially present. The amounts extorted are not mere transfers but entail additional deadweight losses.

Extortion of current gains

In Figure 11.1, underpricing gave consumers of the particular good or service a net gain, measured by PBFP'. The discussion in the prior section treated this area as a simple transfer to users from taxpayers generally. Once the sub-optimal user charge is in place, however, politicians can threaten to reduce benefit area PBFP' by increasing user charges. Rather than suffer loss of benefits, beneficiaries will pay a portion of them over to politicians *not* to impose the higher (optimal) user charges. A portion of the consumer gains is thereby lost, with real resources being expended in the process.

Consider again private use of national forest and national park resources. Invariably, attempts to price these resources more correctly meet with powerful political resistance from users.[8]

> Until modest fee hikes in 1986 and 1987, the weekly fee per vehicle for Yellowstone Park had been stuck at $2.00 since 1916. When the intention to raise fees in 1986 was announced, there was protest from local merchants and several local recreation groups.
>
> (Leal 1990: 42)

Similarly, the American Meat Institute has been active in helping defeat proposals for a user charge to cover the cost of government meat and poultry inspections.[9]

Protests against raising user fees are not registered just by letter. Access to politicians is aided by making contributions to them. If politicians threaten to raise prices for timber lands or ski areas from P' to P, reflecting government's true costs MC$_G$, private beneficiaries would pay up to PBFP' rather than have user fees increased. In effect, another incentive exists for politicians to keep user fees too low: the ability to profit later by threatening to raise them. Politicians who price optimally at P gain nothing thereby; but politicians who price sub-optimally then have something of value – continuation of artificially cheap government goods and services – for which users will pay. The lower the user fee set, the greater the personal benefits available to politicians to keep fees low.

It is important to note that the payments to keep user fees low benefit politicians *personally*. There are many legal ways – contributions to political action committees, payments for speeches, and various in-kind benefits – for private beneficiaries to compensate politicians who forbear from increasing government charges and user fees. Speech honoraria are personal income to the politician; contributions to a political action committee can easily be turned to personal use.[10] Until very recently, Congressional legislators could keep unspent campaign contributions for personal use after leaving Congress. Although the law has been changed to preclude these political 'individual retirement accounts', Congress exempted all members in office as of January 1980 from the change.

This process of threatening increased fees in order to extort contributions applies to taxation as well as to user charges. Threatening to raise excise taxes is a common way for legislators to extort campaign contributions and speech honoraria (McChesney 1987: 115-17). Threatening to raise income taxes also has proven to generate considerable personal gains for politicians (Doernberg and McChesney 1987). These threats go by different names: 'milker bills' are legislative threats to milk political contributions; 'juice bills' similarly squeeze private interests for contributions; 'fetcher bills' are proposed because politicians find they bring in donations.[11] By any name, the extortion strategy is the same.

This aspect of the taxation process has puzzled analysts who work with a public-interest model of excise taxes. Excise taxes have seemed 'too low', given the supposed externalities invoked to justify them. The common justification for 'sin' taxes on goods like alcohol and tobacco, for example, is the claim that consumption of such goods imposes costs on others. At the same time, it is said that when government imposes excises to reflect externalities from consumption of such goods, the tax rates are systematically too low (Pogue and Sgontz 1989). This should not be surprising, however, given the advantages to politicians of selling excise-tax relief in the form of sub-optimal excises.

It is impossible, in effect, to purchase durable government benefits. This point has been brought home by what Shughart (1987) calls the 'annual Washington rite' of income-tax changes.[13] Different groups' taxes are constantly 'up for grabs'. Particularly noteworthy in recent years has been the Congressional practice of legislating tax relief to take place in subsequent years but later threatening not to allow it to go into effect without further political contributions.[14]

But the same problem must bedevil any excise tax or any government user charge. Threatening change is profitable for politicians; it offers the possibility of inducing payments *not* to implement the threatened action. These payments do not represent simple transfers from citizen-taxpayers to politicians. Buying lower taxes and user fees requires labour inputs (lobbyists, lawyers), the opportunity costs of whose time are relatively high. Specific investments that are vulnerable to subsequent extortion will not be made in the first place (McChesney 1987: 108-9). These opportunity costs must be added to the other costs of user fees discussed in the prior section.

Extortion of future funds

One final cost of a user fee system is noteworthy. In the orthodox model of user fees, the charges actually paid are treated as mere transfers. In Figure 11.1, for example, the sum OP'FQ' is just the amount paid into the treasury for use of the good or service produced by government. As a transfer payment, this sum traditionally has been viewed as raising no important allocative issues. As Lee (1985) has noted, however, revenues paid over to government represent potential rewards from politicians to well-organized interest groups, who will spend real resources to have the revenues paid out to them.

> The claimants against revenues raised by market prices are generally well-specified, as is the extent of their claims. This is not true with revenue raised by government through political prices. Additional monies raised by government generally go into the common pool of general revenue. The allocation of these revenues among rival interests is determined through competition for political influence, a competition which requires the use of real resources. To a large extent this represents pure waste, since what is being motivated is zero-sum, rather than positive-sum, competition
>
> (Lee 1985: 732)

The exact fraction of the sum OP'FQ' that will be dissipated by rent seeking is difficult to specify *ex ante*. But, as Lee concludes, '[T]he setting within which the distribution of political benefits are determined will typically motivate a significant amount of resource dissipation, rather than resource transfer, and will therefore be waste.'

It may be argued that the way to avoid the problem is to earmark the revenues. Earmarking of revenues for some specific future use, like road or airport construction, would keep user charges out of the common pool (i.e., the general treasury). Therefore, earmarked taxes and user charges seemingly would prevent competing rent seekers from obtaining access to the earmarked funds, and so avoid the wasteful dissipation that typifies competition for general revenues.

But the apparent advantage of earmarking is in fact illusory, for two reasons. First, as discussed above concerning taxation generally, it is simply impossible to achieve political durability for any system of government revenues. Earmarking revenues for some future use gives the supposed beneficiaries no enforceable property rights in those funds. They are subject to subsequent political expropriation every day that the legislature is in session. Consider the Social Security system, for example. It is funded by an earmarked tax imposed on employers and employees, ultimately for return as retirement benefits to employees. But, throughout its history, the fund created by the earmarked taxes has been imperilled by attempts to shift part of the revenues to other uses. This is particularly a problem when, as at present, the fund has a current surplus being held against later payment obligations. In the early 1970s, Congress considered using Social Security operating surpluses to create a new fund providing students with loans for college. State-worker pension funds have had similar problems, fighting off state politicians who want investment in local public works.[15]

Similar problems beset other earmarked funds. Chairman Dan Rostenkowski of the House Ways and Means Committee has recently proposed the diversion of revenues from the gasoline tax, under current law earmarked for road projects, to various other programmes, especially education.[16] Until Congress banned such fees in 1970, municipalities that owned airports levied taxes on airline tickets that were earmarked for airport construction and maintenance, but then diverted the funds to other city projects like sewers (Wessel and McGinley 1990).

The point is simple, but fundamental. Politicians cannot even bind themselves, much less their successors, to respect the commitments that are made for earmarked funds. What is earmarked for one use today can always be diverted to competing uses tomorrow. Realizing this, of course, competing rent seekers will invest resources to facilitate such diversions.

Even were rent seeking not an issue, earmarking would raise a second problem. Once in the treasury as earmarked for future use, the funds may simply not be spent without further wasteful lobbying activities. Consider the federal 'trust fund', created with earmarked taxes, to finance the construction of airports and related projects. As the demand for these projects has risen, Congress has simply refused to keep its promise to release the money to finance them. 'The trust fund has an uncommitted balance of $7 billion, infuriating airlines, passenger associations and others who want the money spent on aviation projects' (Wessel and McGinley 1990). The supposed beneficiaries of the fund thus have organized several groups to lobby Congress for use of the money as it was intended. As one lobbying group has written,

Every time you or I fly, we pay an 8% surcharge or 'ticket tax' to the federal Airport and Airway Trust Fund. By law, Congress has pledged to spend these funds to improve our air travel system. But Congress has failed to keep its promise and more than six billion dollars in unspent transportation taxes sit idle, while safety and capacity projects go unfunded. . . . The simple fact of the matter is we pay this ticket tax and we elect our Senators. That gives us the right to demand our tax dollars be used for the purpose for which the tax was created – to improve our air transportation system.[17]

In other words, earmarking cannot shield beneficiaries from Congressional 'breach of contract'. Earmarking, if durable, may segregate funds from rent seeking by others. But the supposed beneficiaries of the fund predictably will have to undertake the same kinds of lobbying and other wasteful tasks to hold Congress to its promise. In effect, beneficiaries are made to pay twice for their future benefits. The allocative losses represented by having to repurchase one's own benefits are no different from those of rent seeking by others.

Finally, even when politicians are willing to let earmarked funds be spent for the promised purpose, there is considerable rent seeking among potential recipients for the funds. Earmarking rarely includes specification in advance as to who will get the money or where it will be spent. Thus, potential beneficiaries invest resources to increase their chances of getting the earmarked money. Part of the difficulty for new airport construction, for example, is competition among politicians to have new projects assigned to their jurisdictions.

3 CONCLUSION

The notion of lower-cost government production financed by user charges, or of lower-cost government imposition of excises to correct externalities, seems unobjectionable. But lower-cost government intervention is only a necessary, not a sufficient, condition for efficiency. Government must also set prices correctly once it intervenes.

In the real world of government user charges, this second requirement is systematically violated. User fees are frequently lower than they should be. As explained here, underpricing is quite rational politically. Politicians and bureaucrats gain little, if anything, from setting allocatively correct prices. But they gain votes and monetary contributions from setting user charges inefficiently low. The result is overconsumption: scarce physical resources and user time are both wasted when government goods and services are underpriced. Excess burdens from the additional taxes needed to cover revenue shortfalls increase the deadweight losses.

Further welfare losses arise when user fees are set too low. Politicians can and do subsequently threaten to raise user fees, resulting in lobbying and related rent-seeking costs to avoid imposition of the higher charges. One seeming solution to this problem is earmarking of taxes. Earmarking restricts future uses of tax or user revenues, and so would apparently limit the amount of rent seeking for those revenues.

But earmarking entails its own problems. In particular, future beneficiaries of earmarked taxes have no property right to them. Congress can always tax today for earmarked purposes but subsequently refuse to release the revenues unless new lobbying expenses are incurred and payments made. Several examples of this sort of political opportunism have been observed recently.

In the end, then, the economics of user fees is much more complex than has been realized heretofore. The benefits of government production are straightforward and derive from a single source – lower government costs. But the costs of government production are considerably more subtle, deriving from several different sources. When the costs of overconsumption, queuing, excess burdens, extortion, and double-payment for earmarked funds are all taken into account, there is no reason for the generally sanguine attitude that economists take towards government production with financing via user charges.

NOTES

* Professor of Economics and Robert T. Thompson Professor of Law and Business, Emory University. Helpful comments on an earlier draft were received from Howard Abrams, Peter Aranson, Jennifer Arlen, Louis de Alessi, Richard Doernberg, Paul Rubin, and Richard Wagner.

1 For simplicity, constant marginal costs are assumed for purposes of the exposition here. Of course, high fixed costs and declining marginal costs mean that second-best pricing solutions often must be adopted (Atkinson and Stiglitz 1980: 458–70). That complication does not alter the present analysis.
2 Many excises, of course, have nothing to do with externalities but are simply ways of raising revenue and redistributing income. The standard economic treatment of excises subordinates this positive aspect of taxation and stresses the normative function of using excises to cure externalities. It is the conventional normative analysis that is addressed here.
3 In some cases, for example libraries, marginal costs (including congestion costs) may be zero. But fixed costs are positive, and the ability to exclude would permit charging a fixed fee for access. Yet such fees typically are not charged.
4 See, for example, Atkinson and Stiglitz (1980: 480). The information problem is endogenous, however. It is commonly recognized that with public goods for which exclusion is impossible or impractical (such as national defence)

government actors will have difficulty discerning consumers' true demands. Thus, '[t]he political process may result in serious misallocation because it may fail to interpret preferences correctly' (Due and Friedlander 1973: 99). But no such problem exists for goods for which exclusion, and thus user fees, is possible.

5 There is no important constitutional constraint on politicians' decisions how to finance government production: the government 'has many options and it can do pretty much as it pleases. . . . The only thing that can easily be said about this question is that governments could use special assessments and user fees more than they currently do, but little is known about why and when these devices are used' (Levmore 1989: 4).

6 De Alessi (1975) presents evidence consistent with that of Peltzman. He finds that municipal power companies sell electricity at lower prices than do private companies.

7 As noted in Buchanan's analysis of earmarking, bureaucrats' objective 'is primarily that of expanding the size and importance of the public sector' (Buchanan 1963). For a lengthier discussion of bureaucratic incentives and user fees, see Lee (1990). For historical examples of bureaucratic preference for 'free' government services, see McChesney, 1986; Pashigan 1976; West 1967.

8 The same reactions follow legislative attempts to put a price on pollution (Buchanan and Tullock 1975; Maloney and McCormick 1982; Yandle 1989).

9 See Jaroslovsky 1989: 1.

10 During the Congressional session that produced the Tax Reform Act of 1986 it was reported that politicians had used campaign funds to purchase things like country club memberships, Kentucky Derby tickets, football tickets, liquor, art and other investments (plus insurance for them), golf clubs and trips abroad (see Jackson [1985: 1]). Indeed, by the Technical and Miscellaneous Revenue Act (TAMRA) of 1988, congress has made it even 'easier for legislators to divert political donations for political use' (Ford 1989a: 958). Since that time, records show, campaign contributions have been used for such items as tickets to Broadway shows and travel to Switzerland (Ford 1989b: 959).

11 A recent *Newsweek* report defined 'fetcher bill' as follows: 'What members of the state legislatures call bills introduced solely to draw–fetch–lavish treatment from lobbyists'.

12 For a recent discussion, see Pogue and Sgontz (1989). As the authors note, there is disagreement as to whether any costs of such 'sins' are truly external or whether they are internalized.

13 The 1986 tax changes in particular seemed to engender optimism that increased durability had arrived for income taxation (see Rabushka 1988); for a pessimistic evaluation of the durability of the 1986 changes, see McChesney (1988). For an indication that, at least publicly, the 1986 changes now are perceived as temporary, see Rosenbaum (1989): 'The brief experiment in tax reform seems to be coming to an end. The three-year old law, the dream of generations of academic experts, has fallen victim to political reality . . .'.

14 Following the 1986 legislation of lower individual rates to take effect in later years, Speaker of the House Jim Wright 'proposed freezing the 1987 interim rates instead of letting the lower permanent rates take effect in 1988. . . .

[T]ax reductions promised in the Economic Recovery Tax Act of 1981 were wiped out in 1982 and 1984 legislation before their promised benefits were received' (Doernberg and McChesney 1987: 907–8).
15 See White (1989).
16 See Birnbaum (1990).
17 Letter of 28 November 1989 from the Partnership for Improved Air Travel, asking members to contact politicians and demand release of trust fund money.

REFERENCES

Ahlbrandt, R. 'Efficiency in the Provision of Fire Services'. *Public Choice* 16 (Fall 1973): 1–16.

Atkinson, A.B. and Stiglitz, J.E. *Lectures on Public Economics*. New York: McGraw-Hill, 1980.

Birnbaum, J. 'Rostenkowski Backs Boost in Gas Tax, Would Use Defence Cuts to Trim Deficit'. *Wall Street Journal*, 3 January 1990: A8.

Buchanan, J.M. 'The Economics of Earmarked Taxes'. *Journal of Political Economy* 71 (October 1963): 457–69.

Buchanan, J. and Tullock, G. "Polluters' Profit" and Political Response: Direct Controls versus Taxes'. *American Economic Review* 65 (March 1975): 139–47.

De Alessi, L. 'Some Effects of Ownership on the Wholesale Price of Electric Power'. *Economic Inquiry* (December 1975): 526–38.

Doernberg, R.L. and McChesney, F.S. 'Doing Good or Doing Well? : Congress and the Tax Reform Act of 1986'. *New York University Law Review* (October 1987): 891–926.

Doernberg, R.L. and McChesney, F.S. 'On the Accelerating Rate and Decreasing Durability of Tax Reform'. *Minnesota Law Review* (April 1987): 913–62.

Due, J.F. and Friedlander, A.F. *Government Finance: Economics of the Public Sector* (5th ed.). Homewood, Ill.: Richard D. Irwin, 1973.

Ford, F. 'TAMRA Said to Have Opened Sizeable Loophole in Campaign Spending Rules'. *Tax Notes*, 28 August 1989a: 958.

Ford, F. 'Senate Campaign Funds Spent on Foreign Travel Chauffeur May Still Qualify for Tax Breaks'. *Tax Notes*, 28 August 1989b: 959.

Jackson, 'Congressmen Charge All Kinds of Things to Campaign Chests'. *Wall Street Journal*, 3 December 1985: 1.

Jaroslovsky, R. 'Industries Mobilize to Block Bush's User-Fee Plan'. *Wall Street Journal*, 29 December 1989: 1.

Leal, D. 'Saving an Ecosystem: From Buffer Zone to Private Initiatives', In J.A. Baden and D.Leal, eds, *The Yellowstone Primer*. San Francisco: Pacific Research Institute for Public Policy, 1990.

Lee, D.R. 'Rent Seeking and Its Implications for Taxation'. *Southern Economic Journal* 51 (January 1985): 731–45.

Lee, D.R. 'The Political Economy of User Charges: Some Bureaucratic Implications'. Unpublished manuscript, 1990.

Levmore, S. 'Just Compensation and Just Politics'. Unpublished manuscript, 1989.

McChesney, F.S. 'The Cinderella School of Tax Reform: A Comment on Rabushka'. *Contemporary Policy Issues* (October 1988): 65–9.

McChesney, F.S. 'Rent Extraction and Rent Creation in the Economic Theory of Regulation'. *Journal of Legal Studies* 16 (January 1987): 101–18.

McChesney, F.S. 'Government Prohibitions on Volunteer Fire Fighting in Nineteenth-Century America: A Property Rights Perspective'. *Journal of Legal Studies* 15 (January 1986): 69–92.

Maloney, M.T. and R.E. McCormick. 'A Positive Theory of Environmental Quality Regulations'. *Journal of Law and Economics* 25 (April 1982): 99–123.

Maloney, M.T., McCormick, R.E., and Tollison, R.D. 'Economic Regulation, Competitive Governments, and Specialized Resources'. *Journal of Law and Economics* 27 (October 1984): 329–38.

Pashigian, B.P. 'Consequences and Causes of Public Ownership of Urban Transit Facilities'. *Journal of Political Economy* (December 1976): 1239–59.

Peltzman, S. 'Pricing in Public and Private Enterprises: Electric Utilities in the United States'. *Journal of Law and Economics* 14 (April 1971): 109–47.

Pogue, T.F and Sgontz, L.G. 'Taxing to Control Social Costs: The Case of Alcohol'. *American Economic Review* 79 (March 1989): 235–43.

Rabushka, A. 'The Tax Reform Act of 1986: Concentrated Costs, Diffuse Benefits – An Inversion of Public Choice'. *Contemporary Policy Issues* (October 1988): 50–64.

Rosenbaum, 'The Tax Breaks America Couldn't Give Up'. *New York Times*, 8 October 1989: E1.

Shughart, W.F. II. 'Durable Tax Reform'. *Cato Journal* (Spring–Summer 1987): 273–81.

Wessel, D. and McGinley, L. 'Federal Tax on Air Fares May Climb'. *Wall Street Journal,* 8 January, 1990: B1.

West, E.G. 'The Political Economy of American Public School Legislation'. *Journal of Law and Economics* 10 (April 1967): 101–28.

White, J. 'Pension Funds to Politicians: Hands Off'. *Wall Street Journal,* 5 December 1989: C1.

Yandle, B. 'Taxation, Political Action, and Superfund'. *Cato Journal* 8 (Winter 1989): 751–64.

Yandle, B. 'User Charges, Rent Seeking, and Public Choice'. See Chapter 3 of this volume.

12 User fees and earmarked taxes in constitutional perspective

Richard E. Wagner

The preceding essays have shown how the reality of user fees and earmarked taxes is often strikingly different from the normative justifications commonly advanced in support of those fiscal practices. This divergence between norm and reality is, in turn, an understandable result of the incentives contained within prevailing political systems, as the theory of public choice explains. Once it is recognized that political and fiscal outcomes are governed by the constitutional rules that order political activity, constitutional reform of political processes becomes a significant element in any effort to secure improvement. In this concluding chapter I seek to set forth some of the primary elements of and reasoning behind a constitutional perspective on fiscal processes.

1 THE SOCIAL DILEMMA AND THE CONTRACTARIAN STATE

The primary model that is used to portray the central problems of constitutional order is the social dilemma. This model, which hearkens back to Thomas Hobbes, was first presented in modern dress by Winston Bush (1972), and was developed more fully by Gordon Tullock (1974) and James Buchanan (1975). A simple, two-person version of this model envisions each person as choosing how much of his energies to devote to trading with the other person and how much to devote to predation and defence. The central features of this model are illustrated by Figure 12.1. As shown here, each participant can choose between two rules or principles of conduct. 'Exchange' entails an adherence to the limitations on personal conduct imposed by the rules of property and contract, while 'predation' entails no such adherence and might be thought of as a rule of 'anything goes'.

The structure of the social-dilemma model incorporates the Hobbesian presumption that all participants would prefer to avoid the

	Exchange	Predator
Exchange	2,2	4,1
Predator	1,4	3,3

Figure 12.1 The social dilemma

war of all against all than to engage in that war. As described by Figure 12.1, both participants would be better off if both would refrain from predation, which in turn would eliminate the need for efforts to defend against predation, and would devote their energies fully to trade or exchange.

The avoidance of the joint-predation outcome and its replacement by the joint-exchange outcome can be visualized as the result of an agreement between the participants. In Hobbes's version, the participants granted authority to some sovereign who by definition was not bound by the agreement between the participants, and who could thus capture up to the aggregate gain the participants could otherwise capture by replacing joint predation with joint exchange. The contemporary scholarship on constitutional political economy has sought to explain how those gains might be captured by the participants themselves. For this to happen, there must be some alternative resolution to the dilemma than the Hobbesian recourse to some sovereign authority. Hence, the social-dilemma model can be used to tell a story of the emergence of government through contract – the creation of a contractarian state.

To be sure, this contractarian framework has been subjected to several lines of criticism, many of which, while correct on their own terms, do not really dispute the central features of this approach so much as they raise different questions for exploration. For one thing, the social-dilemma model is a prisoners' dilemma, and such work as that by Axelrod (1984) gives grounds for thinking that in repeated plays the prisoners' dilemma may be resolved, as through the tit-for-tat strategy. If so, order may be preserved through informal processes without any formal process of constitutional construction. But what holds for small numbers of people may not hold for large numbers. With only two participants it is readily apparent if one person departs from exchange to engage in predation. But as the number of participants increase, it may be impossible to determine just who is engaging in predation. Some more explicit formalization of some constitutional agreement may be necessary.

It is also often objected that the record of such contractually grounded government is scanty if not absent entirely. Even the American constitutional founding was far from peaceful and consensual. Much government clearly originates in conquest. Contractarian theories would seem to fare poorly when judged by ordinary explanatory standards, as many critics have noted. But the social-dilemma model is far more normative and didactic than explanatory in purpose. When interpreted as an explanatory model the social-dilemma model is portrayed as characterizing the civilizing of the human beast through some combination of necessity and weariness. But when understood didactically the social-dilemma model does not so much explain the emergence of order out of chaos as it illuminates some of the eternal problems of social life this side of Eden: cooperation allows us to deal more effectively with scarcity, but scarcity also tends to make us look upon our own projects with special favour and threatens to disrupt the cooperative process.

2 PROBLEMS OF CONSTITUTIONAL MAINTENANCE

Donald McCloskey (1985) has reminded us of how fully we think in terms of metaphors and analogies. The principle metaphor in constitutional political economy is that social life is a game. A basketball game, for instance, is an ordered set of relationships among the participants, in which the order is produced through people pursuing their interests within a set of rules. In playing the game the teams are impelled by self-interest considerations. But the actual conduct of play will be shaped by the various rules that govern the game.

With high stakes, the players will also choose referees or umpires to monitor the play of the game and to enforce the rules by which the players have agreed to play. But it is important to note in this respect that it is the players and not the referees who choose the rules that order the play of the game. The referees are simply agents of the players, chosen to enforce the rules the players have adopted. From time to time the players may also choose to change the rules, with those new rules to apply to subsequent rounds of play.

Constitutional political economy sees a constitution as analogous to the rules of a game. A constitution represents a set of rules that order the relationships among the individuals who constitute the society, each of whom subsequently pursues his or her interests within the framework of those rules. With respect to games there is a distinction between two processes: playing the game and choosing the rules of the game. With respect to politics there is an analogous distinction, in which in-period politics represents the playing of the game and constitutional politics represents the choice of the rules of the game.

An important implication of this analogy between governments and referees is that while both act as agents in enforcing rules their principals have adopted, they themselves do not make those rules or revise them. This means that government does not make the rules of the game. Government is not a source of rights, but rather is seen as a reflection of people's uses of their rights. The very *raison d'être* of constitutional government is that government is subject to limits that reside in people's prior rights of person and property, and is not itself the source of those rights or the arbiter of those limits. If two people acting privately cannot legitimately take the property of a third, neither should they be able to do so just because they form a political majority and invoke the name of government on their behalf. For to do otherwise would make government the source of people's rights, rather than being a reflection of people's use of their rights.

To be sure, the order that characterizes social life is more complex than that which characterizes a football game. With ordinary games there is a clear demarcation between when one round of play ends and the next one begins. The play of a game is discontinuous, and this discontinuity makes it possible to limit the applicability of a change in the rules to future rounds of play only. But social life is continuous. Changes in constitutional rules will to some degree be analogous to changing the rules in the very midst of play. Constitutional politics and in-period politics will take place simultaneously. But this difference can also be easily exaggerated. For it is always possible for the outcomes of constitutional politics to take effect some time in the future. By increasing the uncertainty about how particular changes will affect particular positions, the scope for agreeing on changes in the rules can be widened.

It is also often claimed that constitutions involve complex problems of interpretation that do not arise in ordinary games. To be sure, there are constitutional provisions that do not raise questions of interpretation: provisions that the President must be 35 years of age or that each state shall have two senators are illustrations. But equally clearly there are provisions in ordinary games that do raise questions of interpretation. Rules against 'unnecessary roughness' or 'unsports-manlike conduct' are surely as subject to interpretation are are rules against cruel and unusual punishment or imperatives to promote the general welfare. The problem of maintaining the rules against pressures for amendment via 'interpretation' does not seems to be categorically more difficult for constitutions than for ordinary games.

3 'INTERPRETATION', AUTHORITY, AND CONSTITUTIONAL ORDER

Does the necessity that the referees must interpret how the rules are to be applied to the numerous particular situations that will arise mean that those referees will necessarily be involved in revising the rules of the game? If so, the game analogy would border on the incoherent. The conceptual distinction between the players choosing the rules and the referees merely enforcing the rules the players have chosen would be a concept without a referent. The players may have chosen a set of rules once upon a time, but what the rules actually are thence forward will be what the referees through their interpretations have declared them to be.

Consider, for instance, the American constitutional provision (Article I, Section 8) to the effect that the power of the legislature to impose taxes is limited by the requirement that those revenues be spent only on activities that 'promote the general welfare'. The provision entails a possibility that tax revenues could be used to promote the particular welfare of some. In this respect, William Niskanen (1986: 352), remarks that the 'US Constitution ... provides no explicit authority for federal welfare programmes', and goes on to note that the constitutional 'authority' for those programmes was created by the Supreme Court in 1936.[1] Related to this, Richard Epstein (1985: 306–29) argues that the bulk of the transfer programmes of the welfare state are unconstitutional because they violate the anti-taking clause of the Fifth Amendment. In both cases the main point is the same: a programme through which government acts as a partisan of some people's interests to the detriment of other people violates the principles on which the American constitutional order is founded, for it would involve government as a source and extinguisher of rights, and not merely a reflection of people's use of their rights.

It seems clear that there are solid grounds for arguing that transfer programmes are unconstitutional, both in terms of the fifth Amendment's strictures against takings as well as in terms of Article I,

Section 8's requirement that the power to tax is limited by the requirement that appropriations be for the general welfare – as distinct from the welfare of particular people or groups. While the model of the social dilemma describes the gains to the participants from agreeing to a set of rules, such an agreement does nothing to change the nature of the situation. There are tendencies, latent if not manifest, for post-constitutional opportunism to emerge through democratic political processes, eroding the gains from overcoming the social dilemma in the process of violating some people's rights for the benefit of others.

For instance, suppose some people in a city own developed property while others own undeveloped property. If the owners of the developed property could prevent the owners of the undeveloped property from developing their property they could enrich themselves at the expense of the owners of the undeveloped property. The only legitimate way this could be done privately would be for the owners of the developed property to buy the undeveloped property. But the owners of the developed property could accomplish the same thing at lower personal cost if they could enact a zoning ordinance that would declare the undeveloped property to be for agricultural use only, or perhaps suitable only for 5-acre residential lots. By restricting the supply of developed land, the zoning ordinance increases the value of the developed property while lowering the value of the undeveloped property. It enables the owners of the developed property effectively to rob the owners of the undeveloped property, just as surely as the owners of developed land had forcibly prevented the owners of the undeveloped land from developing their land. In this case the police powers of government are used as an instrument of plunder.[2] Likewise, a winning coalition could approve an appropriation of general revenues that was for the benefit of its members only, to the detriment of the remainder of society. This would represent taxation for the welfare of particular people, in contrast to taxation for the general welfare, and would violate Article I, Section 8.

But is it truly so easy to distinguish appropriations that promote the general welfare from those that promote the particular welfare of some to the disadvantage of those others who are forced through taxation to provide the subsidy payments? For instance, do transfer programmes necessarily violate Article I, Section 8, as well as perhaps the fifth Amendment? It is surely possible to fit transfer programmes into a model whereby a majority places burdens on a minority. But are programmes that appear to transfer wealth from some people to others, or that otherwise appear to impose disabilities on some people for the benefit of others, necessarily what they appear to be? And how can such a determination be made? Are there truly no conceivable grounds to justify some transfer programmes as reflecting people's use of their rights and hence being consistent with the injunction to promote the general welfare?

The literature on Pareto optimal redistribution suggests there is.[3] This literature proposes to transform transfer programmes into public goods. It does so by arguing that wealthier people generally value the alleviation of destitution, but that free riding among the well-to-do will prevent them from achieving their desires efficiently through market processes. Some programme of state-supplied transfers is thus seen not as a transfer that violates some people's rights for the benefit of others, but rather as an activity that is consistent with people's rights and which helps people to exploit more fully some of the potential gains from trade.

A welfare or transfer programme can thus be subject to two contending interpretations: first, it represents an unconstitutional taking from some for the benefit of others; and, second, it violates no one's rights, and rather represents the provision of a public good that overcomes what would otherwise be market failure. Is there any way to distinguish between these interpretations? It might seem tempting to argue that it would be straightforward to make this distinction. If a programme promotes the general welfare it should be agreeable to all. Hence, one way of testing a claim about the general welfare would be to give people a standing to sue the legislature on the grounds that they are not receiving worthwhile value from their tax payments. The filing of such suits would be regarded as sufficient evidence that the general welfare requirement was being violated.

However, the free-rider argument predicts that some people would make such a claim even if the claim were false, so long as the making of that claim led to a reduction in tax liability. A claim that someone receives no benefits from a transfer programme is not sufficient basis for accepting that claim, and for rejecting the claim that the programme is consistent with the general welfare limitation. For the free-rider counter-argument is that many people would make such statements even if those statements were false, so long as a reduction in tax liability resulted. Therefore, it is certainly possible for someone to argue that some forms of transfers satisfy requirements of 'public use' or 'general welfare', despite the presence of people who profess the contrary.

In such cases as these, a court-driven process of constitutional maintenance requires a third-party choice between competing truth claims. Since judges in these situations are asked to choose among non-observable conditions, they would seem to have wide scope for ruling as they choose with little fear of falsification. Indeed, the higher the stakes the greater the investment people will make in constructing rationales and developing justificatory arguments. Disputes will surely arise as to how particular constitutional provisions apply, so some process of interpretation and adjudication will be necessary. But it is possible to determine when a particular court decision represents simply an interpretation of what the constitutional contract requires and when it represents a judicially imposed, though perhaps legislatively sanctioned, revision or amendment of that contract? In the absence of considerably more success in searching for just men than Diogenes found, much would seem to ride on who in particular is appointed to the court.

In the light of a general ability to give a justification or rationalization for perhaps almost anything, it would be reasonable to wonder whether or not there is any test to distinguish acts of interpretation from acts of amendment. Or must one person's reasonable interpretation be someone else's (un)constitutional amendment? Recall the earlier comparison of processes of constitutional enforcement as those found in organized athletics.[4] A particular referee may be a partisan of the underdog and call penalties in a biased manner so as to enhance the underdog's chance of winning. In the light of this possibility, how are referees, or judges, to be limited to enforcing rules and restrained from making rules, particularly when irreducible elements of judgement can always lead to some blurring through 'interpretation' of the conceptually clear distinction between making rules and enforcing rules?

Even though interpretation is inescapable, it none the less seems reasonable to conclude that referees do not make the rules but only enforce rules to which the participants have agreed. But what makes this conclusion reasonable has nothing to do with any observation or comparison of the actual rulings made by referees with the rules the participants originally agreed or by which they intended to play. Rather, the reasonableness of this conclusion stems from the *consensual process* by which referees are selected. Not only are they chosen by the agreement of the participants, but also they are subject to periodic and consensual reaffirmation by the participants. If the participants were to disagree over the maintenance of a referee this would mean that the referee was viewed as being an amender and not simply an enforcer of rules.

In other words, the problem of distinguishing reasonable interpretation from unconstitutional amendment via 'interpretation' can be approached from a procedural even if not from a substantive perspective. There are two important elements that make it reasonable to say that referees merely enforce the rules by which the participants have agreed to play, and do not engage in some unconstitutional process of amendment via 'interpretation'. One is that there is some periodic process by which the continued employment of the referees is subject. With respect to judges this might argue for limitations on their tenure. To say this is not to say that they should be subject to periodic election, as I shall note momentarily. But it is to say that the idea of a truly independent judiciary would be to create a position of Hobbesian sovereignty, which in turn would surely and generally engage in unconstitutional amendment. Indeed, the intense interest about, and growing interest-group campaigning over, court appointments suggests that the court is not part of a consensual process of rule interpretation, but rather is a participant in a process of rule amendment via 'interpretation', as a form of continuing constitutional convention.

The second, and surely more important, element is that with games the referees are selected by the *agreement* of the players. This consideration directs attention to the legislative process by which judges are selected. To the extent those processes are capable of reflecting a consensus among the participants those legislators are presumed to represent, the game analogy would seem to work. However, this means, to start, that a system of single-member constituencies is incapable of reflecting such a consensus, regardless of the voting rule by which it operates. And even a system of multi-member constituencies, which would lead to proportional representation, would be capable of reflecting some underlying consensus only to the extent that the legislature operated by consensual voting rules rather than through simple majority voting.

4   ENDOGENOUS POLITICS AND THE PROBLEM OF CONSTITUTIONAL REFORM

Welfare economics emerged within economics during the second quarter of this century as representing the interests of economists to say something systematically and formally about the characteristics of good or desirable governmental policy. With the refinements of the model of a competitive market economy that were taking place, welfare economics emerged as an effort to explore the limits to the proposition that in a market economy it would be impossible to make someone better off without making someone else worse off. The various models of market failure, such as represented by notions of monopoly, externality, and public goods, all characterize situations where the participants in the market process are prevented from exploiting fully the potential gains from trade. It falls to government to enable those participants to realize that potential.[5]

The problem of good government policy was seen fundamentally as one of developing knowledge about the sources and types of market failure. With the development of such knowledge it was presumed, usually more tacitly than explicitly, that that knowledge would be put to good use, as described by the model of the competitive economic process. Knowledge of the good would be sufficient to ensure its attainment through, in this case, right governmental action. Welfare economics represented, in other words, a reasoned and disciplined approach to social reform, with the problem of securing reform being a matter of presenting reasoned argument and evidence to the reforming authorities. Those reforming authorities occupied an exhalted position in welfare economics. While not being treated as omniscient, they were most surely presumed to be benevolent in that they were construed as having a single-minded dedication to promoting the cause of good government. And welfare economics represented a systematic effort to expound the requirements of good government.

Public choice demoted those authorities to the status of ordinary people, which, while not denying the presence of benevolence, treated all people as having a particular affection for their own projects. With self-interest presumed paramount in the organization of human affairs, within the polity as well as within the economy, the enactment of public policy became subject to questions of incentive compatibility. Political processes and their reflection in public policy outcomes became endogenous and subject to economic explanation. The result of this was the elimination of the subject to whom welfare economics could be addressed. Once political outcomes are seen as largely determined by the rules that constrain political processes, welfare economics, at least as it has been traditionally conceptualized, becomes incoherent, for there no longer exists any subject to whom the analytical effort is addressed. Political interventions into the economy will follow an economic logic that is orthogonal to the dictates of welfare economics. How closely particular policy measures will correspond to those dictates will be a matter of willingness to pay, broadly speaking, and not a matter of the analytical cogency of those dictates.

With the unification of political and economic processes, what happens to any residual interest scholars may have in contributing to the creation of a better world? Must Hamilton's query in the *Federalist* 1 – 'whether societies of men are really capable or not of establishing good government from reflection and choice, or whether they are forever destined to depend for their political constitutions on accident and force' – be answered that accident and force rule all?[6] Constitutional political economy represents an effort to articulate a place for reflection and choice; it represents an effort to use economics to contribute to the betterment of life once the presumption of benevolent despotism has been vanquished. While constitutional political economy accepts the proposition that political outcomes conform to an economic logic and are not truly open to choice, it asserts that the rules that constitute a political order *are* open to choice. Or at least it asserts that if there is any scope for reflection and choice, it is at the constitutional level and not the level of in-period politics where it must be exercised.

In opposition to this assertion, it could be argued that the very same economic logic that public-choice scholars have applied to in-period politics can be applied to constitutional choice as well.[7] It could thus be objected that constitutional political economy is likewise rendered incoherent by the endogenization of politics and the annihilation of the benevolent despot that the public-choice revolution brought about. To be sure, there is surely greater scope for people to reach some agreement when the resulting choice is to be applied to a sequence of plays than when it is to be applied only to a single play. None the less, constitutional choices will be longer lived than ordinary political choices, which increases the present value of getting particular constitutional measures enacted. Constitutional choice, in other words, may not be so much a matter of negating rent-seeking politics as it is a matter of raising the stakes involved in such political processes.

The possible incoherence of constitutional political economy depends on what is considered exogenous once politics is treated as endogenous. One possibility is that biology or genetics is the exogenous variable, in which case there would be no scope for bringing reflection and choice to bear on questions of constitutional order. For, in this event, the very effort to articulate and argue for particular constitutional rules would be determined by biological self-interest, and choice would be illusory. Such a world would be the very opposite of the famous statement about John Maynard Keynes, to the effect that ideas dominate interests, let alone Richard Weaver's more moderate claim merely that ideas have consequences.[8]

While it is common to contrast ideas and interests and to think of these as competing explanations, with an increase in the importance given to interests implying a decrease in the scope for ideas to influence social processes, it may be more appropriate to characterize ideas and interests simply as alternative reflections or representations of the same thing. In this case, self-interest would not so much conform to some biological imperative as it would be a mental construction of an individual. If self-interest is something that an individual constructs there is an important place for knowledge to affect outcomes, despite the endogenous character of politics. Hamilton's query in the *Federalist* 1 can thus be answered positively, even though an appropriate constitutional understanding may be necessary to provide a fertile environment for the nurturing of such an activity.

5   FISCAL POLITICS IN CONSTITUTIONAL PERSPECTIVE

There would seem to be a substantial cleavage between the various normative lines of argument often used to support user fees and earmarked taxes, and a consideration of the positive processes through which tax legislation emerges. Even if tax legislation is modelled as the outcome of a benevolent process, the knowledge necessary to impose user fees and earmarked taxes in the manner envisioned by the common normative arguments is unlikely to be present. Furthermore, tax legislation is really the outcome of a self-interested process of interest-group competition. For the most part, the analysis of taxation has been pursued from within the normative perspective of welfare economics. Only recently have economists begun to analyse taxation in terms of positive theories of fiscal politics. And when this is done what often emerges is a realization that actual fiscal outcomes diverge significantly from the characterizations of normative analysis. The standard justifications for user charges and earmarked taxes may have little to do with the actual operation of such practices.

This is not to deny that particular fees and taxes might in some circumstances correspond to what the normative arguments envision. But such a possibility would seem to be a matter of the constitutional rules that govern processes of tax legislation. This point was central to Knut Wicksell's seminal work on democracy, public finance, and constitutional order. In short, the more fully constitutional rules operate to require the consent of taxpayers, such as is envisioned by the benefit principle and as is justified by arguments for user charges and earmarked taxes, the more closely principle and practice will correspond. Regardless of particular analytical details, the incorporation of public-choice insights into a normative concern with tax policy in a democratic political order places in the foreground the constitutional order within which political and fiscal choices are made.

To be sure, it is difficult to make sense of many constitutional provisions without a presumption that government is dominated by self-interest, and that the operation of in-period politics is likely to have undesirable   consequences   without   appropriate   constitutional constraints. The presence of a first amendment guarantee in the American constitution, for instance, embodies the presumption that Congress otherwise would be likely to abridge freedom of the press, religion, and speech. Similarly, the last clause of the Fifth Amendment is inexplicable, save for the presumption that Congress would otherwise be likely to countenance the taking of private property without paying just compensation, and would do so for private and not just for public use.

It is instructive to note the American constitution contains a number of constraints on the use of fiscal authority. The first clause of Article I, Section 8 limits Congress by insisting that tax revenues be used only to 'provide for the *common* defense and *general* welfare', and it requires that 'all duties, imposts and excises shall be *uniform* throughout the United States'. The emphasis should surely be on the adjectives: 'common', 'general', 'uniform', for these suggest a recognition that in-period politics would otherwise be subject to the republican disease. Surely, if there were no presumption that fiscal discrimination would be likely to emerge through ordinary democratic processes, there would have been no point to such a requirement of uniformity. The uniformity clause has been interpreted as applying geographically, particularly as requiring uniform rates of federal taxation throughout the United States. But it is easy to see that without that limitation the use of tax discrimination on a regional basis might have emerged. But budgets are two-sided entities, and expenditure discrimination can substitute for tax discrimination, as noted earlier. In similar fashion, the restrictions provided by the '*common* defense' and the '*general* welfare' can likewise be understood as reflecting a recognition that constitutional constraints on fiscal authority are necessary to control the republican disease.[9]

At the same time, to articulate limitations on governmental processes, out of a recognition that otherwise those processes will undertake the proscribed activities, does not itself assure obedience to those limits, as Wagner (1987) explores. The opportunity for discriminatory taxation points to some severe constitutional questions for democratic political systems. Bruno Leoni (1960) points out that 'no taxation without representation' originally meant no taxation without the consent of the taxpayer. A principle of non-discrimination would seem very much to be a related element of a constitutional approach to taxation, as Hutt (1966) argued in his review essay on *The Calculus of Consent*. While it is reasonable to think of democracy as a process of, among other things, self-taxation, in that we choose to tax ourselves, it is unreasonable to think of it legitimately as a process by which some people choose to tax others. A tax measure that gets a two-thirds majority may be fine when the majority is among the taxpayers. But when the taxes are concentrated among the minority, what may result is a system of a majority choosing to tax not themselves but to tax other people, and a severe conflict with the principles of constitutional government becomes quickly apparent.

The extent to which the tax enactments of actual governments can be reconciled with the normative vision of constitutional government would seem to depend on the extent to which the constitutional rules that constrain political processes prevent the use of government as a means of imposing disabilities on some people for the benefit of others. In short, the more fully constitutional processes work in the direction of requiring the consent of taxpayers, as illustrated by the Wicksellian principle, the more likely it is that normative visions and positive explanations will become congruent.[10]

The less fully constitutional controls operate to constrain the market for tax legislation, the more likely it seems that tax legislation will be an on-going process through which the legislature serves as an arena for brokering wealth transfers. Such legislative activity does, of course, run strongly contrary to the view that one of the most important tasks for government is to provide a framework of stable rules and to secure rights, for the continual churning of the tax code by the legislature injects instability into the economic process, along with associated economic costs, and diminishes the security of individual rights.[11]

NOTES

1 In *United States* v. *Butler* 297 US 1 (1936).
2 For careful examinations of government as an instrument of predation and of the importance of appropriate constitutional protections, see Epstein (1985). Related to this, see Siegan (1980), Aranson (1985), and Anderson and Hill (1980).
3 Initiated by Hochman and Rodgers (1969) and critically surveyed by Pasour (1981).
4 For further elaboration, see Wagner (1987).
5 It is perhaps worth noting that welfare economics developed within, and not in opposition to, liberalism. Welfare economics took individual preferences as its standard of evaluation and sought to describe how government could help people to exploit opportunities for mutual gain more fully than they would otherwise have been able to do.
6 For a careful examination of the principles undergirding the American constitutional creation against the backdrop of Hamilton's query, see Ostrom (1987).
7 This has been done for the federal government by Landes and Posner (1975) and for state governments by Crain and Tollison (1979).

8 For Keynes's statement that 'the power of vested interests is vastly exaggerated compared with the gradual encroachment of ideas', see Keynes (1936: 383). For the claim only that ideas have consequences, see Weaver (1948).

9 Buchanan (1964) argues that a combination of flat-rate taxation and expenditure programmes are of general or common benefit may be one that leads to approximate unanimity about the size of the public-sector.

10 For an examination of the Wicksellian principle in this light, see Wagner (1988).

11 For a careful argument that such churning is an inherent feature of all states, see de Jasay (1985).

REFERENCES

Anderson, T.L. and Hill, P.J. *The Birth of a Transfer Society*. Stanford, CA: Hoover Institution Press, 1980.

Aranson, P.H. 'Judicial Control of the Political Branches: Public Purpose and Public Law'. *Cato Journal* 4 (Winter 1985): 719–82.

Axelrod, R. *The Evolution of Cooperation*. New York: Basic Books, 1984.

Buchanan, J.M. 'Fiscal Institutions and Efficiency in Collective Outlay'. *American Economic Review* 54 (1964) 227–35.

Buchanan, J.M. *The Limits of Liberty: Between Anarchy and Leviathan*. Chicago: University of Chicago Press, 1975.

Buchanan, J. M. and Tullock, G. *The Calculus of Consent: Logical Foundations of Constitutional Democracy*. Ann Arbor: University of Michigan Press, 1962.

Bush, W.C. 'Individual Welfare in Anarchy'. In G. Tullock, ed. *Explorations in the Theory of Anarchy*. Blacksburg: Center for Study of Public Choice, 1972: 5–18.

Crain, W. M. and Tollison, R.D. 'Constitutional Change in an Interest-Group Perspective'. *Journal of Legal Studies* 8 (January 1979): 165–75.

De Jasay, A. *The State*. Oxford: Basil Blackwell 1985.

Epstein, R.A. *Takings: Private Property and the Power of Eminent Domain*. Cambridge: Harvard University Press, 1985.

Hamilton, A. *The Federalist* 1. New York: New American Library (1961): 33.

Hochman, H.M. and Rodgers, J. D. 'Pareto Optimal Redistribution'. *American Economic Review* 59 (September 1969): 542–57.

Hutt, W.H. 'Unanimity Versus Non-Discrimination (As Criteria for Constitutional Validity)'. *South African Journal of Economics* 34 (1966): 133–47.

Keynes, J.M. *The General Theory of Employment, Interest, and Money*. New York: Harcourt Brace, 1936.

Landes, W.M. and Posner, R.A. 'The Independent Judiciary in an Interest-Group Perspective'. *Journal of Law and Economics* 18 (December 1975): 875–901.

Leoni, B. *Freedom and the Law*. Los Angeles: Nash, 1960.

McCloskey, D.N. *The Rhetoric of Economics*. Madison: University of Wisconsin Press, 1985.

Niskanen, W.A. 'A Constitutional Approach to Taxes and Transfers'. *Cato Journal* 6 (Spring 1986): 374–52.

Ostrom, V. *The Political Theory of a Compound Republic*, 2nd ed. Lincoln: University of Nebraska Press, 1987.

Pasour, E.C., Jr. 'Pareto Optimality as a Guide to Income Redistribution'. *Public Choice* 36, (No. 1, 1981): 75–87.

Siegan, B.H. *Economic Liberties and the Constitution*. Chicago: University of Chicago Press, 1980.

Tullock, G. *The Social Dilemma*. Blacksburg, VA: Center for Study of Public Choice, 1974.

Wagner, R.E. 'Parchment, Guns, and the Maintenance of Constitutional Contract'. In Charles K. Rowley, ed. *Democracy and Public Choice: Essays in Honor of Gordon Tullock*. Oxford: Basil Blackwell, 1987: 105–21.

Wagner, R.E. '*The Calculus of Consent*: A Wicksellian Retrospective'. *Public Choice* 56 (1988): 153–66.

Weaver, R.M. *Ideas Have Consequences*. Chicago: University of Chicago Press, 1948.

Wicksell, K. *Finanztheoretische Untersuchungen*. Jena: Gustav Fischer, 1896.

Index

ability to pay principle 1, 11n
Ahlbrandt, R. 167
Airport and Airway Trust Fund 164, 173–4
alcohol tax 126, 171
Anderson, Gary M. 13–29
Atkinson, A.B. and Stiglitz, J.E. 164
Axelrod, R. 180

Barnett, H.C. 54
Baumol, W.J. 62
bureaucracy and user charges 60–73; the bureaucratic environment 62–4; the bureau's ideal user charge 71–3; the importance of user charges 64–9; some qualifications 69–71
Belanger, G. (in Migue, J.L. *et al.*) 63
benefit principle, the 3–7, 112, 141, 153–5, 190; the benevolent fisc 153–5; as computational objective 4–6; and the contract theory of the state 3–4; as outcome of proper political process 6–7
benevolent fisc, the *see* benefit principle, the
Benson, B.L. and Mitchell, J.M. 69
bias, systematic 98–100
Bird, R.M. and Slack, E. 15
Bös, D. 78
Brennan, G. and Buchanan, James M. 115, 122, 160
Browning, E.K. 114–15, 121
Buchanan, James M. 79, 114–15, 125, 141, 152–62, 157, 164, 179; and

Flowers, M.R. 40–1; (in Brennan, G. *et al.*)115, 122, 160; and Stubblebine, W.C. 44–5; and Tullock, G. 49–50, 53, 122
budgetary processes 112–14
budgetary processes, and fiscal politics 114–16
Burbee, C.R. (in McNeil, D.W. *et al.*) 54
Bush, Winston C. 179

Calculus of Consent, The (Brennan and Buchanan) 122, 191
cigarette tax 10, 18, 71–3, 118–21, 126, 171
Coase, Ronald H. 45, 86
Comprehensive Environmental Reclamation and Clean-up Act (1980) 52
Consolidated Omnibus Budget Reconciliation Act (1985) 34
constitutional perspectives 11, 121–2, 152–62, 179–92; the benevolent fisc 153–5; constrained Leviathan 159–60; and earmarking 152–62; endogenous politics and reform 187–90; fiscal exchange 155–7; fiscal politics in perspective 190–2; fiscal transfer 157–9; 'interpretation', authority and order 183–7; problems of constitutional maintenance 181–3; and the social dilemma 179–81; toward fiscal reality 161–2
contractarian theories 2–4, 179–81

Cook, P.J. (in Phelps, C.E. *et al.*) 18
Cordes, J.J. 43
corrective taxes 34, 42–9
cross-subsidization 87, 104–5
Cushman, J.H., Jr. 22

Danzon, P. : (in Flowers, M.R. *et al.*) 158
Demsetz, H. 62
Department of Transportation (DOT) 21–2
disguised taxation 85–6
Doernberg, R.L. and McChesney, Fred S. 171
double-payment 175
Downing, P.B. 49
Due, J.F. and Friedlander, A.F. 164, 167

earmarked taxes 9–11; the fiscal significance of 13–29; and the optimal lobbying strategy 141–50; the political economy of 110–23; the relative importance of 19–21; and rent seeking 125–39, 163–75
Electricité de France (EDF) 90–108; EDF'S justificatory argument 100–2; price determination within EDF 95–7; strategies and group interests 106–8; systematic bias 98–100; who is right? 102–6
Environmental Law Handbook (1985) 52
Environmental Protection Agency, US (EPA) 22–3, 52–5
environmental user fees 20–1, 35, 165; a diagrammatic treatment 46–9; and new public choice perspectives 49–51
EPA *see* Environmental Protection Agency, US
Epstein, Richard A. 8, 183
excises 19, 163–75; alcohol tax 126; cigarette tax 10, 18, 71–3, 118–21, 126
extortion, potential for political 169–74

Federal Communications Commission (FCC) licence sale user fee 25

Federal Pipeline Safety Program 22
'fetcher bills' 171
'fisc', the 152–5; the, 'fiscal brain' 153–4
'fiscal doublespeak' 24
fiscal exchange 155–7
'fiscal illusion' 29
fiscal transfer 157–9
Florida Power and Light v. *NRC* 39
Florio, James J. 54, 55
Flowers, M.R. : and Danzon, P. 158; (in Buchanan, James M. *et al.*) 40–1
Foshee, A.W. : (in McNeil, D.W. *et al.*) 54
free riding 164, 185
Friedlander, A.F. : (in Due, J.F. *et al.*) 164, 167

gasoline tax *see* Highway Trust Fund
Goetz, C.J. 114, 142
government bureaux and user charges 60–73; the bureaucratic environment 62–4; the bureau's ideal user charge 71–3; the impotence of user charges 64–9; some qualifications 69–71
'green taxes' *see* environmental user fees

Hazardous Substance Response (Superfund) 20, 52–5; Superfund Amendments and Reauthorization Act (1986) 54–5
Highway Revenue Act (1956) 145
Highway Trust Fund 9–10, 22, 111, 145–8, 150n, 153, 164
Hutt, W.H. 122, 191

incentives and public pricing 82–5
interest groups 61, 106–8, 125–31, 142, 190
'interpretation', authority and constitutional order 183–7
Irwin, W.A. and Liroff, R.A. 49

Jensen, M. 62

Katzman, M.T. 53
Klott, G.A. 16
Krashinsky, M. 15

Leal, D. 166–7, 170
Lee, Dwight R. 60–73, 172; Kimenyi, S. and Tollison, Robert, D. 141–50; and Tollison, Robert, D. 125–39; and Wagner, Richard E. 110–23
Leoni, Bruno 191
Lepage, Henri 90–108
Leu, R.E. and Schaub, T. 72
Lindahl, E. 155; Lindahl pricing 76
Liroff, R.A.: (in Irwin, W.A. *et al.*) 49
lobbying strategy 141–50; empirical model and results 145–8; and tax institutions 143–4 *see also* special interest groups

Macaulay, Hugh H. 45
McChesney, Fred S. 50–1, 163–75; (in Doernberg, R.L. *et al.*) 171
McCloskey, D.N. 181
McCormick, R.E.: (in Maloney, M.T. *et al.*) 50
McGinley, L.: (in Wessel, D. *et al.*) 173
McMahon, W.W. and Sprenkle, C.M. 110
McNeil, D.W., Foshee, A.W. and Burbee, C.R. 54
majoritarian politics 116–21, 152, 158
Maloney, M.T. and McCormick, R.E. 50
Marchetti, P.K. 38–9
marginal cost pricing 15, 78–9, 90–108; EDF's justificatory argument 100–2; price determination within EDF 95–7; the story in France 91–5; strategies and group interests 106–8; systematic bias 98–100; who is right? 102–6
Marris, R. 62
Mercer, L.J. and Morgan, D.W. 41–2, 49
Migue, J.L. and Belanger, G. 63
'milker bills' 171
Mitchell, J.M.: (in Benson, B.L. *et al.*) 69
monopolies 39–40, 79, 83–4; Electricité de France 90–108
Morgan, D.W.: (in Mercer, L.J. *et al.*) 41–2, 49
motor fuels tax *see* Highway Trust Fund

multi-part pricing 79
Musgrave, R.A. 156

National Park Service 27
Nationalization Act, the 95
Niskanen, William A., Jr. 61, 63, 183
'non-tax revenue enhancement' *see* user charges
Nuclear Regulatory Commission (NRC) 39

Pashigan, B.P. 167
peak-load pricing 83, 101, 113
Peltzman, S. 168–9
Penrose, E. 62
Phelps, C.E. and Cook, P.J. 18
Pigou, A.C. 35, 40, 42, 153–4; and logic 52; and the Pigovian prescription 42–3; and political economy 52–4
Pogue, T.F. and Sgontz, L.G. 171
political economy 52–4, 60–73, 110–23; and the Pigovian prescription 52–4; and tax earmarking 110–23; of user charges 60–73
political extortion, potential for 169–74
pollution, taxing *see* environmental user fees
Posner, R.A. 83
post-equilibrium bargaining 44–5
price determination (within EDF) 95–7
pricing: marginal cost 90–108; public 75–88
property rights 75–88
Public Broadcasting Trust Fund 26
public choice 7, 11, 111, 141, 190; new perspectives 49–51
public pricing 75–88; disguised taxation 85–6; and incentives 82–5; knowledge and rules for 80–2; a simple model 78–80; when should users be charged? 76–7

quasi-pricing 110, 112, 118

Regulation magazine 43
rent seeking 34–56, 87, 125–39,

198 *Index*

163–75; potential for political extortion 169–74; and public choice 34–56; and tax earmarking 125–39, 174; theory and practice/ excises 164–9
revisionists, the 43–5
Rockefeller, S.P. 26
Rothschild, T. 39

Samuel K. Skinner, Secretary of Transportation v. *Mid-America Pipeline Co.* 21, 34
Samuelson, P. 155
Savas, E.S. 13–14
Schaub, T. (in Leu, R.E. *et al.*) 72
sectoral budgeting 152, 155–7, 161
Sgontz, L.G.: (in Pogue, T.F. *et al.*) 171
Shughart, W.F. 171
'sin' tax *see* alcohol tax; cigarette tax
Singh, N. and Thomas, R. 15
Slack, E.: (in Bird, R.M. *et al.*) 15
social dilemma, the 179–81
social efficiency 132–5
Social Security Trust Fund 20
special interest groups 61, 106–8, 125–31, 142, 190
Sprenkle, C.M.: (in McMahon, W.W. *et al.*) 110
Stiglitz, J.E.: (in Atkinson, A.B. *et al.*) 164
strategies and group interests 106–8
Stubblebine, William Craig: (in Buchanan, James M. *et al.*) 44–5
subjective cost 75–88
Superfund Amendments and Reauthorization Act (1986) 54–5
'Superfund' (Hazardous Substance Response) 20, 52–5

tariffs and user charges 22
Tax Foundation 19
taxes 163–75; corrective 34, 42–9; earmarked *see* earmarked taxes; institutions and lobbying 143–4; norms 1–11; in a rent seeking model 163–75; and user fees compared 14–18

telecommunications and user fees 25–6
Thomas, R. (in Singh, N. *et al.*) 15
tie-in sales 156
Tollison, Robert, D. 169; Kimenyi, S. and Lee, Dwight R. 141–50; and Lee, Dwight R. 125–39
toxic wastes and user fees *see* environmental user fees
trade and purposeful behaviour 36–7
Tuerck, D. 158
Tullock, G. 179; in Buchanan, James, M. *et al.*) 49–50, 53, 122
Turvey, R. 43

underpricing 168, 174
uniform pricing 83
US Congress 50
US EPA 55
US General Accounting Office 53
user charges 13–29, 60–73; and excises 164–9; from feudalism to capitalism 36–8; other thoughts on 38–42; in principle and practice 7–9; proposed fees 24–9; the relative importance of 19–21; a survey of schemes 21–4; and taxes compared 14–18
user fees *see* user charges

voluntary exchange theory 155–7

Wagner, Richard E. 1–11, 75–88, 179–92; and Lee, Dwight, R. 110–23
welfare economics 11, 82
Wessel, D. and McGinley, L. 173
West, E.G. 167
White, S.D. 37
Wicksell, Knut 3, 7, 111, 115–16, 121, 156, 157, 190
Wilson, P.W. 69

Yandle, Bruce 34–56; and Young, E. 51
Young, E.: (in Yandle, Bruce *et al.*) 51